IDEOLOGY AND THE IMAGINATION
FRED INGLIS

CAMBRIDGE UNIVERSITY PRESS

Published by the Syndics of the Cambridge University Press
Bentley House, 200 Euston Road, London NW1 2DB
American Branch: 32 East 57th Street, New York, N.Y. 10022

© Cambridge University Press 1975

Library of Congress Catalogue Card Number: 74–82220

ISBN 0 521 20540 9 (hard covers)
ISBN 0 521 09886 6 (paperback)

Printed in Great Britain
by The Anchor Press Ltd, Tiptree, Essex

for Liz Drury
and for Basil Bernstein

What is the price of experience? do men buy it for a song?
Or wisdom for a dance in the street? No, it is bought with the price
Of all that a man hath, his house, his wife, his children.
William Blake

I turn away and shut the door, and on the stair
Wonder how many times I could have proved my worth
In something that all others understand or share;
But O! ambitious heart, had such a proof drawn forth
A company of friends, a conscience set at ease,
It had but made us pine the more. The abstract joy,
The half-read wisdom of daemonic images,
Suffice the ageing man as once the growing boy.
W. B. Yeats

Contents

Thanks and acknowledgements

An introduction is what it purports to be: the author inviting his reader to shake hands with his book, and providing – as politely and clearly as he may – some details about the book and its previous history. I make such introduction in the first pages, but there are these few, important remarks to make first. To publish a book is to open a conversation with many people. It is therefore right that those readers who are most directly spoken to in the book should be called out as affectionately and gracefully as possible for the way in which their prior conversations with me, and my knowledge of their attention, have helped me to tell the truth and, where it can be done, to decide what it is important to think about.

It always seems odd that such tributes tend to be made *after* the more commonplace acknowledgements to hospitable but distant journals and their editors. I would rather begin by thanking the two friends to whom the book is dedicated: Liz Drury, to whom I would simply quote John Stuart Mill's magnificent words,

> There are certainly few persons living who are capable of doing so much good by their indirect and unconscious influence as you are and I do not believe you have ever had an adequate conception of the extent of influence you possess and the quantity of good which you produce by it. Even by your mere existence you do more good than many by their laborious exertions.[1]

That influence is alive in such of those pages which follow which may work for good. Basil Bernstein, as he will see, has given me on many occasions the analytic structures I needed if the argument was to be any more than a heap of insights. Since he is, I am sure,

[1] *Collected Letters*, 29th May 1844.

the most creative sociologist now at work in this country, I would like to pay my debt with a proper obviousness, especially since *his* gifts have made him unduly liable to the attentions of intellectual cutpurses, to their jealousy, and to their vindictiveness. Thirdly, and as ever, much from me is due to Quentin Skinner, the most generous of scholars and friends, as well as the most luminous. Lastly, I must thank both my students and colleagues in the Division of Advanced Studies at the University of Bristol School of Education, who between them have provided the space and the active, energising debate necessary for me to write the book. Where it is wrong, it is wrong; the book is not offered as a point of view, nor as a corner of society seen through a temperament. I intend to describe the world truthfully as well as, no doubt, to change it in certain ways.

I owe acknowledgements to the editors and publishers of the following journals for permission to use material which has already appeared in one form or another in their pages: *The Journal of Curriculum Studies* and William Collins Ltd, *English in Education* and NATE, *Children's Literature in Education* and Ward Lock Ltd, Penguin Books and Mr Denys Thompson, editor of *Discrimination and Popular Culture*, *Tract* and Mr Peter Abbs.

Introduction

This book has a single theme. It studies those moments at which the imaginative life of society either reaffirms the lines of an old ideology, or challenges it with a new declaration. It attempts to mark out the way a social group or class or a society tends and cherishes its imagination, and, from that creative process, comes to understand its own public identity. That sense of public identity is what I mean by ideology. The subject of this book is the way in which ideology transpires from values as they live and change in the imaginations of society.

The book is therefore a series of studies in the formation of consciousness. This definition entails the study of formal and informal education – the study of the way society provides officially and precisely for the formation of consciousness among its newer members. I have tried therefore to stand at the intersection of social ideology and social imagination; it is inevitable that those roads will often cross in schools.

Even there, the acquisition of consciousness is riven by contradictions and incoherence. Schools commend to their members values and beliefs which the children and the teachers can only live with by holding them apart, or from which they escape into that half-world between politics and mythology where the social consciousness of our present history lies asleep.

We still lack an adequate theory to explain these processes. The available explanations will hardly do to understand how people learn their values and live with them. Faced as it is with wholesale political ignorance and the deep social roots to often hateful class ideology, classical Marxism is helpless to diagnose the present. Its predictions have been falsified. In the face of the destructiveness and brutal expansion of the industrial West, its historical predictions look random and threadbare. In Britain, the traditional refuge of historians, social scientists, and philosophers has been the no less Victorian religion of liberalism. But that frame of belief has also been strained beyond bearing. In a human history become beyond any doubt world history, with the systematic re-creation of waste and poverty and starvation visible on every television screen in the world, the liberal and individualist tradition has badly overdrawn its moral account. To live private lives has come to look dishonourable, even if it is not clear what else you can do. Some measure that people feel such dishonour is the fairly widespread and, no doubt, salutary guilt that is sometimes felt in the rich West about its riches. Now the criticism of both these beliefs – Marxism and Individualism – in Britain is not at all new, but it is still small-voiced. This book aims to help bring that criticism up to date.

But the absence of a body of cultural and political theory – a way of accounting for the present state of affairs – has forced a particular method and shape upon this book. Such an absence has meant that the cultural and political critic has to raid what areas of culture he can, and see what patterns recur, what corners of the living culture – its institutions, arts, symbols, and language – compose a structure of belief and value. There can be, in other words, no straightforward approach, no set of instruments with which to anatomise a cultural imagination. Consequently, I rely on a number of terms taking their precise definition from the way I have approached each context, each report from the culture. The key terms include: consciousness, ideology, politics, imagination, identity, values, institutions. The terms may be usefully thought of as set in a triangular matrix whose three corners are identity, culture, education.

Yet a two-dimensional diagram will not do. That it will, is still the illusion held by a too schematic and positivist social science. On the contrary, these key terms take their meaning from my attempt to recreate them in a concrete study of the life in question. I have taken the three corners of the triangle of forces: first, personal identity and reading literature; second, social culture and townscape, or mass communications; third, education and the details of curricula as they are actually taught and examined in schools, and as the certificates are exchanged in the job-market place. Because there is no agreed way to map out the relations of ideology to the imagination, of politics to culture, these inquiries have been occasional; they spring, as they must, from the idiosyncrasies of one man's subjective attention. Any grander ambitions, as we have learned from the desolate aridities of semiology and the structuralism of the *Collège de France*, lead in the present conditions to mystification. As things are, to lay claim to a theory which *can* pull together all parts of a culture, is to fake the case.

Yet nobody stands intellectually naked; everyone brings some pieces of theoretical clothing with him from the past. Anybody who is serious about trying to understand the Englishman and his history tries to do so from a particular tradition and cherishes particular pieties. The great tradition of Western socialism is barely 150 years old; in many ways it has not touched the consciousness of people in Britain. One great strength socialism has had since it struck root here has been its strong sense of country. The Marxist claims that socialism must be an international movement have, rightly or wrongly, come to sound over the years more and more thin. And certainly the thick network of defensive positions[1] into which British socialism has dug itself has been at times insular to a philistine degree. But I do not think this has been too high a price to pay for its nationalism, its robust sense of the texture of things at home. The language of struggle, resistance, of stubborn courage, as well as of victory, success, advance, humanness, has been made out of the stuff of *our* life – all that unbelievably vivid, dense and local living has gone to make a picture of the world and its meanings of a very practical, concrete kind. There are no doubt things to be said against such a picture: against its insensitivity to intellectualism, to bold theorising and to any great gust of popular enthusiasm, against its over-scepticism, and rather biting, sardonic closeness of fist and mouth.

In spite of all these proper criticisms of British socialism, its traditions and its language are still strong and moving. I have tried in this book to extend that tradition in Britain and British education, and this at a time when there are too many gaps between like-minded people in schools and universities and colleges. For we are joined in some sort of common purpose, united in the strife which divides us. Yet in these days when the raw evils of industrialism, the waste and callousness of its social policies, more than ever need the critical resistance of teachers in all institutions, the education

[1] Edward Thompson's phrase in 'The Peculiarities of the English', *Socialist Register*, 1965.

systems revolve in mild disharmony and a signal lack of grip upon either precept or behaviour. That is what I meant when I spoke of the half world between politics and mythology, the twilit zone where people get by without any sense of the way the world goes. Both their thought and their action go forward in vastly foreshortened relation to one another. Thinkers and actors take in nothing like enough of the other's washing. In Collingwood's great *Autobiography*,[2] he speaks stirringly of 'the way historical events impinged upon myself and broke up my pose of detached professional thinker'. He went on: 'I know that all my life I have been engaged unawares in a political struggle, fighting against these things in the dark. Henceforth I shall fight in the daylight.' The study of culture and education is not the business of 'detached professional thinkers'. It is the study of the meaning life has in a particular history. The arid English division between theory and practice simply shuts out the daylight needed to prevent one's having 'to fight against these things in the dark'.

All history is at least partly in the dark. It is messy and obscure. Yet, as I say several times in the pages that follow, there seems to me a historical opportunity to capture. A few of the 400,000 teachers in Britain are emerging at last from their long subordination to the exigencies of the job-market and their function as child-minders. The gradual growth of the National Union of Teachers[3] as a force to be reckoned with is one very rough measure of the coming to a social consciousness of teachers in and out of school. The links of schools with colleges and of both with universities, though still frail and suspicious – and in the minds of universities viewed often with a much too seigneurial remoteness – embody the active possibility of 'cities of reason', the great Renaissance vision of a community of learning. The potentiality is, in Britain, stronger now perhaps than it has ever been. That is the nature of the opportunity. Whether it is taken or missed turns on whether teachers as a group – and a group whose leadership is the national intelligentsia – recognise the chance, and take their decisions accordingly.

'The city of reason'. The metaphor of a city is a rich one. It has a long history. Paradise is a city; it is a *place*. I am trying in this

[2] Oxford 1939, p. 167.
[3] A history not very well described by R. Manzer in *Teachers and Politics*, 1969.

4

book, in its predecessors *The Englishness of English Teaching* and *The Imagery of Power*, and in its successors, to help take the opportunity I have named; to find and make the social identity, the social consciousness. One way of putting it, satisfactory enough for the time being, is to say that teachers must map out and rebuild their city: its routes and its communities. And, indeed, its membership. Who shall be its citizens, free to come and go?

The book, then, is part of that long, common effort – a labour, as the powerful old saw has it, a labour of love. Common effort requires a common speech, and such speech requires a spokesman. Of course, a spokesman's authority comes only from the people who recognise him.

Part I

Knowledge and values

I

Towards a politics of education

The educational system pulls strongly towards the centre of gravity in its society. Inevitably, a national institution tends to express the main stability of its parent society. Any education – especially at secondary schools level – has to arrange for the nation's children to enter the social structure at the right level and in the right numbers; the schools are charged with so providing skilled and unskilled manpower that to each is given according to his expectations. Too great expectations, and you lose your grip on the social controls; too low, and your growth rates drop below par. Just right, and there seems to be no reason why the English class system should not contain and express its technology for ever. No evolution; no poverty; gentle social reform and the end of ideology. The quickness of the hand deceives the eye.

Within this largely respectable edifice, there has been, to its credit, an always vigorous and dissenting minority. This minority has itself been made up of different factions. They have largely spoken up for two sorts of criticism of the way things are: one has criticised the limitations of social access in education, access to institutions and to knowledge; the other has criticised the constraints upon separate individuals which have stifled their personal growth and stunted their creativity. The first has worked for democratic forms of education, the second for forms which will express the love so glaringly absent from the workings of the parent system. The idea of this first section of the book is to clarify the present contexts and details of this critical tradition. It aims also to bring together the social and individual critiques and to give them purchase upon the present situation. Finally, this section attempts to identify the political elements which lie below many of the particular arguments and are, by a peculiarly English (rather than Scots or Welsh) suppression, left out of the argument, since to bring in the

9

politics of culture is so often held to be a hopelessly partisan act, a characteristic only of the rabid Left.

Part I works through the following sections. First, an account of things aiming to show how much like-minded spirits need to stand together; second, the section 'The End of an Ideology' offers a criticism of the educational system of values which *only* looked to save the souls of individuals, one at a time, and had no social vision of its own importance. In 'The Sociology of Powerlessness', I go on to link this frame of mind to the widespread view that saving individuals is the best you can do because everyone is irrevocably conditioned by his home life; although I then point out how some teachers have resisted this view. 'The Genteel Radicals' is a brief history of this resistance, and leads into a definition of 'The Missing Centre' as being, in these radicals' case, the absent belief in positive human (and extra-human) ends. That is, they have no consciousness of their own social and political strength.

In these circumstances, the teachers have tried, honourably, to cope with the facts of class and cultural divisions by trying to provide a *recognisable* curriculum for different social classes. The danger, outlined in 'Salvation and Middle-Class Culture', is that the curriculum is stratified once again in the old class terms; class becomes not a home but a prison. The alternative is to rewrite our understanding of culture – and this is 'On Behalf of Schooling' – so that it becomes an interclass possession, the property of a people.

To see the need for this, we must look again at 'The State of the Nations' and place our perspective upon our own culture against our picture of world history. However little we can *do* about world famine and cruelty, we cannot pretend they are not there as measures of our own lives. Education, to be truthful, must see what its knowledge and values can do about the world. The American teachers' and students' reaction to the war in Asia provides an example of how a national educational system – anyway, in its critical minority – may act to rouse its nation's conscience. Considering this example returns us to opposing the idea that teachers, or indeed any group of people, are politically helpless. It returns us to the coincidence of knowledge and values, to the politics of education.

Such a politics implies large upheavals in the nature of education. 'The Idea of a Common Culture' and 'Culture and the Curriculum' aim to understand what such an upheaval means, and to show how ordinary everyday experience ('culture') becomes studied, educated knowledge ('curriculum'). And the last section, 'The Teacher as Maker', models a social image for the teacher. The idea is to give life to the dead sociological phrase, 'the role of the teacher', and to account for the extraordinary variety of actions expected of him.

In all this, I want to speak from the possibilities of *what is really there*. The writing of political theory is successful when people can say with Dr Johnson, 'I have never seen the notions in any other place; yet he that reads them here, persuades himself that he has always felt them.' The theory, that is, tells them where they are when until that moment they did not know.

SOLITUDE AND COMMUNITY

What you know fixes in part what you become. As a man's way of perceiving and organising knowledge changes, so does his identity.

> Though leaves are many, the root is one;
> Through all the lying days of my youth
> I swayed my leaves and flowers in the sun;
> Now I may wither into the truth.[1]

If wisdom came with time to Yeats, the change of identity as another man grows older doesn't mean that he gets wiser. There is no happy causal relationship either between erudition and truth or between maturity and truth. And yet in your experience, certain preoccupations recur, certain landmarks stand out; you revisit those memories which give significance and shape to your life. When you come to find that other men walk those places, that the same ghosts people shades of other imaginations than yours, then you feel displaced; you feel unwelcome and retreat. You feel the release as private anxieties disperse in a common pool of living; and you feel the invasion of the self by lives you can't control, lives which invade your intimate reflections and fantasies. The long, multiple shock is the shock of history – the discovery that a man really is a part of his world and what he thought was his own turned out to be other men's as well. The discovery becomes the subscription paid to the social group which shares that view of the landscape, these landmarks, these events, this shape of life.

[1] 'The Coming of Wisdom with Time' from *The Green Helmet* by W. B. Yeats (1910).

This essay attempts to identify some of the events and perceptions which characterise a distinctive social group. The attempt inevitably commits me to a good deal of generality and an involuntary discourtesy. There will be points at which a sympathetic reader – one who it may be recognises himself in the description – will want to pull back and disclaim the identity. But at a time of social fragmentation – particularly in the way in which people see themselves – it is important to discover and announce such connections as may be there. Then it may be that the announcement is mistaken; because it is made one-sidedly, it is bound to be in part mistaken. Someone has said, 'We feel this way'; and others reply, 'No we don't'. So he begins again. And then, 'that's better; but . . .'. And by this stage, conversation is joined. A different social consciousness is in the making.

Iris Murdoch seems absolutely right when she asserts that 'reflection rightly tends to unify the moral world, and that increasing moral sophistication reveals increasing unity. What is it like to be just? We come to understand this as we come to understand the relationship between justice and other virtues. Such a reflection requires and generates a rich and diversified vocabulary for naming aspects of goodness.'[2]

Now it may be in the end true that the effort to see the world as one and still to see it whole is doomed, that one can only (though gradually) give up monism.

> And though one says that one is part of everything,
> There is a conflict, there is a resistance involved;
> And being part is an exertion that declines :
> One feels the life of that which gives life as it is.[3]

Yet the struggle to recover meaning does not require the recovery of absolute claims, the point most forgotten by the moral sceptic. The sceptic says: 'Your view of [say] human love would have meant nothing to a Bedouin. *Therefore* [and it's this that doesn't follow] that view of love is simply an expression of your personal preferences. It means nothing to me.' Well, moral terms take their meaning from a given history, but this relative condition does not collapse morality into meaninglessness. Why should it? Love and

---

2 *The Sovereignty of Good* (Routledge 1970), p. 58.
3 Wallace Stevens, 'The Course of a Particular', in *Opus Posthumus* (Faber & Faber 1957).

goodness are what they are when men and women act in certain ways. But the general precepts, Be Good, Love Thy Neighbour, are nonetheless valid for all that. The problem is to translate precept into behaviour, belief into action. (The first is the ground of the second.) And so,

> If ever the search for a tranquil belief should end
> The future might stop emerging out of the past . . .

There's the dialectic for you. And the certain fact that the future will not stop ('here it comes again') does not make the search a waste of time.

The effort to recover significance for life in the face of the dreadfulness of history is another name for the creative impulse. A moral sense is that which, in the face of the present grim prospect, ministers to life. What can a good man believe in? What are the common dreams? The good man has always been an elusive figure and his dreams take many forms. But if it were impossible to think that at least among teachers and their students there remain some good men and true, then the straits would indeed be bad. Because the calling of a teacher is still honourable and the duties assigned to him by society increasingly impossible to discharge, I shall try to identify what a good teacher might believe in; what he might look out for and how he might think about his society now and again; such an identification, if it works, will at least make possible the plausible use of the pronoun 'we'. In a culture badly gone in the teeth, its sane affirmative speech almost inaudible, to speak of what 'we' might do and think is a poor show of communality; whistling in the dark to stop your teeth rattling. Even so, there are still a few groups who might expect to share some consciousness about what is happening. When everybody insists upon these differences between men, it is only thrifty to share out what you can. In a bitter aphorism :

> There are only three kinds of person : those who, having found God, seek Him; those who, not having found Him, spend their time seeking Him; and those who live without having found Him and without seeking for Him either. The first are both blessed and reasonable, the last both mad and unhappy, and the second unhappy but reasonable.[4]

---

[4] Pascal, *Pensées*, fragment 257.

THE END OF AN IDEOLOGY

The least that teachers can do is to recover their reason. At the moment they work, by and large, within a view of the world and a set of justifications for their work which increasingly fail to meet the realities of everyday. Take some instances. Much of modern education appeals for its value to master-symbols of personal development and fulfilment, images of individual growth and freedom and richness. It is these qualities which teachers seek to develop. At the same time the immense research efforts of the past thirty years have insisted upon the truth and omnipresence of facts which the teachers' conception of society (their frame of mind) prevented them from seeing.

That frame of mind tends only to see its society piecemeal: as an aggregate of individual success and failure. It doesn't see the structural conditions which set a limit to what a child is, and can do. The research has marked out time and again the educational privilege and support which are unfailingly made available to that minority of children which already possesses inordinate advantage. The facts of inequality within one country are now easily learned. But equality is not a simple condition. When Lawrence speaks of 'the passion for equality' as being 'the last great religious passion left on earth' he reduces a vast historical movement[5] to a single emotion and forgets the daring and scope of his own political definitions: definitions both of equality and of democracy. He makes his best sense when he says

> Society, or Democracy, or any Political State or Community
> exists not for the sake of the individual, nor should ever exist
> for the sake of the individual, but simply to establish the
> Average, in order to make living together possible: that is,
> to make proper facilities for every man's clothing, feeding,
> housing himself, working, sleeping, mating, playing, according
> to his necessity as a common unit, an average. Everything
> beyond that common necessity depends on himself alone.[6]

These are the boldest claims for individualism. And his point is that equality on those terms, though we do not begin to have it, is not

---

[5] Represented in *Women in Love* by Thomas Crich's striking miners.
[6] 'Democracy', in *Phoenix* (Heinemann 1936), pp. 699–718.

'what men ultimately live for'. On this argument, one shall, with Lawrence, 'see free men in the streets' only when

> the people of the world have finally got over the state of giddy idealising of governments, nations, inter-nations, politics, democracies, empires, and so forth; when they really understand that their collective activities are only cook-housemaid to their sheer individual activities; (and) when they at last calmly accept a business concern for what it is . . .

Equality at the mundane level is to do with straightening out fairly all we need to live in comfort. After that – 'our sheer individual activities' – for which a condition of equality is the essential ground.

Something like that account would fit how the teachers might describe their main values. 'Get things handed out fairly', they might say, 'and then we reach the business which really counts – the education of the unfettered self, unimpeded by poverty and wrong opportunity.' Well, it has been a decent hope; it has graced with a sufficient light many hours of honest teaching; and it will no longer pass. Why not?

It no longer passes because it is now so clear that it never worked for very many. For a hope to remain hope, it must be the case that it is one day capable of realisation. This particular hope – that, one day, education can be so equitably arranged that all children and students will, as they say, realise their own potential and develop their special attributes – this hope, it is now clear, never worked nor could work for very many. And the criterion of its feasibility is not utilitarian – 'the greatest good of the greatest number'. Indeed, I hope that this first part of the book will offer an alternative set of bearings for the lapsed utilitarian, the honest liberal for whom the inadequacy of utilitarian concepts like 'material good', 'welfare', 'satisfaction', and so on, has become rightly intolerable.

What went wrong with this hope – what was always wrong with it – was that the moral measure was not intrinsic, but just the consequence of the chosen action. By this way of measuring, eating people is not wrong in itself, but only wrong if (for example) someone gets hurt by being eaten. On the contrary, the problem about the failure of universal liberal education is not one simply about numbers. Few men will ever win access to the fullest images of beauty, truth and goodness; no doubt as few as won access in a past when, it is at least possible to *imagine* (and therefore in some

15

sense to imitate), there obtained a seamless and shared culture. The failure of liberal education is, like all such problems, one of consciousness. It has failed, because it is now known to have failed. And failure was a condition of seeing that the teaching and the education could not countervail what the society did to children. Indeed, the education on its worse mornings seemed, in the forms of its control, of its thinking, its shaping the lives of its student members, to act clean contrary to the individualist ethic. Instead of liberating pupils, it seemed too often to constrict and stifle them in the interests of docility and a quiet life.

It is becoming clear to more and more teachers, from changes in the structure of the school and from much telling research, that their efforts on behalf of individual fulfilment could hardly counter the grinding disinheritance of community, language and culture. Not only that. Those best efforts were themselves distorting the humanity they worked with. Understandably, when faced with the blank incomprehension of their pupils, teachers have in their turn failed to find in themselves an essential *recognition* of the humanity and the experience which their pupils brought to school with them. Without common recognition, no art and no culture is possible. It is the first, indispensable, and remains the central experience in a continuing education.

Largely denied that recognition, thousands upon thousands of school-children have suffered the assaults of an alien speech and symbolism as an impersonal violence against which they have closed their shutters and remained in hiding until the noise outside went away.

This disjuncture is one which many teachers have lived with. The bitter experience has tired the life out of many, and made not a few dead with cynicism;[7] a few saints have kept the old lamps alight. As the rent between what was hoped for and what was possible has become more obvious, however, certain lines of response have become apparent amongst teachers and educationalists.

They have first made even more of the greatest successes amongst the children. They have then extended the hierarchy of success, so that those who have been previously excluded from success are now allocated success at, in the grisly language, 'their own level'

---

[7] I am trying here to develop what I have said of literature teachers in *The Englishness of English Teaching* (Longman 1969) into a more general account.

(generally according to examinations) and according to their various gifts. And, for all that this has been an effort to humanise schooling trapped within the old inhuman framework, the effort has not been trivial and the benefits are real. They are manifest in the new aspirations of new certificate holders, in the rate of sixth-form increase, in the extension of subjects taught and taken (examined, too).

THE SOCIOLOGY OF POWERLESSNESS

These changes have resulted in the increasing strain now placed upon the educational system in its efforts to guarantee returns upon the pupils' investment of themselves, their commitment, time, and lost earnings. That strain is causing new cracks to appear in the system. For the moment, however, the first expediency has worked. The opportunity for various kinds of success has been expanded. The relation between education and social mobility has been made pretty close. As in Michael Young's brilliant prophecy of how things would work, the meritocracy has inherited the earth. That is to say, a new technology required a flexible and highly differentiated manpower. An old society provided antique social forms to contain the manpower. It was and remains the function of the schools to accommodate this state of affairs. Thus and thus the school confirms the class divisions which the society passes on to it. The close relation between school success and social privilege turns less upon innate merit than upon the provisions made by parents and home to fit their children for success.

Teachers have made two responses to this condition. First, they came to see themselves as increasingly powerless; as convinced that the school can barely affect what it is the child brings with it, and that the results of education which can be clearly separated from the harsh determinants of social structure are narrowly a matter of the transmission of skills and information. 'With the best will in the world', some would say, 'you can hardly affect the children during school hours.' This doctrine is of a piece with a much larger view of individual helplessness in the world of public and political action, and it helps to confirm a very general feeling amongst teachers that the only remedy for their social ineffectiveness is to cherish as devotedly as possible their individual relationships with their pupils and their colleagues. The second response to the discovery that schools help to confirm whatever it is that children bring to school from their homes has been the effort to reduce that confirmation by altering the structure of the school. It is held or hoped that changes in access to educational institutions will repair major cultural cleavages.[8] Thus, the 11+ examination is abandoned, and primary and secondary schools adopt less inflexible systems of streaming and stratification. This increased looseness of structure sorted well with the changes becoming necessary in new curricula and teaching methods, although it is a mistake frequently made to suppose that there is any causal connection between egalitarian impulses and team-teaching in a latter-day humanities project. Nonetheless, in the face of so much evidence and opinion telling teachers either that what they did was ineffectual, or that it was all too effective in strengthening the strong and holding down the weak, the teachers have honourably responded by trying to reverse the terms of the paradox. They have tried to repair the ravages of poverty single-handed,[9] and to oppose a different set of controls to those by which their society maintained its structure and dispositions.

This has led them to a new barrier and to the discovery of the next stage of the regress. (It seems impossible for a single element in a social organism to alter its essential structure.) Thus, the attempt by school-teachers to stop social class divisions being clearly reflected in the simpler divisions into ability in a school resulted in the reappearance of the social class boundaries in a less obvious pattern. When the studies of streaming made it clear that primary schools began to dictate their future life styles to children at the age of seven then the necessity for change pressed itself upon the primary teachers ('you've got to find out who's any good and seven's the age to do it. You can spot the nits by then'[10]). But in spite of the large-scale movement towards unstreaming in primary schools, the teachers and trainers and administrators reckoned without the power of their own social consciousness. In the unstreamed classes,

---

[8] A point taken from Ioan Davies' very useful paper 'The Management of Knowledge', *Sociology*, 1, 4, January 1970.

[9] Poverty is rendered by the euphemism 'disadvantage'; if you are 'disadvantaged' you come last in the Handicap. See *Crossed with Adversity: the education of socially disadvantaged children* (Schools Council with Methuen Educational 1969).

[10] Quoted in Brian Jackson's singlehanded and courageous *Streaming: an Education System in Miniature* (1964). This pioneering study cleared the way for NFER's mammoth *Streaming in Primary Schools*, Joan Barker Lunn *et al.* (1970).

18

invisible forces created the camps and ghettoes which kept the old lines of social class, intelligence, and opportunity, less regularly drawn but hardly less pervasive. Not only do the fluent, lively and well-mannered children move together, but the teachers – and faced by classes of forty-odd noisy, self-willed, energetic eight-year-olds, which of us would not? – smile upon the children who smile back, write neatly, read novels, and walk meekly in the ways of Parnassus.

The same thing happened in the secondary school. The dogged faith that change in access to opportunity would effect great changes of mind and heart, which cancelled the 11+ and unstreamed the primary schools, now has set to work in the comprehensive schools. Already it seems that, as a conservative might tell us, these schools also can no more eradicate their own social class structure than a raw mineral can change the veining of its crystals.[11] The old lines remain under the new agriculture. Thus GCE 'A' and 'O' levels, the CSE, or the Higher and Ordinary Diploma, the City and Guilds examinations, all mark out the intellectual landscape in such a way as to make minor administrative changes negligible. Furthermore, within these boundaries, areas of study are themselves distributed in such a way as to confirm the old streaming. Within 'A' or 'O' level, within the CSE, some subjects or areas are regularly seen as more 'suitable' to 'academic' children, and others for the 'practical' ones. Well, things being what they are for the moment, it perhaps *does* make sense that fifteen-year-old girls from bookless homes should make dresses and queen cakes for domestic science and pre-pare projects on pop music for English, but if those are general assumptions about what it is proper for those teenagers to study, no one could pretend such practices are likely to change history and culture very much. It is at this point that those people committed to the ideal of social change as a consequence of educational change have invested a lot of effort and hope in new forms of teaching, new subject matter and a reduced emphasis on the teacher's control. They saw that to change the way pupils learn subjects is to change the pupils. The traditional hierarchies of school subjects have forced them to acknowledge that, within those subjects, the traditionally

---

[11] This generalisation has so far only limited research to back it up. Julienne Ford's *Social Class and the Comprehensive School* (Routledge & Kegan Paul 1969) is far too hasty and ill-put-together to make it much more than a guess. But other evidence is piling up. See e.g. T. G. Monks, *Comprehensive Education in Action* (NFER 1970); D. A. Pidgeon, *Expectations and Pupil Performance* (NFER 1970).

successful virtues – hard individual work, disciplined reading, articulateness, and that amiable combination of obligingness and shrewd self-seeking which has marked the middle-class medal-winners since the 1944 Education Act – these virtues will always come out best. The subjects are not only matters of a body of knowledge and of autonomous ideas;[12] they themselves dictate some at least of the terms on which they shall be known. The way in which a subject shall be known – always allowing for the radical change in such knowing at the onset of either genius or social upheaval – entails the development of certain qualities and habits in the knower. To be any good at history or physics in school, it follows that you must show these qualities. Lacking these qualities, it becomes the conventional wisdom to say, why, there can surely be no point in studying the subject? And so a situation comes into play in which, in order to become recognised as competent in a given subject, you display a successful mastery of the appropriate range of skills and qualities. The attainment of intellectual identity is a matter of entering a particular society and of gaining acceptance by sharing and making your own (internalising) its social signals. A part of becoming a person in the intellectual as in any other sense is to make yourself recognisable, and if you defy that society and flout its signals, then of course you pay the intellectual costs of isolation and oddity. Such costs have always made intellectual (or political) change very expensive for those whose discoveries have made them into subversives. The role of novice in the process of *initiation*[13] which is so heavily emphasised in a system dominated by the filters of selection, tends to ensure unsubversiveness amongst those who enrol for admission to the mysteries.

THE GENTEEL RADICALS

This state of affairs quite a number of teachers have correctly diagnosed, as they tracked their way back through the series of edu-

---

12 As defined by Paul Hirst in 'Liberal Education and the Nature of Knowledge' in R. D. Archambault, *Philosophical Analysis and Education* (Routledge & Kegan Paul 1965). Hirst, however, fails to attend to any *ideological* (as opposed to epistemological) origins in a 'realm of knowledge'.

13 This is Richard Peters' explicit metaphor to describe how a person becomes educated. See *Ethics and Education* (Allen & Unwin 1966). It is a version of education which leaves out the movement of history, and therefore makes politics into a neuter.

cational chambers which enclose and shape the minds and imaginations of every pupil in schools. They have seen that not only does success in this process depend upon the atmosphere and training of a home over which the teachers can have no influence, it also fosters rapacious and competitive feelings which are often hurtful to real imaginative energy. The process requires a student to see himself as acquirer and possessor of his own knowledge, and that knowledge as so much currency for conversion into certificates, diplomas and degrees – paper which in turn is convertible into compound interest. The same impulse which pushed through the changes in access – the 11+ and so forth – is now attempting to unfreeze the lines and rites of transmission and initiation. The teachers hope to see a co-operative spirit informing the works of groups of pupils and not individuals. They create projects of work which ask that the students work out the areas of inquiry and collect the essential data for themselves. It is easy to be sardonic at the expense of such labours. Much of the work is infantile; much more is badly directed, or the effort is launched upon trivial topics (the triviality often picked up as contagion from those banal, sentimental primary school projects and topic work with 'the beach', 'the post office' or 'breakfast'). Such faults are remediable. It is a number of other difficulties which go unremarked by the advocates of teaching by teams and across (in the cant) the 'subject-barriers'. For the new curricula involve the following changes.[14] First, that teaching is conducted with one's colleagues present and that consequently there must be a good deal of agreement about the point of it all.

Second, that because there is no set subject area (history, biology, religious knowledge, etc.) it is impossible to specify a given intellectual identity and the process of socialisation which goes with it. That is, without definable ways of knowing and states of knowledge, you cannot work from the security of certain boundaries of discourse: a shared vocabulary and its values.

Third, and consequent upon this, that without such a shared and transmitted identity, students will tend even more strongly to create their identity in relation to their peer-group life. The grain

---

[14] See Basil Bernstein's paper (much cited in these pages) 'On the Classification and Framing of Educational Knowledge', in *Class, Codes, Control* (Routledge & Kegan Paul 1971); see also an early version of this, 'Ritual in Education', *Philosophical Transactions of the Royal Society of London* B 772 vol. 251.

of its culture and its forms of information will be the main influence on them rather than their educational experience.

Fourth, that in order to maintain control in a situation in which the sanctions of traditional authority have lapsed, the teachers must instead construct a delicate anatomy of personal control. This control depends upon the maintenance of many individual relationships and conversations. It will be essential to such control that such teachers be popular,[15] or at least intelligible, for it does not depend on external 'authority' (however demonstrated) and its sanctions. If it is to work, the pupils must allow this invasion of their sensibility to act as the structure of control within which they live as school-children. These doubts about informality can easily lead onto a bland affirmation of rigorously Etonian (or Borstalian) conditions – 'we find the boys like strict rules: they know where they are' and 'they prefer to have their offences caned off, it's much less bother than impositions'. Nonetheless, it remains true that the new curricula enforce exceedingly elaborate, pale, anxious, and ambiguous systems of control. And they make difficult the sort of teaching which (for example) Norman Malcolm reports so vividly from Wittgenstein's classes in philosophy:

> Wittgenstein sat in a plain wooden chair in the centre of the room. Here he carried on a visible struggle with his thoughts. He often felt that he was confused, and said so. Frequently he said things like 'I'm a fool!', 'You have a dreadful teacher!' 'I'm just too stupid today'. Sometimes he expressed a doubt that he would be able to continue the lecture, but only rarely did he give up before seven o'clock.
>
> It is hardly correct to speak of these meetings as 'lectures', although this is what Wittgenstein called them. For one thing, he was carrying on original research in these meetings. He was thinking about certain problems in a way that he could have done had he been alone. For another thing, the meetings were largely conversation. Wittgenstein commonly directed questions at various people present and reacted to their replies. Often the meetings consisted mainly of dialogue. Sometimes, however, when he was trying to draw a thought

---

[15] The importance of popularity as a main curricular factor is something I tried first to bring out in my *The Englishness of English Teaching* (Longman 1969), p. 178. Its significance is much more complicated than it looks.

out of himself, he would prohibit, with a peremptory
motion of the hand, any questions or remarks. There were
frequent and prolonged periods of silence, with only an
occasional mutter from Wittgenstein, and the stillest attention
from the others. During these silences, Wittgenstein was
extremely tense and active. His gaze was concentrated; his
face was alive; his hands made arresting movements; his
expression was stern. One knew that one was in the presence
of extreme seriousness, absorption, and force of intellect.

Wittgenstein's personality dominated these meetings. I
doubt that anyone in the class failed to be influenced by him
in some way. Few of us could keep from acquiring imitations
of his mannerisms, gestures, intonations, exclamations. These
imitations could easily appear ridiculous when compared
with their original.

Wittgenstein was a frightening person at these classes. He
was very impatient and easily angered. If someone felt an
objection to what he was saying he was fiercely insistent that
the objection should be stated.

Wittgenstein's severity was connected, I think, with his
passionate love of truth. He was constantly fighting with the
deepest philosophical problems. The solution of one problem
led to another problem. Wittgenstein was uncompromising;
he had to have *complete* understanding. He drove himself
fiercely. His whole being was under a tension. No one at the
lectures could fail to perceive that he strained his will, as
well as his intellect, to the utmost. This was one aspect of his
absolute, relentless honesty. Primarily, what made him an
awesome and even terrible person, both as a teacher and in
personal relationships, was his ruthless integrity, which did
not spare himself or anyone else.[16]

Well, this is a genius at work. Few indeed are the teachers who ever
taught at anything like this pitch. But public teaching and the atten-
dant necessity of public agreement about what is taught mean that
teaching like Wittgenstein's, which depends as much upon the play
of fierce intellect and vivid imaginative reach as it does upon *privacy*, that is, upon one teacher with a very few pupils, is very hard

[16] *Ludwig Wittgenstein: A Memoir* by Norman Malcolm (Oxford 1958),
pp. 26–7.

to practise. This in turn means that the seriousness and harsh dedication to truth and goodness which mark such teaching for the rare and necessary thing it is, qualities which always show themselves in a very small number of students, become acutely less important in the climate which forms the main intellectual styles of the country.

THE MISSING CENTRE

I have named four consequences of the move to more loose-limbed methods of teaching and of running schools. Those are: teaching takes place by teams rather than individuals; intellectual identities are much more shadowy; pupils identify therefore with their peers and not their school; to deal with these informal conditions systems of control have to be highly personalised. Like any institutional and structural changes, these changes are at the same time moral and conceptual as well. That is, the structure of administration carries moral meanings. And the morality of an informal, personal and unstratified sort of school is institutionally incapable of living seriously in the modern world. I do not mean that such schools dispatch spineless layabouts into society – the Black Paper outlook. What I mean is that the heavy emphasis on personal relationships cuts down the social horizon to your close friends. The thematic and pupil-directed forms of inquiry make knowledge into the balance of opinion, and not the uncovering of truth. The specialised and individual nature of the work, the casual forms of ceremony, reduce the expressive and ritual nature of school experience, and tend also to make little appeal to a collective morality. There is no notion of a destiny. Its intellectual style – its dominant styles of speech, gesture, ceremony and organisation – is such as to make seriousness seem austere, and dedication of spirit into priggishness.

The sources of such incapacity need describing. They are not really those which the voice of the conservative Right would identify. That voice would point to the lapse in continuity, in received authority, in respect for traditional wisdom and custom. And he would be right; the lapses are there, and every bit as much the concern of a socialist as of anyone else. But the conservative[17] would

---

[17] Not, of course, in any narrowly party sense. By conservative I mean what the word says. There is a sad lack in education, as in politics, of conservative argument of the kind which must be taken seriously.

see the lack of seriousness in intellectual life as a result of senti-mentalising human inequalities. On this view only a few people will ever have access to the good and the true, and to disinherit those few by insisting they drop their sights from the highest pinnacles of aspiration in the interests of keeping up human solidarity is to be-tray the human mind. The view holds at its best that you can only keep in touch with sweating, banal, incorrigibly trivial-minded and self-interested humanity, by letting go of a harsher and higher hope of perfection. You tolerate, in other words, the intolerable by all settling for fifth best. In the face of this telling attack, the spokes-man of the liberal Left has found himself increasingly speechless. The virtues which his new educational structures embody are rationality, tolerance, self-awareness, honest puzzlement and sincer-ity. These virtues are real and they are indispensable; they are also on their own a recipe for ineffectiveness. For as the changes in con-sciousness have taken place, it has become clear that these virtues are themselves part of a particular world-view and that they are intimately enmeshed in a particular set of social relations.

That set of social relations both makes and is made by its techno-logy, its wealth, its power system. So, tolerance, sincerity, and so on, are celebrated in a society where individual freedom is more highly valued than social vision (sincerity); where the classes have compromised their differences rather than gone to war (pragmat-ism); where moral disagreement has made confusion inevitable (tolerance). The trouble is that these virtues,[18] real and timeless enough in themselves, but tied here to a particular time and place, are invoked as master symbols to justify much less than virtuous forms of behaviour, especially in politics. For while the social con-tract only ties you to the state of which you are a citizen, the uni-versal knowledge we have of the world circulated through television makes it impossible not to know something of how awful the world is. And then to avoid convicting ourselves of callousness and smug insensitivity, we have to get clear what, however small, we *can* do about the state of the nations, and how we shall regard the facts of our helplessness. It is in the effort to justify a greater helplessness than is really imposed by their degrees of freedom, that people say, 'You can't judge until you've been there', or, 'the South African

[18] I try to uncover precisely the way these virtues get into the curriculum in the chapter 'Ideology and the Curriculum'.

25

guerrillas are as bad as the white police', or 'What difference does it make if we do settle with Rhodesia. They get on without us.'

Tolerance then is invoked as a defence against the clearly intolerable sufferings of parts of the world; injustice is relocated as plurality. Self-awareness becomes a justification for inaction; it permits the confirmation of impotence. Sincerity and puzzlement walk demurely hand-in-hand; since no man has access to all the truth, only deluded and terrorising fanatics can be full of passionate intensity. Most crippling of all, rationality is cut down to common-sense and cut off from speculation. And so, the socially conscientious man and the honest radical come to a pass in which the only politics they can believe in is the politics of the enclave. (A stockade not a barricade.) Within the enclave they will do what they can; outside, the accelerating forces of destruction drive on to their completion. The details of this self-imposed powerlessness in a history which is racing by are brilliantly summarised by George Lukács:

> if from the vantage point of a particular class, the totality of existing society is not visible; if a class thinks the thoughts imputable to it and which bear upon its interests right through to their logical conclusion and yet fails to strike at the heart of that totality, then such a class is doomed to play only a subordinate role. It can never influence the course of history in either a conservative or progressive direction. Such classes are normally condemned to passivity, to an unstable oscillation between the ruling and the revolutionary classes, and if perchance they do erupt then such explosions are purely elemental and aimless.[19]

In some ways, what Lukács says is true for this whole country, insofar as Britain is one of the richer countries in the world. But for the purposes of this essay I am simply trying to identify teachers and intellectuals as a social group; at the least, to describe what a British intelligentsia, conscious of itself, might be able to believe in.[20] Such belief requires us to put a larger interpretation on Lukács' word 'interests' than is commonly applied to the phrase 'class in-

---

[19] In 'Class Consciousness' from *History and Class Consciousness*, first published in German 1930 (Merlin Press, London, 1971). See pp. 50–2 ff.

[20] I do not want to underestimate the difficulties. The absence of any conceivable intelligentsia has crippled British politics since 1921. I still think it plausible at least to conceive of its creation at the present. For a long time, however, it will be factious and fragmentary.

terest' and to recognise on his tip, that 'consciousness and self-interest then are mutually incompatible'.[21] The consciousness which is necessary in order that teachers shall vindicate what they do is one that must go right beyond its present recognition of powerlessness to imagine the total social order of which it is part and which potentially it could alter beyond recognition. The inquiry which educators need to share is that inquiry which would indeed lead them 'to think the thoughts imputable to them . . . right through to their logical conclusion', and this would lead to making a frame of mind adequate to the reality of world politics. It is precisely the refusal to make this effort which has disillusioned liberals and radicals about the social strength of education, and led them to support de-schooling and to doubt that schools and universities are good for anything. The liberal belief, which developed in the nineteenth century, that universal education would lead gradually and naturally to universal enlightenment and which took no account of the deep social roots to bigotry and ignorance, has collapsed of malnutrition. Unable to think the thoughts which would take them beyond their own ideology, the liberal and socialist camps of Western education are in a few, temporarily fashionable cases renouncing the faith which sustained them, in a childish fury against the institutions which they see as having betrayed them.[22] On the arguments which are rehearsed here, the schools have helped to reinforce those social pressures which it was intended that one of their main functions should be to modify and resist.

Now there is no society which could sanction that one of its main institutions should set itself headlong against the mainstream of social values. Institutions tend naturally to reinforce society, unless that society is in dissolution. But a great strength of liberal society has been the institutionalising of reason in its education system : the universities, and to a lesser extent the schools, are such institutions. Since, further, the function of reason, after Hume and Hegel, has been defined as profoundly critical, education has come to see itself as the corrective conscience of its society. The nonconformist

21 *History and Class Consciousness*, p. 61.
22 In, most famously, Ivan Illich, *Celebration of Awareness* (Calder & Boyars 1970), *Deschooling Society* (1971). See also E. Reimer, *School is Dead* (Penguin 1971), N. Postgartner, *Teaching is a Subversive Activity*, T. Pateman (ed.), *Counter Course* (Penguin 1971, 1972), N. Keddie, 'Classroom Knowledge', in *Knowledge and Control*, M. Young (ed.) (Open University and Routledge & Kegan Paul 1972).

Dissenting Academies were the first in a line of critical, dissident curriculum-builders. When our society has worked against some of its own latter-day master-symbols, such as freedom or justice or equality, a minority of its teachers have seen their own perfectly legitimate function as being to work, in their turn, against that tendency of their society. It isn't a surprise that such teachers have been a minority. Any social group will only contain a smallish number of people who will speak up against received authority and wisdom. There is a story Trotsky tells in his autobiography about leading a demonstration against an unpopular teacher from which he drew the simple truth:

> Such was my first political test, as it were. The class was henceforth divided into two distinct groups: the tale-bearers and envious on one side, the frank and courageous boys on the other, and the neutral and vacillating mass in the middle. These three groups never quite disappeared even in later years.

When all is said and done about the determination of morality by social relations, men hold fast to such classless values as honour, courage, frankness.

Hence, the critics have argued against permitting harmful and unjust social pressures to work on the life of schools. The alternative, more hopeful effort, as my synopsis goes, has been to loosen and render informal the structure and rituals of schooling. The danger is then that the formative experience of school may well be reduced to the acquisition of the skills and attitudes suitable to the jobs which the pupils' class and state of consciousness make it likely that they will manage to hold down. So a sizeable minority of children, in their anxious, effortful way, achieve the success and accept with relief the rewards doled out to them by a careful bureaucracy, and all that numberless host which remains, faced with the unblinkable facts of their own incomprehension, get on, cheerfully and doggedly enough, with making their own satisfaction in their own ways out of the small areas of life and the curriculum in which they are left to be their own men and women.

SALVATION AND MIDDLE-CLASS CULTURE

It is in these latter areas that working-class culture lies. And much of the debate about educational opportunity and social equality has turned upon contradictory interpretations of this phrase 'working-class culture'. On the one hand that culture has been an important and identifiable cause of inadequacy in, so to speak, public living: that is, at work, in politics, on television, or in court. It has provided insufficient practice in ways of speech which any man must learn fluently if he is to be his own master in a bureaucracy. This deficiency in language is not, as some educationalist of the piecemeal might say, 'only' a matter of language. Nor is the deficiency, in any way answering to a simple Left diagnosis, a matter of the expropriation of the people's own culture. And, as Basil Bernstein has pointed out time and again,[23] to misrepresenters of the work which has gone so far to identify just these inadequacies,[24] not to possess a certain mode of speech code is not a god-sent exemption, nor a disqualification from the status of human being. It is a consequence of exclusion from the language of public reality, from government, jurisprudence, and therefore from politics. Such exclusion violates the right of access to politics, the grounds of which are that all men are equally gifted with the faculty of all modes of speech. Their habitual forms of speech are therefore a consequence of the experience to which they can win access. Without other forms of speech, other names for experience and structures of life within which the names have a living context and meaning, men and women cannot understand what happens to them in these public arenas. Such an absence in the centre of social and personal life is more than linguistic, as the teachers know. It is more than a case of social injustice. The nature of working-class speech and culture requires teachers to sort out again what it is they mean by equality, and what part the conscientiously anxious cliches about privilege play in knowing where they stand. It is more than a matter of saying: 'Our pupils must learn to talk properly'. Access to middle-class language, culture and politics, certainly. But general access would

[23] E.g. in *Class, Codes, Control*, 'A Critique of the Concept of Compensatory Education' at pp. 190 ff.
[24] See also W. Labov, 'The Logic of Non-Standard English' in P. Giglioni (ed.), *Language and Social Context* (Penguin 1970).

mean a deep structural change in that language and politics. To change education in this way really would be to change the society. The justice of the case against teachers that they failed to recognise and understand the culture and the history that working-class children bring to school is in a philistine way often recognised. A commonplace of the criticisms made of, say, new television series, curricular schemes or novels for children is that 'they are much too middle-class',[25] and there have been specific efforts to provide, for example, basic literacy programmes in which the material and stories are deliberately placed in a working-class environment.[26]

At the same time, especially in the curricula prepared for the humanities or for social studies, there is the planned exclusion of such 'self-evidently unsuitable' materials as the works of Charles Dickens, Shakespeare's plays,[27] of all poems and music written before 1920, or any painting rather than any photograph.[28] Hard-headed practicality of this kind is only a step away from the cultural stratifications of the BBC wavelengths. The preparation of school curricula along the lines recommended by the Newsom report in 1963[29] is of a piece with the same tendency. Finally, a number of cultural prophets of the new[30] rest their case on the assertion that the old culture is dead and gone, good only for the museum, and that the new, technetronic, decibel culture of television, rock

25 An example at random : 'But the old authors (and) the excellent new ones . . . all remind how thoroughly middle class children's books are. They appeal to an ordered, imaginative, adjusted, slightly introverted type of child . . .' *The Guardian*, 22 August 1972.
26 E.g. Leila Berg's Penguin series, *Nippers*. See also the Schools Council Literacy programme *Breakthrough to Literacy* (Schools Council with Longman 1971). Of course these are not only much better technically, they are incomparably more wholesome than the Ladybird stories, because less genteel and pastel-shaded and anaesthetic. The much quoted and very moving stories of Paulo Freire's political literacy programme in Brazil make the same point with a very topical urgency. But my point against the Ladybird books is not that they are middle-class but that they are dead.
27 E.g. best-selling volumes of English textbooks such as Rowe's and Emmence's five-volume series *English Through Experience* (Blond), John Watts' five-volume series *Encounters* (Longman), Fowler's and Dick's five-decker *English 11-16* (Allen & Unwin). See also the most used Class Readers listed in K. Calthrop's *Reading Together* (Heinemann 1972), a survey of the texts.
28 See note 25 and the Schools Council Humanities Project material.
29 Especially at paras 461 ff.
30 E.g. A. Alverez, *Beyond All This Fiddle* (Allen Lane, The Penguin Press 1968); E. Leach, *A Runaway World* (BBC Publications 1968); most recently G. Steiner, *In Bluebeard's Castle* (Faber & Faber 1971).

music, cassettes and pulsing lights is what speaks up for the authentic soul of the kids.

Each of these impulses goes to confirm the separations which undoubtedly exist between class cultures, and to petrify working-class culture in its present condition, often from an exaggerated respect for its real but narrow virtues. Those virtues include the rich, diverse expressiveness of *local* life,[31] its handiwork and practical busyness, the communitarian strengths[32] and the unembittered humour. But the costs of the deficiencies are terrible. They include a brutal disregard for the sufferings of alien societies, a hateful and mean-minded dislike of foreign peoples in Britain, destructiveness towards many non-human forms of life, and a mistrust of things of the mind so complete as almost to deny its authors the idea of liberation.

Failure to see and name these traits in the working classes of Western capitalism makes the analysis of culture and politics impossible. Not that these traits, in different, ugly forms, are any less obvious in other classes. What remains as the function and meaning of teachers and their intelligentsia cannot therefore be that in some grisly parody of Marx's *The Holy Family* they suppose that the salvation of all men lies in adopting the life-styles and speech of the bourgeoisie. Nor in its present constricted condition can proletarian culture offer much in the way of redemption; to commend it as it is, is to turn a people's home into its prison. What is needed is so to understand the shape and texture of modern cultural life, that the recapture of the people's inheritance on the people's terms is at least imaginable.

Those terms could not remain as they are in any sufficient and dignified politics. The recapture of culture, as Trotsky saw, is never an optimistic affair, a trustful populism[33] which would simply hand over the instruments of culture – the battered books and broken statues – and hope for the best. Trotsky wrote on this score:

Because of too much individualism, a section of the pre-

---

31 Unforgettably recorded in Richard Hoggart's *The Uses of Literacy* (Chatto & Windus 1957).
32 Emphasised throughout Raymond Williams' work; see particularly *Culture and Society* (Chatto & Windus 1958), pp. 295 ff, and his novel *Border Country* (1960).
33 Such as one finds sentimentally voiced in Jack Newfield's and Jeff Greenfield's *A Populist Manifesto: The Making of a New Majority* (Praegar, New York 1973).

revolutionary intelligentsia threw itself into mysticism, but another section moved along the chaotic lines of Futurism and, caught by the Revolution – to their honour be it said – came nearer to the proletariat. But when they who came nearer because their teeth were set on edge by individualism, carry their feeling over to the proletariat, they show themselves guilty of egocentrism, that is, of extreme individualism. The trouble is that the average proletarian is lacking in this very quality. In the mass, proletarian individuality has not been sufficiently formed and differentiated . . . What the worker will take from Shakespeare, Goethe, Pushkin or Dostoievsky, will be a more complex idea of human personality, of its passions and feelings, a deeper and profounder understanding of its phychic forces and of the role of the subconscious, etc . . . (His) class cannot begin the construction of a new culture without absorbing and assimilating the elements of the old cultures . . . a new class cannot move forward without regard to the most important landmarks of the past.[34]

'Recapture' of course is a bit of a slogan necessary because properly militant. But what you recapture is *never* what you had before. It needs new, brand new settlements and negotiations and government. Trotsky's remarks give us the lead – as do Leavis' no less revolutionary but more congenially and, as things are, realistically English adjurations,[35] to work out from the concrete illustrations (in this case T. S. Eliot; elsewhere Blake and Dickens) to the fostering of new cultural life. Leavis' faith that the university is itself the mighty institution which can offer its society this culture is both stirring and compelling. Such faith and resolution would also give direction and meaning to the larger educational system too often torn by jealousies of privilege and status to draw largely upon the rich credit stored in the university for the good of all men. Leavis writes:

[34] Leon Trotsky, *Literature and Revolutions* (1924, reissued by the University of Michigan Press 1960, translated by Rose Strunsky, pp. 225–6).

[35] Leavis' relevance in the remaking of a national culture is something I try to show in detail in chapter 10 'Human Studies and the Social Crisis'. This quotation comes from *Nor Shall My Sword: Discourses on Pluralism, Compassion and Social Hope* (Chatto & Windus 1972), p. 124. See especially his tribute to the University of York, p. 193.

I have raised the supremely important head of *liaison*. Its importance is not to be measured by the amount of time I give to it. In fact, the quantitative criterion has no authority in the realm of our essential concern, life – life itself, which, not being able to engage on it, the invoker of the criterion always leaves out as not really real, or too important to matter, or too axiomatic to count. What we stand for, being (to put it negatively) non-specialist, is, positively, something of which in a university milieu we can with proper optimism say that everyone stands humanly, and that is vitally, in need of . . . I'm not preaching wild optimism. I don't for a moment suppose that you can leaven the whole quantitative lump of a university. But where there is the vital centre I'm envisaging, and the fostered transcending of departmental boundaries, you will have beyond the boundaries some understanding of why the centre is vital. Shading outwards beyond that there will be some awareness that humanity can't safely ignore *humanitas*, and further out still, shading off into not unkindly near-indifference, some tacit and vague respect. What I am describing – and don't take it for a Utopian dream – is a university that tells in the life of the country as itself a centre of the informed and responsible opinion that an educated public would make into a climate in which politicians, bureaucrats, Vice-Chancellors' committees and Ministers of Education had to do their planning, negotiating and performing.

ON BEHALF OF SCHOOLING

The first problem is to see where we are. It is to show how culture and politics penetrate one another deeply and to create a language which will express these ambiguous relationships. At a time when such efforts are unlikely to be concerted, such creation is sure to be scrappy and inexact. But that is the inevitable stage of inquiry. The second stage – which is complementary and certainly goes on at the same time as the first – involves the creation of concepts and interpretations for the recapture (the revaluation, let's say) of culture. Dickens, Shakespeare, Verdi, Brueghel, Brunelleschi, were the products of a popular as well as an aristocratic or a bourgeois culture. The task is to recreate ways of seeing this high art and its relation to everyday life in such a way that it confers its significance on the lives of all men and women in its society today. The task is at least partly to see this art in its relation to industrialism and the social relations it creates. The cubist painters (Gris, Picasso), the pioneers of modernism in architecture, domestic and industrial design (Le Corbusier, Gropius, Mies van der Rohe), the early geniuses of modern industrial music (Shostakovitch, Copland, Stravinsky) expressed their hopes on behalf of the poor and brutalised for a future made far more free and abundant by the triumphs of man-made machinery. This rise of modern mass movements created the hope for these men that the poor and the wretched might inherit the earth. The sixty years of slaughter from 1916 via the death camps and Hiroshima to Vietnam and the B52 bombers have crippled that hope. It is now only possible. The tasks I have named – the two stages of the same recreative heroism – to diagnose the present, and to provide new unities for seeing its achievements – go far beyond the capacities of a single institution, even one as vast and powerful as education.

You can't make culture out of the cheerful (or the dogged) will to do it. A culture expresses the deep movement of a nation's life – and it doesn't always do *that*. (No one, for example, could have guessed at the bread riots of 1790 from the servile broadsheets of the years before.) There is always a gap between being and culture. The study of expressive culture, which has at least the merit of standing still to be looked at, will only provide us with a rough index of what is going on. People may be deferential and still resent bitterly the occasions for deference. Working from cultural evidence, especially of a formal sort (like art or education) we must hesitate before we put too much emphasis on how actively or how hazily they felt this way. Very well. We can say that what happens in education in part helps shape how people express themselves and in part *is* how they express themselves. How deep the shaping movement goes we don't and can't know. Changes in educational consciousness – changes of mind, if you like – express *and* affect changes elsewhere. Consequently, one main inquiry, in this and other books, takes us into the formation of such consciousness. Another takes us into the way curricula might be changed in order to both affect and respond to the movements of history apparent in the intellectual and imaginative life of teachers and students. Finally, it is the creative function of education in all its empire to look to the life of its society in the present. To identify when it is alive and when it is dead. To see what might be done to maintain life. And at these points the study of culture becomes the debate about what a man or woman shall do in order to keep faith with the creative life he has found in himself. He has to provide some justification for his beliefs and his aspirations. At that moment, the analysis of consciousness is the analysis of his ideology and his imaginative life as these abstractions live concretely in the times.

As it stands, that culture largely endorses its power politics. To understand this, teachers need to aspire to 'thoughts they cannot think'. The knowledge to release such thinking is now available. What you know sets the limits to what you can think.

THE STATE OF THE NATIONS

It is increasingly clear that there is a close fit between the filtering system which works in British education and the grades of servants within the nation's economy; there is a no less embarrassingly wide gap between the official value system and ideology ('equality of opportunity', 'personal growth', etc.) and educational reality. Ruling-class children dominate the access to high-status education. The structure of education provides in roughly estimated quantities the right personnel for a given set of occupational positions. (The estimates are subject to drastic revision in the light of the trade figures, as witness the reduction in the student-teacher force in 1973–8.) The frame of mind built up by all pupils in these circumstances[36] responds with surprising docility to the pressures which enforce compliance, helplessness, and an assertively legalist frame of mind (especially amongst boys). All of which sit easily beside and perpetuate the authoritarianism rather often found in the English working class.

Linked with these characteristics, broadly and continuously expressed through them, is the poverty of speech which makes it so hard for the class to find and know another consciousness.[37] A simi-

---

[36] See Hilde Himmelweit and Betty Swift, 'A Model for the Understanding of School as a Socialising Agent', in *Trends and Issues in Developmental Psychology*, Paul H. Mussen *et al.* (eds.) (Holt, Rinehart & Winston 1969).

[37] These thoughts are suggested by a long line of texts in the analysis of popular speech and culture. They start out, I suppose, from Ezra Pound's *How to Read* (1930), go on via *Scrutiny*, the journal of English letters published in Cambridge from 1932 until 1953, to John Berger's magnicent book, *A Fortunate Man* (Allen Lane, The Penguin Press 1967).

lar poverty afflicts the untheoretical sectors of the middle classes, and hence *their* language and concepts are called to express and justify a state of affairs whose apparent timelessness it well suits their privileges not to be able to imagine otherwise. In either case, the listener hears a language which has very little proverbial or traditional strength; the metaphors and cadences of a racial memory which could explain and give meaning to unhappiness have gone. Nor has that language vivid individual creativeness; a person cannot make up anything but a stoical, grim world for himself because he does not have the language. The essential concepts with which the imagination must be able to make ready play are only used to reflect the world as it is.

That is to say, the language which we have in general use cannot easily be made to imagine other worlds. It is not a language with which a Blake or a Yeats could readily work, and create images of rich and resonant possibility – images of life as it *could be*. The best public language, which I should say is now to be found spoken by a handful of Trade Unionists, is built upon such qualities as toughness, understatement, steady reasonableness. It is a flat style, and its appeal is to the virtues of struggle, endurance, rational debate, doggedness. For its purposes, well enough. But, for all its conviction, its absences reflect a more general absence in the language of the times. The language makes the times, and the times make the language. We do not have a politics capable of speaking as though men have souls. It cannot speak of love, or generosity, or tenderness. Its most dignified terms are 'rights' and 'justice' – good names both, but not enough with which to imagine a brave new world.

We cannot will such words back with the common language. But if they are not used, the concepts which the words signify suffer drastic famine. If you lack the word, you cannot name the experience. If you cannot name it, you can give it no meaning. Thus, politics is diminished to the House of Commons; history to the museum; revolution to teenage fantasy; freedom to Speakers' Corner,[38] erotic love to orgasm, domestic love to kindness. These are the human and moral meanings of so much educational research into deprivation and disadvantage, into achievement motivation and peer-group integration, and the rest of that bankrupt jargon.

The only shared feeling which sometimes seems to be held in

[38] The point of John Berger's novel, *Corker's Freedom* (Panther 1966).

common amongst both working and middle class in the industrial West is one of public impotence. Most people feel helpless, and helplessness either accompanies or turns into indifference. The American dissenters were a minority and they became desperately tired, and fell away. Fatigue is a familiar note in all the writings of the British Left. In this waste and frightfulness, perhaps the only recourse could have been to withdraw a little way, into pity and detachment. And this, one supposes, is where the best teachers are now. They keep themselves going in an enclave. They talk to the small number who can and who will listen. The comfort and the danger about enclaves is that you never go outside.

Such a withdrawal gives us, I suggest, a metaphor for the present politics of education. But because England is not becalmed in history, the metaphor becomes out of date as soon as I write it down. Even now, when social hope is more scattered than for a long time, dispersed through a thousand minor projects, a ragged and sporadic movement of dissent is making itself felt. By and large, most teachers would say that politics should be kept out of education. What is meant by politics in this essay – the nature of relationships in schools, colleges and universities, the formation of consciousness there – they see as the non-ideological stuff of everyday life.

They have tried as far as possible to separate that stuff from the fabric of social life, and to make of it a pattern suffused with only personal and private colours. The values teachers bravely affirm in the face of a terrible and indifferent world are local, intimate, staunchly individual. They are the values of a tenacious liberalism. Yet, as knowledge of world reality grows, and, in tension with the world, knowledge of the social forces that shape the contours of the self and the self's intimacies grows also, the values of liberalism come to stand in a more and more compromised and dishonoured relation to the world. There is a shrinking point in cherishing individual fulfilment if you cannot see in what ways the individual can possibly make his fulfilment engage with his life and times later. One embattled response has been to construct an ideology out of this solitude. By this token,[39] only 'an armed and conscious' minority can keep alive the personal and individual values which must be

---

[39] Best expressed, I imagine, in Dr Q. D. Leavis, *Fiction and the Reading Public* (Chatto & Windus 1930). Popularised by G. H. Bantock in *Education in an Industrial Society* (Faber & Faber 1963), and in many of his later books and pamphleteering.

37

kept alive if cultural continuity is not to lapse for ever, and modern consciousness to grow up barbarous and amnesiac. Well, any intelligentsia will always remain a minority; but the minority on this ideology is in danger of keeping itself alive simply in order to talk to itself. The easy charge of élitism is negligible; an intelligentsia is by definition an élite, and needs to be in order to tell in any society. What counts, however, is how it tells. 'Minority culture' may not tell at all; it may simply survive in a refrigerated state. Ostensibly alive like culture in the Weimar Republic, in the Versailles of the late eighteenth century, or Confucianism in the mandarinate of the Kuomintang in 1927 – but all without weight in the life of their society. So the central questions for a politics of education are these two:

1. How shall the minority make culture tell at large in its society?
2. How shall the individual teachers relate their teaching to a world which desecrates its values?

THE IDEA OF A COMMON CULTURE

It is impossible to justify the world as it is. 'In the last days, perilous times shall come; evil men and seducers shall wax worse . . .' If you try to explain the world as it is by saying that things were always so hateful, you have to accept the idea that some men are bound to starve to death or be bombed to pieces. You have to say that some men are bound to scorch, raze and devastate the lives of other men. It is in the nature of things. And it always will be. And to believe this, you have to strip yourselves of the values which you inherited from your history. You become fatalists.

The alternative course is to protest your helplessness. Things are bad but there is nothing you can do about it. To believe this you have once more to abandon historical values – the affirmations of courage, selflessness, persistence, thought, which live and glow in the innumerable examples from the past of men and women who kept faith with a small brotherhood, and toppled mighty enemies. You have to pull back into your enclave and stay there; the politics of the back garden. To practise a doctrine of helplessness, you have to keep yourself ignorant.

To decline both courses commits a teacher to re-entering politics. This is not a matter, as the campus radicals believe, of taking to the Welsh hills with a rifle. The teacher's efforts need to go towards a much less glamorous, more patient and laborious effort to make a new consciousness. It is just possible that the minor explosions of neighbourhood dissent which are visible today indicate the changes from which such a consciousness might grow. But in any case, the teacher's effort will go to create an imaginative body of experience and a state of consciousness the richness and diversity of which make real and celebrate the freedom and community of men and women. Whereas now, our educational consciousness and imagination work to perpetrate imprisonment and separation.

What does such a generalisation mean? How do teachers 'create a body of experience', 'a consciousness'? The ultimate aim is to realise the century-old vision of a common and equal culture. First, though, it is important to get clear what this does *not* mean. Thinking of D. H. Lawrence's essay on 'Democracy', it does not mean some forced and awful uniformity of experience.

> You can't make an *idea* of the living self: hence it can never become an idea. Thank heaven for that. There it is, an inscrutable, unfindable, vivid quick, giving us off as a life-issue . . . The quick of the self is *there*. You needn't try to get behind it. As leave try to get behind the sun. You needn't try to idealise it . . .
> Where each thing is unique in itself, there can be no comparison made. One man is neither equal nor unequal to another man. When I stand in the presence of another man, and I am my own pure self, am I aware of the presence of an equal, or of an inferior, or of a superior? I am only aware of a Presence, and of the strange reality of Otherness. There is me, and there is *another being*.[40]

The quotation will do to suggest the essential force of the blossoming self (no 'fancy little homunculus' either) in the socialist idea of a common culture. The commoness and equality reside precisely in the power of individual fulfilment such a culture provides. But this fulfilment also grows from a shared and social experience. The culture itself is not deliberately portioned out in such a way that it teaches divisiveness. Most marvellous and moving of all, the variety of a living culture provides every man – in school, every boy and girl – with the chance of recognition. It is not a monologue, dumbly heard, endless and incomprehensible. For as we know now, much

[40] D. H. Lawrence, 'Democracy', *Phoenix* (Heinemann 1936), pp. 712–13.

of what most children hear in school *is* incomprehensible, or else only snatches of what they hear remain in their imagination. And the stuff of their imaginative life has had little official recognition. At best, the official culture has allowed for the admission of some superficial stylistic details – fashion and pop music – but little of the recognition which is the essential experience of a culture. It is the experience Dr Johnson describes when he writes of Gray's *Elegy in a Country Churchyard* that it 'abounds with images which find a mirror in every mind, and with sentiments to which every bosom returns an echo'. But the experience is not only a matter of finding a *reflection* of yourself. Johnson goes on, 'The four stanzas beginning "Yet even these bones" are to me original : I have never seen the notions in any other place; yet he that reads them here, persuades himself that he has always felt them . . .'[41]

A living culture would make this access of confirmation and growth available in all its parts. While it is undoubtedly true that such a culture can hardly be planned from a bureaucracy, the frame of mind in which educationists organise the lives of schools can at least make the idea of a common culture more possible.

These are the conditions asked for. First, that educational life present children with the continuous experience of *recognition*. That is, they should find in the life of the school images which give reality to the living but unspoken and, until the right moment, unspeakable areas of their lives. Johnson's image of a mirror is too simple a metaphor to go far but it stresses the two-sidedness of the process. Even though the imagination is not blank, the culture must still make its reflection there. It must be possible for school-children to retain the images given them. In this way, something nameless and imageless finds its own shape. The image received gives man or woman, girl or boy, terms in which they can understand and think about what they know. This is the traditional justification for the study of art and literature. The literature provides examples of moral and imaginative life in which events comparable (and different) to those of the reader–spectator's life are sorted and judged and given meaning. Without these examples, the people who live in imaginative poverty have no means of naming and understanding their lives. They have no images in which to render their lives comprehensible by giving them external and metaphoric

41 Samuel Johnson, *Lives of the poets*, 'Gray', Vol. II (1781).

reality. Once, religion supplied these images and metaphors : religion and the cosmic explanations implicit within a seasonal agriculture and a localised economy. Since the destruction of this symbolism and the spoken tradition of saw and proverb which made it articulate, there has been no secular imagery to replace what is lost. Other, that is, than the largely rootless imagery of mass communications.[42]

Deprived of an imagery, the people of England have been unable to create a new politics. For the presence of a shared imagery, one which takes its meaning from a social mythology, is a necessary condition for the creation of a new politics. Lévi-Strauss says somewhere that modern mythologies express the shape of politics, and he writes,

> Images cannot be ideas but they can play the part of signs,
> or, to be more precise, coexist with ideas in signs and, if
> ideas are not yet present, they can keep their future place
> open for them and make its contours apparent negatively.
> Images are fixed, linked in a single way to the mental act
> which accompanies them. Signs, and images which have
> acquired significance . . . unlike concepts . . . do not *yet*
> possess simultaneous and theoretically unlimited relations
> with other entities of the same kind.

If this generalisation is true, there is an important consequence for the conventional wisdom of cultural theorists. The consequence follows through into education. For a familiar English theory goes that bookish, intellectual culture is qualitatively different to aural, visual folk-culture, and that members of this sort of culture cannot deal in abstract ideas. The two ways of thinking – peasant and courtier, intellectual and labourer, academic and practical man – once sprang from a single cosmogeny, and abstract ideas lived in popular images and ritual. But first the two became separated and thought became scientific reason and images became poetry. And then, with the onset of industrialism, the folk (now the urban peasantry) lost touch with both. The only thing is to make the best of two widely separate worlds by experiencing them in education.

The advantage of this scheme of the world is that it provides a decent enough justification for keeping the disinherited without

---

[42] An argument I try to develop in my book *The Imagery of Power* (Heinemann 1972).

culture, and therefore lost, blind and speechless. In this condition, they turn inevitably to the construction of an ignorant and reach-me-down ideology which, without any dynamic place for history and imagination, can only fight to keep things as they are. It is this ideology which marks both the English middle and working classes. Turning to the only material in general circulation – television – people create a social mythology and its imagery compounded equally of the mystifying short change of news bulletins ('the pound was again selling below parity in Bonn'), the destruction of reason by instant opinionising ('Now perhaps you'll give us your views on . . .') and the grotesque agglomerate of superstition, sentimentality and nostalgic conservatism which transpires from most of the rest.[43]

Against this condition of immobilised deprivation, the idea that imaginative experience is a basis for theory gives education a purchase point on politics. All men imagine. The vast circulation of pulp and televised fantasy makes that truism unforgettable. But

> We had fed the heart on fantasies,
> The heart's grown brutal from the fare . . .[44]

We have a brutal culture, half-starved by fantasies which circle further and further from the world, and offer sustenance to no real imaginative flight. But if we found other forms for the imagination to take, it would be possible in the ensuing conversations, the shared experiences of the culture, to imagine new ideas of men, new explanations of their whereabouts, growing onwards from the images which were brought forward as new creations for study.

CULTURE AND THE CURRICULUM

Consider how this might happen.

> In the dream in which every epoch sees in images the epoch
> which is to succeed it, the latter appears coupled with
> elements of prehistory – that is to say of a classless society.
> The experiences of this society, which have their store place
> in the collective unconscious, interact with the new to give

[43] I try to provide a more systematic structure for these generalities in the chapter 'Public communications and consumer culture',

[44] W. B. Yeats, 'Meditations in Time of Civil War', *Collected Poems* (Macmillan 1939)

birth to the utopias which leave their traces in a thousand configurations of life, from permanent buildings to ephemeral fashions.[45]

The experiences of a society are not so much hidden in 'a collective unconscious' as recorded in the social memory to be retrieved as and when a society needs them, or when its rulers see fit to open them up. Redrawing the curricula of schools involves a different picture of knowledge and its distribution : different according to whether teachers or rulers write them. The curricula which teachers now have the chance to draw should set their boundaries along the frames of a common culture.

'Common' here cannot possibly mean 'universally known'. Modern technological culture is too impossibly various and growing at too fast a rate for that. 'Common' here indicates the common possibility of access to discovery and definition. That is to say, such a culture gives everyone a chance to recognise his own experience and to judge it. To judge it so that he is able to give it meaning against the shape and movement of society. To know, in however provisional a way, what his life is worth to himself and to his people. And knowing what a man's life is worth, it is necessary that he understand what he does and where he lives within its structure. To say this is to return to a statement of Plato's in the *Republic* that 'the worst of evils for a state is injustice',[46] and questions of justice certainly turn about questions of the distribution of knowledge and culture.

What clearly happens at the moment is that the most prestigious forms of knowledge and culture are apportioned according to the lines of success which follow the lines of class. What might happen instead is that every man and woman should be allowed to exercise their equal right to the knowledge which belongs to all men. This would mean that canoeing and domestic science are not kept for the ineducable, and that solitary, acquisitive bookwork is not confined to the intelligent and privileged. Knowledge is traditionally kept mysterious. People are kept out of the ultimate mysteries until they are fully initiated. The old priestly sequence of learning roles – novitiate, initiate, priest-but-sworn-to-secrecy – still works busily

[45] Walter Benjamin, 'Paris—Capital of the 19th Century', *New Left Review* 48, March–April 1968.
[46] *Republic* v 3, 434.

43

away, and serves to keep out strangers and intruders who might pollute the sacrament of wisdom.

Learning does not have to follow such a sequence. Learning may certainly be difficult; it may be easy. Some forms of knowledge, studied at certain levels, are undoubtedly very difficult indeed. But that does not make them into a mystery, and access to the mystery should not be allowed to guarantee social status and wealth. (Possession of difficult knowledge is bound to guarantee its own privileges.) It is a question of how learning and knowledge are *seen*. The way teachers see and teach these things will deeply affect the mind and spirit of a people. The greater openness which everyone has noted about the forms of knowledge and teaching can as well lead to a bland pointlessness as it can serve the just and good society.

What the new openness needs to serve is an idea of freedom which is not confined to the private individual; a sense of collective destiny which is greater than that of private interests. That sense lives in genuine popular arts. Such arts would be the antithesis of the narrow nostalgia and the sentimental statements of the private soul which defraud and console the people of industrial Britain. The consumer culture of the chainstores, the car lots, the TV and the supermarket disc bargains are a fraud, an anaesthetic fraud. Instead, imagine an expression of authentic popular art; like a great public park.[47] A park with a bit of heath in it, like Richmond Park, Hampstead Heath, Chatsworth Park, Sutton Coldfield Park. Some of it the gift of rich local worthies. Mostly the creation of a really good series of municipal officers and councillors. It would include public sculpture, wild flowers, playing fields, playgrounds, arboreta, as well as little pockets of natural wilderness. A zoo. An open theatre. Like all parks, it would bear the signatures of the eighteenth-century country houses and their prospects, in which garden ran out into farmland. None of our latter-day munificence though, in which Dukes, purporting to relieve killing death duties, rake in a quarter of a million pounds per year. A national park. *Nationalised* parks, if you like. Threading their way up the country, so that using them was natural and easy, and you wouldn't have to drive to them.

The park would be like a common ancestor to the people. Not an appeal; nor a declaration of national and civic strength. Nor misty nor patrician; not melodramatic. The park or the culture made

[47] Chapter 8 'Public Townscape and Popular Culture' tries to develop this point much further.

up of these arts would be like a great cathedral or a great mountain; it would be surprising. It would allow all men and women, all lovers, and all boys and girls, to discover what it was they had gone to find. It would give permanent reality to the image which troubles the mind of every industrial society, 'a day in the country' It would permit conversation with history.

THE TEACHER AS MAKER

Metaphors, in a good poem, enact their meaning. My public park is a metaphor for the common culture. A school could aspire to be such a park. (Work goes on in parks.) In the wantingness of present experience, one of the few forms of public life which carries some associations of freedom and justice – and others of the cardinal virtues like courage and discipline – is public sport. One finds on the football field and the running track – in amongst the egotism and bullying – the emblems of grace and beauty which keep alive a public art. But sport is obviously too tiny an activity to sustain such an effort singlehanded. It is only one form of life in a park.

Yet the lesser metaphor may help. In sport, people are quite clear who is good and who is bad. They can recognise and name the virtues and vices. Sports have their artists and artisans, their executives, teachers, legislators and archivists. Like any public institution, they reflect their society in their structure. What marks them out as a form of public culture is that no one is denied admission. Anyone can play; and there will be a place for him to play.

Teachers could be the artists – the makers and creators – of public culture. (I am thinking of any teacher.) What would this mean? A maker is a free man. A free woman. What he makes renders the meaning of his life. A teacher is a man and he makes the consciousness of his pupils and students. He tends their imagination and their beliefs. This is cultivation; this is the process of culture. What happens at the moment in this country is that that consciousness – the skills, the values, the sensibility and power of mind which go to make it up – is treated as a commodity on the market like any other commodity. You sell your mind (or your hands) for what it will fetch.

It is this state of affairs which cannot last. Or which, if it lasts, can only become more shameful and wretched for those who uphold it by teaching for it. And a different teacher will not have to

45

sail before the mast to Havana or Peking in order to make things otherwise.

The best teachers will be like artists in this way. They will help towards expression the impulses of freedom and justice which men everywhere are trying to control. They will bring the impulse to life. And that 'help towards expression', the 'bringing the impulse to life', is in a short term. Freedom and justice, those great names, have meaning here and now. As someone said, 'the trouble with revolutionaries is that they see light at the end of a long tunnel. But a lot of people live and die in the tunnel.' The threats of war, famine, and poison are too lurid and ghastly for any long avenues of hope. Thus a teacher needs to measure the visions of freedom against the lives of the children and the grown-ups now in front of him. What the teacher makes means what it does in the inter-section of private lives with history. These infants playing, these students painting, these housewives reading, express in their studies the changing condition of men and women. The common endur-ance. The resistance. The common delights.

The gap between the effort by the teacher to bring this con-sciousness to life and the obdurate stuff of oblivion is regularly enormous. The strain, as things are, to stretch the whole way by himself, would break many hearts. It does break them. Pain and wrong continue. The teacher gets to the end of his strength and he has to pull back for his own survival. But at best – on the best days and in the best lives – a teacher, first, provides recognition for his students. He recognises what they bring to their education and he lets it speak. He gives it speech. Then he makes the line between that experience and the possibilities of other experience. He offers the pupils the recovery of their lost chances to seize the life of their imagination and make it command the vacancy of the world. He helps to turn images into theories.

To work like this would be, like a popular artist, to become spokesman for a people. Not their leader, but their representative. There is no question that such a man or woman will know every-thing. Instead, he will know how to negotiate what others want to know. A teacher or a student may become master of his craft but may not close his shop. The teacher would stand not so much for the specialism but as the representative of humanness.

In this, he would reconnect with a long and admirable European tradition, the image of the complete man : not a priest, but guardian

46

of his students' records and memories; he would then stand at the many gates of possibility. The gate is the simplest metaphor of access to freedom.

A familiar difficulty for the radical is that, without a suitable social opportunity, there is no radical change. Without such opportunity, he is reduced to moral exhortation and to recommending that success waits upon will-power. (Hegelian Will walks again.) Moral exhortation is generally unappealing. With this in mind, it will have to do, to point out that the gate anywhere is only a point of departure, and freedom matters only as the necessary condition of achieving, in a cliché which retains great moral force, a life worth living. That life remains a mystery which it is the point of demystification, of patient discovery and revelation, to celebrate. Free men and women in the streets, educated men and women, would know what was worth keeping secret.

Part 2

Knowledge as power: who learns what?

2
Ideology and the curriculum

I

I would like in this chapter to take up the general description of Part I and apply it in the following four particular ways. First, to offer a rapid description of three styles of thought dominant in powerful institutions in society. Second, to discover how these three styles, or certain of their characteristics, enter the planning of national curricula, and to set out some of their latent contradictions and deficiencies. Third, I would also like to counterpose against what may be called the *public* styles of thought, examples of the teachers' typically *private* styles and characteristics – styles which have of course different absences and defects. Fourth and last I would like to indicate some points of growth in the private styles, and one or two ways in which privacy may usefully return to public life. Such a return and the process of reconnection which it implies, may affect our teaching both in its social relations and its specific content. What I have to say has, I hope, quite practical consequences for the making of a human curriculum. The chapter, then, takes up the main themes of the book: 'public' as opposed to 'private' being and the value of each as they bear upon the forms of educational knowledge.

I I

The first style of thought which dominates curricular and educational planning is directly a product of modern technocracies. It appeals to a model of reason whose terms derive from the coarse utilitarianism developed for the administration of social welfare in a mass competitive and consumer society. This model defines practical objectives and aims to calculate probable human responses to them. Such models cannot, as I hope to show, answer tests of rationality, but pass themselves off as rational because they answer the criteria of cost, productivity, growth and efficiency as defined by the input–output economists and investment accountants who uphold the systems of planning in Whitehall and the corporations. In the absence of opposition, these criteria now provide the instructional models for the control and evaluation of public knowledge. A condition of the latter-day utilitarianism which this style of thought expresses is that society is held to be static, and that the extension of benefits follows from increased economic growth and the elimination of conflict by legislation. The model implies the end of ideology[1] and the eradication of history. It celebrates the complex divisions of labour in a technocracy as offering the best vehicle for social variety, social opportunity, and social progress. In this non-ideological climate the managers preoccupy themselves with questions of means and efficiency; the point is then to work out how best to run a system which so clearly works to create the best of all possible worlds.

The techniques devised on the basis of this model run counter to a strong tradition in educational thinking which has also been vigorously critical of that same specialisation, and the industrialism which produced it. Yet the techniques themselves deeply penetrate the official forms of educational thought. It is easy to find operational management manuals which provide curriculum models of this sort:[2]

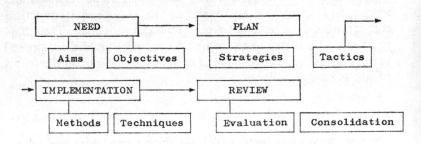

[1] The title, of course, of Daniel Bell's now notorious apologia, first published in 1961, just about the moment when the argument became incredible.

[2] Quoted from John Merritt, Professor of Educational Studies, The Open University, 'Priorities in Curriculum Design' in *Journal of the Institute of Education of the Universities of Newcastle upon Tyne and Durham*, Nov. 1970, vol. 22, 110.

The model is offered in the interests of rationalisation. Professor Merritt then applies the model.[3]

> Let us first look at the simple sequence which may be observed in any complete action. Motivation Plan Implementation Review. We may remember the initials: MPIR. There is no action without motivation, no satisfaction without a plan that is then implemented, no satisfactory profit from experience without review ... It is not enough that a child should have knowledge of his needs, he must be able to weigh one need against another and determine his priorities. To do this, he must first distinguish between his aims and his objectives. His aims are those states of body or mind which he wishes to attain. His objectives are the environmental correlates of those aims. Thus, the satisfaction of hunger may be an aim. A plate of steak might be the correlated objective.

It is in the first place much too reductive to describe all human action as impelled by 'need', unless 'need' is to turn out on examination to be a hopelessly elastic and slippery term. The model supposes that all action is intended to bring about the reduction of 'need'. But in what sense can we say that we teach in order to satisfy 'need' – and whose need? The teacher's or the child's? Inasmuch as the term 'need' may be ascribed either to behaviour which follows certain rules *or* to behaviour which has no conscious structure (dreams, psychosis, randomness) it is not clear what connections there are between our needs and our aims and objectives. Indeed it cannot be shown that there are *any* connections between 'need' and 'aim' unless you adopt a theory of such flaccidity as 'all behaviour stems from the need to reduce tensions'.

This disjunction, the product of a vulgar-minded failure to think the application of operational management to education right through, penetrates the model. It seems to derive from the same

---

[3] *The Curriculum, Context Design and Development*—'Reading and the Curriculum', R. Hooper (ed.) (Oliver and Boyd for the Open University 1971), pp. 216–31. For similar enterprises see John F. Kerr's synopsis of the necromancers in *Changing the Curiculum*, J. F. Kerr (ed.) (University of London Press 1965). First in the field was Ralph Tyler, *Basic Principles of Curriculum and Institutions* (University of Chicago 1947). The other main hornbook in College and Department of Education curricular courses is Hilda Taba, *Curriculum Development: theory and practice* (Harcourt Brace Jovanovich 1962).

submerged and universalised theory of homeostasis: that you do something to satisfy your needs and then check that you can do it again. No doubt this model is true for simple forms of locomotor co-ordination. The trouble is that psychologists of learning have then applied the same paradigm to all kinds of situations. In learning, we are confronted with obstacles. We overcome them. We feel satisfaction. We do it all again. But how does this routinised behaviour apply to playing football? Or reading a novel? Or talking with our friends? In no sense is that satisfaction usefully to be fitted into the homeostatic or pleasure-principle model.[4] It does not follow that the flow chart fits all, or indeed any of the non-repeatable situations which compose most of our lives. But it is a characteristic of this thought-form that it predicates *all* human actions as of this type. It derives from modern theories of organisation which define efficiency as obtainable by dividing tasks into units – goals, aims, objectives – and arranging these in regular taxonomies. In this way the sorting and control of input, the process of transformation, and the quantification of output can allegedly be scrutinised and regulated. The means are broken down and organised for the optimisation (as they say) of the ends. It is held that the school fits this model.

As in many other institutions (including assembly-line plants) the appropriateness of the flow-chart model to education may be refuted on three grounds. First, the objectivity of assessment and prediction which is a supreme factor in the effective application of means–end planning is logically impossible to achieve since the teachers are required to *bring about* their own predictions. (The most bitter example of this is the requirement that teachers predict the exact number of 11 + successes which the grammar school can take.) Second, individual actions have no experiential relationship to flow-chart rationality. In Alasdair MacIntyre's words,[5] 'Institutions are milieux within which people live their lives.' The terms of the curriculum flow chart are not terms in which any agent would or could explain and give reasons for his actions. It won't do to say that objectives-planning just helps people to concentrate when they would normally go ahead without thinking. For it is held to be the *point* of the flow chart that all means are directed towards ends,

---

[4] I derive here some points from R. S. Peters *The Concept of Motivation*, (Routledge 1958), pp. 27–52.
[5] To whose unpublished paper on rationalisation I am immensely in debt.

and that therefore you must follow the arrows in the right order. Some actions, however (especially at school), may *be* their own ends (playing cricket, reading *Jane Eyre*); others may have no ends at all (taking a class of infants for a walk); others again may not at all admit the application of operational analysis (listening to *Cosi Fan Tutte*[6]) nor the schematic division into a hierarchy of behaviours which it involves. The third and most damaging objection to the planning of a curriculum by this model is that the flow chart is itself irrational. Modern demographic movement and organisations being what they are, all individuals must be substitutable, and all regulations adjusted to the lowest common multiple of the participants. Stupid people must be able to take over from clever ones. In spite of the rules, however, the system is always breaking down because the flow of information is sporadic and inaccurate. Consequently, modern organisations require as well as dull or strict adherence to routines, a prompt show of initiative, flexibility, spontaneity and audacity. It is of course logically impossible to supply both, so many people are required to spend much of their time reconciling deep-seated contradictions which curriculum development on this model can only exacerbate. And there's no way out of this dead end by arguing for the free play of individual and curriculum ('idiographic' and 'nomothetic' in the cant). It is, again, the *point* of the flow chart that it moves steadily towards the specific objective and ignores all the attractive eccentricities on the way.

III

The second style of thought which has so deeply marked curricular planning is of a piece with the 'ideology of no ideology' which is so strong in systems analysis and management techniques. The problems the style poses are more a challenge to the sociology of ignorance than anything else. The stylists in question are the philosophers of education, amongst whom the best known, as well as the most graceful wearers of the style, are Richard Peters and Paul Hirst. I do not wish to be misunderstood here. I am considering

---

[6] Trying to provide operational justification for this makes it clear, I think, just how limited is the use to which one may put D. R. Krathwohl, B. S. Bloom, and B. B. Masia, *Taxonomy of Education Objectives: the classification of educational goals — Handbook II: the Affective Domain* (David McKay, and Longman's 1964).

their work because it is clearly important in its own right; they have done a lot to clear up all sorts of confusions in educational thinking; they have attacked sentimentality and spoken up for a proper and valuable sense of traditional purposes and pieties. But they have also defended without naming it a hidden policy of, so to speak, liberal non-intervention. In their useful primer *The Logic of Education*[7] Hirst and Peters enter what has become a liturgical caveat about the relevance of philosophy to education. Philosophy, they say, 'is an activity which is distinguished by its concern with certain types of second-order questions . . . Philosophy, in brief, is concerned with questions about the analysis of concepts and with questions about the grounds of knowledge, beliefs, actions and activities'. It is this latter-day definition of analytic philosophy which permits its authors to leave unexamined certain main validating premisses. Technically they are right; practically, 'second-order' permits them to leave out essential questions about the relationship between 'grounds' and morality, and between both these and social structures. When O'Connor[8] declares that 'philosophy is not in the ordinary sense of the phrase a body of knowledge, but rather an activity of criticism or clarification . . . it is not a kind of superior science . . . to answer difficult and important questions about human life', he joins the others in rendering up contemporary philosophy as that essential adjunct of the rational liberal. And the rational liberal in the absence of any other contender becomes the good man.

These accents, and the vast efforts made in their name in philosophy of education courses, keep in circulation the idea of philosopher as handmaid, practical not purposive, the tidier up of confusions. The idea is strongly criticised by Peter Winch for resting on a *mistake*[9]; it was rejected with patrician scorn by Collingwood[10] as a dereliction of duty thirty-five years ago. His stirring condemnation of a philosophy which denied that a pupil would find in it any guidance for his life would strike chords in the hearts of Peters and his men. But they have left themselves with no explicit justification for such a response. Instead they leave the way open for, in Collingwood's phrase, 'the adventurers in politics', the desperados who

[7] Students' Library of Education (Routledge & Kegan Paul 1970), pp. 2–3.
[8] In *An Introduction to the Philosophy of Education* (1957), p. 4.
[9] In *The Idea of a Social Science* (Routledge & Kegan Paul 1967).
[10] In *An Autobiography* (Oxford 1939), pp. 38–9.

are quite happy to see their own apologia set out in these genteel cadences :

> In both senses of the 'public interest' the school is obviously concerned with promoting it; for the training of technicians, typists, and countless other forms of skilled workers necessary to the viability of the economy of an industrialized society. Unless the wheels of industry keep turning the conditions will be absent which will prevent any man from pursuing a multitude of individual interests. And keeping the wheels of industry turning is a policy that favours no particular sectional interest. This is what leads economists to speak of money spent on schools as a public investment.[11]

Richard Dearden echoes Peters in this when, speaking of 'Values in the Curriculum', he emphasises that in a 'pluralist' society 'there does remain an . . . acceptable consensus on what is valuable for social competence in our form of life'. 'To begin with, there is the importance of being economically viable . . .' These easy-going statements leave out of account question as to whether things should be as they are, and further questions about how things came to be that way. The philosophers admit that the conceptual analysis entails moral argument, but they do not pursue the argument and its inevitable tangle with politics, for fear of muddying what they take to be their 'realist' function. To refuse the pursuit, it has been a political platitude to say since the *Theses on Feuerbach*, is to leave things as they are. The main charge against the philosophers is that they have cast themselves as quietist celebrators of the-way-things-are. This comes out most sharply when Paul Hirst speaks[12] of each subject as being defined by an autonomous body of knowledge and a set of concepts peculiar to its nature. Hirst never analyses the inner connections between ideology and the map of knowledge. He provides no account of the *history* of knowledge, of the philosophic analysis which would identify the distributions of knowledge as in part the product of an antecedent and impermanent epistemology,[13] and in part the way things are. For all Hirst has to say

11 R. S. Peters, *Ethics and Education* (Allen & Unwin 1966), p. 170

12 In 'Liberal Education and the Nature of Knowledge', contributed to *Philosophical Analysis and Education*, R. D. Archambault (ed.) (Routledge & Kegan Paul 1965), pp. 113–38.

13 Marjorie Grene, in her remarkable *The Knower and the Known* (Faber & Faber 1965), is the text here.

57

about the contingencies and overlapping of the 'forms of knowledge', he puts in circulation a disembodied version of knowledge without history, change, or social and ideological roots. There seems no reason why there should not be more or less than seven forms and many of the forms are themselves porous in a way which is not allowed for by Hirst's map of the 'domains'.[14] What he has to say about 'coming to look at things in a certain way' can only have meaning if the education in question looks also at the origins of this process. His education does not. His description of the forms of knowledge is as much an autobiography of willing imprisonment as anything: 'initiation' (Peter's key concept, of course[15]) becomes the process of socialisation into a given intellectual identity.[16] There seems then to be no way for new modes of thought to arise (the novel, for instance) nor for individuals to create for themselves radically different intellectual identities – the process so unforgettably described in, say, Keats' or Constable's or Mill's *Collected Letters*. The special aridity of Hirst's argument is brought out in a paper allegedly refuting Hirst, in which the writer[17] paints himself into a corner where he says that literary criticism is a form of knowledge, but painting isn't. So much the worse for the forms of knowledge.

In practising this style of thought, the philosophers do their considerable bit to make more trivial the study of education. I do not mean that they ought to be political scientists, but that although the nature of their philosophic inquiry is irredeemably moral, they sever themselves from its root. The point is not the same as Marcuse's silly objection to Wittgenstein and John Austin, that they described and did not change the world. (They changed it utterly by describing it differently.) The point is that Peters and Hirst do not describe the world sufficiently. They deprive the educational world of its history, ideology, and social origins.

14 Cf. also his contribution 'Educational Theory' to *The Study of Education*, J. W. Tibble (ed.) (Students' Library of Education, Routledge & Kegan Paul 1966), especially pp. 42 ff.
15 See *Ethics and Education passim*, but especially pp. 54–5, 259–63. See also Michael Oakeshott in *Rationalism in Politics and Other Essays* (Methuen 1962).
16 The term is Basil Bernstein's. More than anyone in England Bernstein has unlocked those mysteries, and uncovered the connections between knowledge and power. Not that there's any easy solace for Left or Right in the revelation.
17 J. Gribble, 'Forms of Knowledge', in *Educational Philosophy and Theory*, vol. 2, no. 1, March 1970, pp. 3–14.

IV

Many comparable omissions and silences occur when one turns to the work of the curriculum builders themselves. (I am referring here to general or liberal studies curricula rather than to specific disciplinary equipment like the Nuffield Science scheme or SMP.) Jerome Bruner's famous and exciting 'Man – a Course of Study' is probably the most influential scheme and it prefigures much of the combined curricular studies in this country, among which the Schools Council Humanities Project is probably the best known. But the excitement is not the point. Bruner's scheme, the intentions and plan of which he sets out in *Toward a Theory of Instruction*[18] is crippled on two counts.[19] The scheme sets out a study of man for ten-year-olds which moves from simple transformational grammar to the growth of technology and on to the analysis of the role structure of society (yes, it *does*). Much of this is achieved by the study of alien cultures in the present day – the Bushmen, the Eskimos. The first, radical absence is of any sense that societies are made and changed by men, that conflicts occur, and that class or ethnic interests are often bitterly at odds. One could never guess from this thrilling, varied, multi-media pack of equipment that men have beliefs, that they fight about them, and that some men dominate other men. The pack is the product of the end-of-ideology ideology which marked America in the early 1960s, and which is so strongly present in the two styles of thought already described: the managerial and the philosophic–educational.

Now Bruner is a psychologist. The second main characteristic of his style of thought is his partiality for a specific version of cognitive development. The version would be congenial to managerial thought and to Hirst's 'forms of knowing'. In a transcript from a discussion amongst teachers about a film of Eskimo life shown to children, the consultant psychologist said:

> They learned a lot about technology. On that we're agreed.
> And they had a good exercise of the cognitive skills involved
> in concept attainment: focussed observation, identification,

[18] Belknap Harvard 1962, pp. 73–102.
[19] He concedes, rather crossly, some of the charges in his contribution to *The Radical Alternative*, Tri-University Project in Elementary Education (New Orleans 1970).

59

categorization, classification, generalization, analytical thought, objectivity, and the rest. Good. They also had a healthy exercise in the emotional skills necessary to support such cognitive activities : control, containment, postponement.[20]

Yet it is not enough to object by saying that Bruner is all cognitive skills and misses out the soul. That is true. What psychologist, in his ready play with cognition and development, would ever use the idea of a soul? But the stock response is to add a new section to the pack which takes care of the soul.

This is to commit the classical heresy of modern technocracies. It was J. S. Mill's in the first place, and it has been most teachers' since. The heresy sees correctly that modern scientific thought, with its stress on 'objectivity' and sense-datum empiricism, misses out something. It then supposes that what you do is create a reserve area – 'the culture of the feelings' (Mill's phrase, picked up by David Holbrook) – where you look after that something. The mind is one thing, and thinks, decides, takes actions; the feelings are another, but must be tended. Art and literature serve this purpose and are therefore necessary to keep the plain practical technocrat civilised. Art and the study of the thick texture of its culture then becomes one of the agreeable graces – needful to be sure, but in no sense a dominant mode of thought.

This view of art as an emollient addition to the tough cognitions which really make the world of knowledge and power what it is, is deeply unattractive. What is absent in all three styles of thought is an account of man in his culture which resists these merely contingent splits in his consciousness, and which restores some sense of the interrelation as well as the divisions of labour; an account which will, in turn, permit us at least an idea of the complete man. The idea has been central to Western educational traditions.

Such a call to intellectual action returns us to the first and most central criticism of Bruner's curriculum – it is static. It includes no mention of change or conflict. It has no politics. But of course to profess no politics, to believe in the end-of-ideology, is itself a political and ideological act. This comes out very clearly in a consideration of the Schools Council Humanities pack. The most serious

---

20 See Richard M. Jones in *Fantasy and Feeling in Education* (University of London Press 1968), who quotes the psychologist and proposes the solution criticised here.

disservice these materials do to education is to eliminate the truth. Their main assumptions are organised by the sociology of mass communications about the central and articulating assumption, that morality is choice, and free choice is displayed and vindicated by the free expression of opinion. That contemporary style of thought – consensus achieved by committee discussion – dominates such curricula.[21] It springs from the liberal supposition that you may choose all your values and ascribe them to the social facts as a function of your existential self. The concept of 'balance', learned painlessly and all the time from current affairs programmes on radio and television and all the other forums of instant banality. turns out to mean something more like a balancing act, a nimble dodging along a myriad points of view. If a man says anything, let another man say the opposite. Thus we will discover the 'balanced' position. It is a necessary part of such a curriculum that its contents will be on the whole brief quotations from *New Society* and *The Guardian*, or passages of black-and-white social-realist literature with a distinct bias. The view of rationality as judicious moderation which transpires from the packs, sorts well with English notions of the free agent as freely discussing, moderate and middle-of-the-road, agnostic but humane. The notion of 'balance' as poise, as the clairvoyant goodness of an artist in the full and frightening exercise of his powers, is simply not available. Just as importantly the truth of an argument in the sense of its irrefutability – the truth that it cannot be a matter of choice that there is or is not a God, or that England is or is not an unjust country, or that all men have or have not a right to the education they ask for – *this* sense of truth vanishes in the quest for consensus which is the latent ideology of liberal-minded group discussion. The model of the group is a microcosm of the society, a plural, self-correcting play of minority forces keeping themselves in a state of tensile equilibrium. Once more, the model eliminates change, and conflict as leading to change. It completes the arc of meaning drawn by the flow chartists and the philosophers by confining the terms of discussion to the limits of party politics and the limits of intelligence to the liberal, tax-paying, punctual and orderly voter.

[21] Cf. also these Schools Council projects and kits : Projects for the Integration of the Humanities; Social Education Project; The Arts and the Adolescent; General Studies Project; Moral Education Curriculum Project; the Whole Curriculum for the Middle Years of Schooling.

V

Curriculum theory and practical development of this kind strengthen the grip of the dominant thought-forms. The training of cognition and the rationalisation of learning combine in the mythology of modern technology, the opiate of the intellectuals. The technology creates its own systems, and the construction of systems is its own politics. The point of such systems is to eradicate as far as possible the multiple idiosyncrasies and deviances of human behaviour.

Certain sections of the education system – certain ways of teaching, certain subject-matters, certain relationships – have long represented themselves to themselves as resisters of the rationaliser. What these teachers have done who have seen themselves as providing a dissident form of consciousness is cultivate the private soul; they have cherished the unofficial, the sporting, the creative, the poetic and personal. They have created forms of curricula which act as enclosures within public thought-forms and morality and affirm the private, the impromptu, the normal and rhythmic texture of human life.

Within these enclaves, such teaching has made possible alternative relationships which simply by their presence can be seen, consciously or not, as criticising the official rituals of relationship within schools. It has, for example, long been an acknowledged technique for controlling difficult low-stream boys that teachers take them out of the school on various expeditions whose ideological intention lies somewhere between the Newsom report and *Scouting for Boys*. Taken out of the precise situation of school, and its multiple emphasis on the classroom relationship of teacher and taught, completely other points of human access open up. It is every probationer's experience. 'Why aren't they always like that?' The change makes suddenly possible for the teacher and the pupil alike much deeper penetration of the other's feelings and attitudes. However well advanced (*pace* Basil Bernstein) the change may be from *positional* (sc. 'authoritarian') to *personal* forms of control in the school, the difference between a camping expedition and the progressive project-bound curriculum is obviously enormous. These small outings may have many intentions: a main, simple one is often to get to know a group of difficult, violent, inarticulate children better. Similarly, the intentions of such 'enclave activities' as a school play may be officially far more to do with the corporate, public face of the school than with looking after childish or intimate things. And yet . . . Within the chaos, bloody-mindedness, and staff-room or PTA rancour which surrounds the school play, the producer and his colleagues almost always succeed in creating a novel, rich network of relationships which flourishes in a consciously non-curricular way. It is a network of lunch-hours and late nights, of unused corners of the school and improbable curricular combinations – electric circuits, dressmaking, *Romeo and Juliet*, brought together in decidedly unintegrated but nonetheless intense, formative ways. These are some of the private and often dissident ways of thinking which importantly resist – are seen by the practitioners as resisting – the implications of more technical planning.

Many of the same points could be made about sport, and its central function as a hinge between official and unofficial cultures in schools.[22] With a more deliberate defiance, the art and music rooms have long been a refuge for handfuls of a school outlawry, and, in particular, English teaching for the past fifteen or so years has mounted a fragmentary but not ineffective campaign against the public world and some of its blander features. The English teacher's lesson on advertising, on a politician's prose, on school rules, connects with the long and honourable tradition of radical dissidence in his subject matter, literature. Falstaff at the Battle of Shrewsbury, Pip helping the escaped Magwitch on the Essex marshes, Huck Finn lighting out for the territory, all these speak up for the private, the critical, the uncompliant voice which gets relegated hearing in the roll-calls of the objectives.

But, as the foregoing analysis suggests, the cultivation of our own souls has left public life, history and politics untenanted by teachers. Liberal ideology, which places the individual at the fount of all value, has no point of insertion into systems technology. It stands helpless. For it is not only a defect, it is a principle that liberalism cannot tell us what to do. We choose for ourselves in all circumstances. And yet this inactivity clearly leads to the steady relinquishing of freedoms until it is only in our play and our cultivated leisure[23] that we make a stand and say, 'Here, on this ground, I'm

---

[22] I suggest this in my *The Englishness of English Teaching* (Longman 1970), p. 180.
[23] Which is all that G. H. Bantock would want to make of the English literature he purportedly admires. He rests easily upon the *status quo*

my own man'. What can be salvaged from this refusal to believe, and to act?

Liberalism acknowledges that the freely choosing individual must be rational; this is the clue we need. A necessary part of the scheme of things must be the preservation of reason, especially since its nominal custodians have made such a mess of things. To consider what it is to be rational returns us to the consideration of what it is to be moral and to be good, terms the omission of which has made contemptible and frivolous so much of recent discussions of moral education and of curricular developments. To consider rationality is to reconsider those qualities which we are taught rational men should admire.

Contemporary rationality is largely content with the positivist model which sets up an easy victory for social calculus over social intuitions. Anyone who objects to this version of reason as narrow and disgusting is then branded as Luddite or clock-reverser. But vast areas of human and extra-human life have been and are being – quite literally – stripped, burned, and devastated for ever by this kind of reason. It is *not* reasonable to live in the present way, and moral disgust *is* a reasonable reaction. It is to resist the alleged rationality of the rationalisers with their own key weapon, reason-ableness, to talk in this way, and it is the least we may expect of an education system.

Such reasonableness, however, cannot stop there. As I said, to consider what it is reasonable to admire is to debate what we ought to do. It is to inquire into the good. Not, 'be ye therefore rational'; but, 'be ye therefore perfect, as . . .'. The worst office of the styles of thought which I have criticised has been to foreclose any dis-cussion of the moral ends of education. The moral tradition that a man's ends are his own business has been, in the politics of today's world, overdrawn beyond the point of bankruptcy. The present relations of the curriculum and ideology work busily to keep it solvent. Systems analysts, analytic philosophers, cognitive psycho-logists, and teacher-as-TV chairman combine to recommend the ideal modern man as responsible, sincere, self-aware, puzzled and helpless.

The moral ends are no longer digestible by such a weak stomach.

and hands over the creative writing in order that the working class will be kept quiet. See particularly his 'Towards a Theory of Popular Education', *Times Educational Supplement*, 12 and 19 March 1971.

One can hardly suggest in a paragraph or two what the ends might be. But it is at this point that the effort is needed to define the affirmations of the private and impromptu in such a way as to give our 'cultivation of the soul' historical point and purchase. It is likely that a large number of teachers feel that present ways of thinking are disastrously not enough to cope with the world. A number, in their different ways, acknowledge and press home the counter-claims of the 'unofficial' styles of thinking. To teach in this way the commonplace lessons of secondary schools – the English teacher on advertising, on *Great Expectations*, on school uniform, the history teacher on Peterloo, the geography teacher's traffic count and the music teacher's lesson on the *Pastoral Symphony* or the *Eroica* – is to see how mighty is the force of an alternative map of knowledge and culture. Pressing home these implicit claims is likely to cause conflict, in and out of school. That is a perfectly understandable reason for having softened the pressure. But it is not a rhetorical flourish by now to say that the values of our education have lost substance and honour by avoiding conflict.

The education community could recover some of that lost honour by setting all its members the task of discovering to what extent they are their own men and women.

3

How not to do things with words: a critique of a language curriculum

I

In the last chapter I have drawn some connections between dominant thought-forms and ways of thinking about education. I suggest very briefly there how on these terms a particular curriculum programme might be looked at for its latent ideological content. This suggestion may now be taken rather further. The Schools Council financed between 1967 and 1972 a five-year programme for the provision of a practical curriculum in secondary school linguistics.[1] The resulting handbook, *Language in Use*,[2] offers itself primarily to the English teacher, although it has sensible recommendations to make on the old issue of the teaching of English by every teacher in the school. The fact that it is teachers of English who will first use the book provides a useful illustration of a clash of ideologies amongst a group of teachers. For it will be my argument that the Schools Council document embodies a latter-day educational ideology; that this ideology serves the interests of social changelessness and individual docility far more than it does those of freedom and justice, though quite without realising it; and finally that both the theory and the practice conflict sharply with what has been the ideology of the surprisingly independent and critical group of teachers who will use the programme first. What it is important to decide is whether this critical tradition or an over-developed respect for planned and tested innovation will command the most support amongst the teachers of the book. To move towards this

---

[1] The estimated costs of which are as follows (including the language programme for infants *Breakthrough to Literacy*, Longman 1970): £156,700, 1967–71, estimate dated 1969, *Schools Council Report* (Evans and Methuen 1970).

[2] By Peter Doughty, John Pearce, Geoffrey Thornton (Arnold 1972). See also *Exploring Language* (Arnold 1973), by the same team.

decision, it is first necessary to look at some of the recent history of English teaching in Britain.

Up to the early sixties the strongest energy in school English teaching derived essentially from the astonishing and brilliant re-statement of liberal individualism which came from the Cambridge English school. Leavis and *Scrutiny* developed an ideology which met the feelings of the times, and his students went out to the schools to spread that account of things. A distinctive movement gathered identity and direction from these beginnings, and during the period of rapid educational change after 1944 – rapid at least in the development of new curricula – this movement found its voice and spoke up for dissidence. In textbooks and in ideological statements,[3] teachers of English criticised the movement of indus-trial civilisation and tried to extend the benefits of a cultivated and literate education further through society than it had ever gone before. In 1965 these teachers formed their own association, the National Association for the Teaching of English (NATE), and it was followed by proper institutionalisation; a periodical, an annual conference, a transatlantic talk-*Fest*.

At about the same time, the honest spokesmen for literature and values began to find their assumptions necessarily tangling with those of men with very different doctrines for the study of lang-uage. The sudden advance of the literature teachers into social and cultural debate overreached their strength. The confident pre-miss 'the study of language has no boundaries' found stern oppon-ents and persuasive revisionists. Linguists and sociologists of both a specialist and an eclectic sort came into the conversation. The excitement and the simplifications of the literature teachers lost their pace and conviction in the face of unlearned and technical languages, alien explanations and an unfamiliar insistence upon allegations of objectivity and relativism which was deeply uncon-genial to the former radicalism.

The conflict, on the following analysis, can be seen as between two peaceful contenders in education, and beyond that, in society at large. A main emphasis in many of the new curricula, as in books about new teaching methods and their ideology, is on the

[3] E.g. from all Denys Thompson's splendid work: *Voice of Civilization, Between the Lines, Reading and Discrimination*, to David Holbrook's classics (they deserve the title) *English for Maturity* and *English for the Rejected*.

need for educational peace and quiet. It is, heaven knows, a sympathetic aim. It is an emphasis on personalised forms of teaching and authority. The emphasis comes out in arguments for flexible systems of learning, for personal and interiorised systems of discipline and control, for self-sufficiency, 'coming to terms with life' and for 'personal adequacy'. The vast new provision for counselling is a product of a decent concern for individual welfare.

That concern can be seen by the other camp as the further institutionalisation of failure. A necessary consequence of the first set of attitudes, and the system of ideas which justifies that view of social reality, is that it supposes that things will continue much as they are. It teaches children the virtues of a flexible compliance. 'Coming to terms with life' turns out to mean, the other camp says, doing as you are told with a good grace. Their counter-claims go that far too much educational knowledge flows one way only; that children are merely objects to the process; that their school experience ought not to be an elaborate grading for the job-market; and that what must count is to provide ways of self-discovery and self-assertion by children, even if this means they *won't* do as they're told, either by teachers or by employers.

The lasting hope of English education is that the two views – putting it simply, the individualist and the conformist – can be kept in a reasonable equilibrium. In the important statement he brought back from the Dartmouth (USA) seminar which discussed English teaching on either side of the Atlantic, John Dixon[4] tried to strike a resolution of this sort between the contradictions of the existing states of mind. The last chapter of this book is also a very intelligent account of what is likely to happen. It misses out, however, the social and ideological consequences of thinking differently. The argument, to say it again, has no politics. He writes:

> The excited response of many young people to 'experience-based' work has encouraged teachers to develop and extend current experiments. How an 'experienced-based curriculum' relates to a curriculum that is subject-based is a further issue.
>
> Clearly English as defined in this report stands as a bridge between the two: our subject is experience, wherever language is needed to penetrate and bring it into a new and satisfying order. But equally our specialist knowledge of how

4 *Growth Through English* (NATE 1967, Oxford 1970).

language relates to experience and society is just beginning to take on a real cutting edge. English will be pulled in two directions, and in resolving the tension we may gain a new clarification of our work. Is a new model for education struggling to emerge, just at the point when we have spelt out for ourselve the fuller implications of a model based on personal growth? Very well. The limits of the present model *will* be reached, that is certain, and thus a new model will be needed to transcend its descriptive power – and in so doing to redirect our attention to life as it really is.

What he gives us is a dialectical model of intellectual change: that is, a resolution in new directions of the tension between opposing forces. The publication of John Dixon's book in 1967 marked the moment at which it is convenient to say that language study of a certain, English kind entered the debate about English studies. Two versions of English teaching – the linguistic and the paediatric – (or language v. child-centred) have since been strong contenders for dominance. Karl Mannheim spotted the generative power of competition in ideas several years ago, and his explanatory framework is useful by way of accommodating the resistance put up to modern linguistics by radical English studies.

I think a consistent application of the method of sociological analysis to mental life will show that many phenomena originally diagnosed as manifestations of immanent laws of the mind may be explained in terms of the prevailing structure pattern of determination within society. It seems to me, then, that I am not following a false trail if I assume that the so-called 'dialectical' (as distinct from the unilinear, continuous) form of evolution and change in mental life can be largely traced back to two very simple structural determinants of social character: to the existence of generations, and to the existence of the phenomenon of competition with which it is our task to deal here.

Now for the problem: what are we maintaining as our thesis? Firstly, that in thought (from now on, this term always means existentially-determined thought) competition can be shown to operate; and secondly, that it can be shown to be a co-determinant in the process of its formation. The first question which confronts us as we try to develop these theses is the following: does the process of thinking involve at all a competition?[5]

Mannheim reminds us that ideological opposition is positively useful; it forces the counter-formulation which will lead eventually to 'thinking new thoughts' – to getting beyond one frame of mind and making a novel consciousness, one which can command instead of defer to, the new forms of social reality.

The arrival of language study ought at least to mean that the argument for an alternative version of English defines itself far more sharply than it has done so far, if there is to be any dialectical resolution of the kind Dixon expects. At the same time we now need a much more careful and thoroughgoing critique of the characteristically English kind of applied linguistics (tautologically known as 'context of situation'), especially as applied to English teaching, and to suggest some of its drastic practical and conceptual limitations.

The problem is then to keep enough defences up against premature dismissal as One of the Enemy. Perhaps an anecdote makes this clear. During this scheme after a number of department heads had met a representative from the Schools Council linguistic unit, one department head – an extremely intelligent card-carrying literature-for-the-sensibility man – wrote expostulating with the unit about the programme carried in *Language in Use*. With heroic innocence he appealed to its authors, 'the book is terribly boring – you must know that', and went on to defend his view of English as being the training of moral perception and the deepening of experience through literary study. It was a long letter, and powerfully felt. He received this reply.

Dear Mr X,
    I shall treasure your letter. It seems to me representative in the worst possible way of the influence of Leavis and his followers upon English teaching.

The problem in offering a critique of language study is to avoid being cast as a Peking Leavisite, and therefore to miss the chance of being heard through. Arguing with one or two linguists is often like arguing with some RCs, or Marxists, or Freudians. After a certain

[5] 'Competition as a Cultural Phenomenon', *The Sociology of Knowledge* (Routledge & Kegan Paul 1952), pp. 192–4.

point they look at you and say 'how interesting that you can't accept what we say' (or 'what a glaring case of false consciousness'!). To mount certain kinds of critique is for the other camp to *be* Luddite, Leavisite, irrationalist.

Certain general tendencies are the cause of increased interest in linguistics. I have mentioned the inevitable encounter of teachers interested in both the state of society and the role of language with sociologists and linguists. This has coincided with the increasing un-certainty of teachers of the appreciation of literature about the status of their value judgements.[6] More and more they have felt the force of objectors who see the study of great art as a riot of opinion, hopelessly subjective, unverifiable and all the rest. In these circumstances the deceptive neutrality of linguists and the socio-logy of language has come to seem confidently and clinically accur-ate. Positivist and empiricist ways of thinking join hands with em-phases I mentioned earlier : emphases on vocational training, obedi-ence and flexibility of role in a rapidly changing technology. No flexibility, no jobs. The plain blunt teacher who emerges from these admonitions can speak with a good deal of condescension; it comes out at the end of Peter Doughty's useful pamphlet *The Relevance of Linguistics to the Teacher of English* :

> In conclusion, it is worth mentioning once again a theme that
> has recurred throughout this introduction, the unenviable
> position in which an inexperienced teacher of English is placed
> by the current habits of professional discussion in the subject.
> When so many different voices are ready to offer him
> guidance, and when so often they seem to speak with radically
> conflicting views, then a teacher new to the subject has a very
> particular and practical need for some rational and objective
> basis by which to judge their value. He can only come to
> judge in this way, if he is in possession of the facts. In his
> situation, the facts can only be arrived at through the
> appropriate use of adequate critical tools. He must be able to
> judge equally the charismatic influence of professional seers
> like Holbrook, and the grey ethos of practical survival he is
> only too likely to find pervading his first staff room. Almost
> certainly his basic studies will have been literary, and
> they will not provide him with the tools he requires, because

[6] See below, p. 106.

first and foremost, his tasks are with language, language in
all its complexity, and variety, and not merely the highly
idiosyncratic form of literature. It is the aim and hope of this
programme that it will be able to supply some of the needs
that become apparent, once it is clear that, however necessary
for a part of work in English, a training in literature is not
sufficient to meet them.[7]

We do not in fact need very developed tools to weigh up the hono-
rific loading in the phrases 'rational and objective', 'possession of
the facts', 'appropriate use of adequate critical tools' and the telling prefix *'not merely'*, 'the *highly idiosyncratic* form of literature'
(my italics). Of course this is a form of polemic we're now used
to: 'literature as one register amongst many', and such is the con-
sistency among the supporters of this position that opposition
almost inevitably has come to be stereotyped. Over there, the language men, the new Wellsians, with the future in their bones: over
here, the 'damned and despised literati', backward-looking, romantic, individualised, dissident, muddled old admirers of D. H. Lawrence: the old battle lines, the new men. I emphasise here that these
are stereotypes and I pay the cost[8] of using them. But it is in those
forms that the argument goes forward.

I want to argue that the appropriation of the terms 'rational and
objective', 'highly idiosyncratic', and a certain self-satisfaction in
this subsequent quotation make either platitudinous or undefended
assertions about the role of language teaching and its relation to
literature. These are, however, assertions badly in need of more
precise refutation than primitive rallying cries among the faithful
students of literature.

From the point of view of the pupil's needs as a whole,
however, the limitations of (Holbrook's) assumption(s)
should be apparent. One of its most unfortunate effects is the
degree to which it ignores the nature and function of technical
varieties of English, that is the working language of a complex
industrial society. One aspect of this is the lack of interest
shown by many teachers of English in the problems that
arise from the large number of specific varieties of English

[7] Longman 1968, p. 71. Restated in a more general version in *Exploring
Language* by P. Doughty *et al.* (Arnold 1973).
[8] Very sharply debited to my account in a paper by Don Salter in
English in Education, vol. 7 no. 1., 1972.

required for the pursuit of subjects within the curriculum. Even if the curriculum is dismantled, and the very notion of the subject swept away, the hard fact remains that it is necessary for a student to master the variety of English appropriate to physics if he wishes to do more than play with apparatus.[9]

Now it is clearly true that 'the very culture of the feelings' and 'the education of the life-flame' have *not* provided English teachers with a sufficient framework within which to work. I shall come back to this. But the point for now is that 'teaching mastery of the appropriate register' is of a piece with the 'flexible conformism' which I earlier remarked on as being an unnamed objective of so much curriculum development. The phrase is of a piece with the means–end rationality of this way of thought which I looked at briefly in Chapter 2, and it is first in this context that one may consider linguistics teaching generally and *Language in Use* in particular. Such consideration sorts well with a discussion of English as posing most sharply the split in education between genuine moral ends and questions of skill and technique. Once more, 'aims and objectives' or 'intentions and purposes'. Means or ends?

II

I wish to argue that neither term will be of much use to us. But I think the authors of *Language in Use* would prefer to answer 'means.[10] The emphasis throughout the manual rests on language as a skill and teaching language as an 'extension of resources'. A 'means' view of English subordinates the study to second-order questions; that is, a subject which can provide no notion of the purpose to which its use can be put, but only an account of how purposes may be directed, once they have been chosen. In this view, language has become technique. I have to generalise very blankly here, but I think it is fair to see *Language in Use* as a product of the technician's, the means–end habit of mind – what Michael Oakeshott calls the rationalist. The book is a manual in linguistic engineering, organised according to hierarchical criteria of goals, roles and efficiency. This view of language is not the pro-

---

[9] Doughty, p. 66.
[10] Cf. Doughty's paper, p. 66, already cited, and *Language in Use*, *passim*.

duct of either Wittgenstein's or Chomsky's philosophy (though he is extensively quoted in *Exploring Language*) so much as the product of post-industrial sociology, or the cost-effective divisions of labour.[11] On this view, the manager or teacher procures efficiency by dividing tasks into units according to certain goals and hierarchies of techniques. It is a process become familiar in the taxonomies of teacher objectives and the flow-diagrams of curriculum development.

At this point it is worth summarising the objections to this form of organisational thought put in the chapter 'Ideology and the Curriculum'. In the first place, the various means and ends of educational activity simply cannot be aligned by any input–transformation–output model. We do not live in that ruthlessly selective way. Although the *notion* of rationally chosen means directed towards a clearly seen end is a necessary mythology in all modern institutions (including educational ones), day-to-day behaviour does not work by these criteria. And this failure is not in that familiar bogey, normal irrational man (who can be put right by good planners) but in the alleged norms of this version of rationality itself. To come directly to our day-to-day work : there can be no means–end rationality possible in much of the curriculum because people do not see their lives like that. The rectilinear pattern of flow-diagrams does not answer the multifoliate shape of human intentions, though these may be perfectly reasonable. *Language in Use*, like so much curriculum development, rests upon experiential and logical mistakes. We do not have goals of any 'basic' (cf. p. 6) kind; or if we do, these are not subject to the operational criteria which inform the curriculum developers' thought-forms.

On the other hand, the authors of this curriculum may seek to balance their emphasis on means – language as skills and competences – by speaking of the work as developing an undefinable 'awareness' which explicitly resists operational structures. They would propose their work as source book (and thus ignore the considerable ideological prestige of their project) and leave the teacher to make of it what he or she will. In this, they are trapped between the two positions I have parodied. They try to be agents of both

---

[11] In support of this analysis it is worth pointing out how often the words 'competence' and 'technique' appear in the books.
See particularly the chapter in *Exploring Language*, 'Language and Society'. 'Competence' means, quite untechnically, just that.

the needs of the technocracy[12] and the liberal imagination. They fail in this, just as they fail to understand the historical point of modern English teaching. Their mistakes depend upon a strategy of non-alignment with existing ideologies – a perhaps wilful or irresponsible strategy; certainly one that involves error.

1. *The mistake about intentions in teaching literature.* In Mr Doughty's *Paper 5*, 'Linguistics and the Teaching of Literature' (1968), there is an extremely fluent account of how literary study goes forward (either as text-, information-, or experience-based), but he fails to diagnose the intentions behind this work. (Intentions not being at all the same as goals, aims or objectives.) These would be (I take it) to discover the quality or *value* latent in the language, and the language as the symbolic rendering of the experience. This is presumably the point (*sc.* intention) of all Mr Doughty's three kinds of English teaching: as education of 'the life-flame' (Holbrook),[13] of the social conscience (Fred Flower),[14] of the creative writer (Marjorie Hourd).[15] They hope in their various ways to answer Leavis' famous questions – 'what for? what ultimately for? What do men live by?' Where does the essential life of a society flow? And in answering such questions, the English teachers will take up all kinds of language – TV, advertising, newspapers, are familiar examples.

2. *The mistake about literature as 'merely one highly idiosyncratic form'.* What does this mean? In a history without the blessings of the camera and electronic circuitry, writing (black marks on white paper) is bound to be our main source of information. In that case does the 'literature' of the seventeenth century include the Levellers' pamphlets, Lilburne's defence, the Putney debates? Or does the nineteenth century include, as well as *The Mask of Anarchy* (oh yes, that's a poem), the Chartist hymns, Engels' 1844 report from Manchester, or Captain Swing's great circular:

> Sir your name is down among the Black hearts in the Black book and this is to advise you and the like of you who are parson justasses, to make your wills. Ye have been the black-

---

[12] One of them has, in a reply to an earlier draft of this chapter. See Mr Doughty's paper 'Children also Use Language to Live', *English in Education*, Spring 1972.

[13] E.g. in *English for Maturity* (Cambridge 1961).

[14] F. D. Flower, *Language and Education* (Longman 1966).

[15] M. L. Hourd, *The Education of the Poetic Spirit* (Heinemann 1949).

guard enemies of the people on all occasions, ye have not
done as ye ought. Swing.

Does, finally, the twentieth century include *The British Gazette* for
May 1926, or the issue of *Picture Post* after the Beveridge Report,
or *A Propos of Lady Chatterley's Lover*, or Kennedy's speech to
the nation on 17 October 1962, or Chomsky on Vietnam?; or indeed, to go beyond literature to creative forms very familiar to the
English teacher, does it include *Ashes and Diamonds* or the 1964
election *Panorama* (none of which is exactly an accidental choice).
Which of these things is 'merely one, highly idiosyncratic form'?

I choose an eclectic variety to stress that I am not standing in the
boots of the innocent reactionary (though better there than in the
boots of the flow-chartists). The objection I make stands on its own:
it is that what literature means as a specialist term is not what it
means in our lives. The elaborate classifications learned by heart
for the examiners – the taxonomies of genre: picaresque and social
realist novels, sonnets and *vers libre*, revenge and character tragedy
– these are the results of taking art to the market for purchase. Dead
for a docket. The uses of literacy are many, and the boundary between *True Confessions* and Esther Summerson's true confessions
in *Bleak House* is not marked by a simple brick wall. But the objection that literature is more than a scholarly specialism is also linked
to the first mistake. The intention in the study of literature is to
register and agree upon the relative significance of the experience
rendered in the words. Leavis again: 'where does this come?' 'How
does it stand in relation to . . .' That is to say, a 'narrow' concentra-
tion on literature may be merely the arid application of a disinherited scholiast or it may be a consistent effort to define a satisfactory language of values – an effort which will *necessarily* concentrate on the most intense and serious occasions upon which
men have tried to say what they mean (*sic*). This leads directly to
the third mistake.

3. *The mistake about narrowness.* The efforts of the English
teachers, even in their charismatic or Holbrookian robes, have represented a decisive response to the culture. They have resisted the
divisions of labour encoded in the different technical grammars of
the culture by attempting to find and speak up for 'a central, a
truly human point of view'. They have – under the impulse, no
doubt, of *Scrutiny* – located that centrality in the suburban back

garden of liberal individualism. There are worse places for it to be. These teachers have taught the primacy of the individual sensibility, the unflinching need to keep your private self your own and clear, spontaneous, intelligible, and full of life. They have carried forward such teaching with some antique conceptual weaponry, picked up from Wordsworth here and J. S. Mill there, but it is a more than historical accident that this ideology has suggested a mode of dissent from late capitalist and industrial society and a purchase point for the individual sensibility upon the smooth, impassive surfaces of technology.

To call this approach 'restricted' is to misread its cultural bearings. The position has radical shortcomings, but it is deliberate and it gives the work of the English teacher meaning.

4. *The omission of meaning and morality.* The fourth, central objection to *Language in Use* is that it can supply no such meaning. I do not mean what the anonymous teacher I quoted meant when he called the books 'terribly boring'. My criticism is that although every page of the suggested exercises is heavily value-laden (values which are never arraigned for interrogation), there is no proposal to study *how* it is that language carries its values, or how that coding changes. Obviously the authors know that language carries values; the decision not to study the morphology of these values must therefore have been conscious. But why? It is not a matter of keeping the work 'value-free', for one can describe values and their changes without espousing them. It looks like simple timidity. In the study of values we are in the very difficult and creatively human zone where the conservative codings of language are retrieved and transformed by unprecedented and radical groupings.[16] If he ignores this form of action, and the reservoirs of social experience which it both expends *and* replenishes, the language teacher frees himself from anything but technical training. His ignorance empties language of morality.

5. *The omission of the agent.* Of course the authors may object that they know language is value-heavy but that 'it is not their position to impose' any value-picture. They may say that the work proposed gives any amount of opportunity for the exercise of the individual teacher's value-judgements but 'they have no right' etc. to insist on these. This would be to dodge the issue. For they have

---

[16] This is an extremely compressed account of Osgood's theory about the dialectic of language and social values.

already smuggled a contraband value-system and world picture into the structure of concepts and assumptions which order the work so firmly. In order to evacuate their programme of a value-system they are obliged to suppress certain key inquiries, about how roles are assigned, and how they may be rejected. That they understand the possibility of rejection is notified by the remark

> [the school] will certainly give to any pupil a strong sense
> of the kinds of classroom participation that go with different
> systems of verbal control that are to be found within it. The
> English Department frequently feels the force of this, just
> because the teaching of literature is likely to encourage
> vigorous departures from the ways of speaking that pupils
> will have come to expect.[17]

But their theory of language (so far as I can see) gives no such point of departure for breaking with the expectations. The whole bent of this work is, like so much liberal sociology (and this sort of linguistics is a sociology of language), deeply determinist. It is even genteel. We are in a Durkheimian world where, just as they enforce the distribution of suicide, the changeless divisions of labour enforce the changeless modes of speech.

In this world the preoccupation with appropriateness which transpires from so much of the work looks more like a latter-day preoccupation with 'talking properly', a sort of technocrat's elocution lesson, than an adequate model of language and its transformations. It is precisely this series of specialisms which the English teacher, in trying to build a human idiom with his pupils, is resisting. On these terms the unit of work for the study of religious language (for example) has no means of telling the difference between Alan Bennett's sermon in *Beyond the Fringe* and John Donne's at Whitehall. Work of this kind *endorses* the perpetuation of stereotypes. And its hierarchies of 'competence' leave no place for a directness of utterance which subverts or flouts the given roles.

Such directness can come from a child's conversation with an adult. (What is it for that register to be appropriate? What questions does the rule of thumb dodge away from?) It can come from literature. This quotation hardly sounds as though it comes from the greatest work of philosophy of the last twenty-five years (the

---

[17] 'Linguistics and the teaching of literature', p. 81.

questions it asks are much to the point of these criticisms of linguistics):

> Someone tells me 'Wait for me by the bank'. Question: Did
> you *as you were saying the word,* mean this bank? – This
> question is of the same kind as 'Did you intend to say such-
> and-such to him on your way to meet him?'. It refers to a
> definite time (the time of walking, as the former question refers
> to the time of speaking) – but not to an experience during
> that time. Meaning is as little an experience as intending.
> But what distinguishes them from experience? They have
> no experience content. For the contents (images for instance)
> which accompany and illustrate them are not the meaning
> or intending. The intention *with which* one acts does not
> 'accompany' the action any more than the thought 'accom-
> panies' speech. Thought and intention are neither 'articulated'
> nor 'non-articulated'; to be compared neither with a single
> note which sounds during the acting or speaking, nor with
> a tune. 'Talking' (whether out loud or silently) and 'thinking'
> are not concepts of the same kind; even though they are in
> closest connection.[18]

These remarks about the relations of intending to meaning in an utterance, and of both to experience, provide the moment to generalise out of these two or three manuals about language in the fourth and fifth years of secondary school to the whole study of our systems of communication which is the real subject of this book. The discussion of communications (in the slippery phrase, the mass media) in both everyday and educational contexts makes little regular place for the study of the intentionality without which an object cannot have meaning. It cannot signify. Significance, therefore, both in the sense of transmitted meaning and of received value, is the issue (*sic*) of communications. The tradition of English social science which has best understood this, and developed ways of studying intentionality, has been literary and cultural criticism. Its practitioners have now a lot to learn from modern philosophers as well as communication theorists of all sorts, but especially in schools they have held tight on to the 'disciplined and mature preoccupation with value' in speech as being the defining characteristic

[18] Ludwig Wittgenstein, *Philosophical Investigations* (Basil Blackwell 1953), ll. 217e.

as well as the point of their work. What Wittgenstein says and the way he says it sharpen this point enormously. His way of writing breaks decisively with normative philosophy (compare Russell's patrician prose). Expression is changed in the *Investigations* by a man of genius; so also is the way we see the world. This is how T. S. Eliot put it, and he is another example of genius changing language and therefore the world.

In short, what is left out of the linguists' scheme of language is the human agent as agent and not role selector. (What classical role theory leaves out of account is how a person makes choices among the multiplicity of roles available.) Think of Lawrence's kind of encounter, instead of Erving Goffman's. Nothing self-conscious here about the presentation of self in everyday life. So –

> I feel I'm the superior of most men I meet. Not in birth,
> because I never had a great-grandfather. Not in money
> because I've got none. Not in education, because I'm merely
> scrappy. And certainly not in beauty or manly strength.
>   Well, what then?
>   Just in myself.
>   When I'm challenged, I do feel myself superior to most of
> the men I meet. Just a natural superiority. But not till there
> enters an element of challenge. When I meet another man, and
> he is just himself – even if he is an ignorant Mexican pitted
> with smallpox – then there is no question between us of
> superiority or inferiority. He is a man and I am a man. We
> are ourselves. There is no question between us. But let a
> question arise, let there be a challenge, and then I feel he
> should do reverence to the gods in me, because they are more
> than the gods in him. And he should give reverence to the
> very me, because it is more at one with the gods than is his
> very self.
>   If this is conceit, I am sorry. But it's the gods in me that
> matter. And in other men. As for me, I am glad to salute the
> brave, reckless gods in another man. So glad to meet a man
> who will abide by his very self. Ideas! Ideals! All this paper
> between us. What a weariness. If only people would meet in
> their very selves, without wanting to put some ideas over one
> another, or some ideal. Damn all ideas and all ideals. Damn
> all the false stress, and the pins.

I am I. Here am I. Where are you? Ah, there you are!
That's my idea of democracy, if you can call it an idea.[19]

To speak like this is to speak as a free man. Language, class and self-consciousness have become one. But such speech is hardly a matter of appropriateness in the society and the education reflected by *Language in Use*; it is omitted from the curriculum by the programme. This cancellation from the map of speech demoralises the language at its centre.

6. *The omission of history.* It is logically necessary that if speech is thus frozen stiff in its roles, it is emptied not only of human agency, and therefore of morality, but also of history. This is the last and most radical criticism. *Language in Use* is atemporal. There is therefore the added objection to the moral emasculation of Shakespeare or George Eliot, searched out for speech strategies, that they are also offered as ready meat for an ahistorical sociology. Not 'what could their lives have meant to them?' but 'how does small talk structure the diversity of experience in *Hamlet*?' (E7).

Language in Use has no use for history.[20] This is not just punning. The uses of literacy are a product of our history, and to ignore the changes in that history is to commit a moral error. It is to ransack the past for our present purposes. But the omission is consistent. A demoralised language is by definition placed out of reach of time, because time coded the language with its values.

I I I

I am trying to indicate some central contradictions and conceptual errors in a complete ideology. Language studies in various forms propose a very complete revision of the English teacher's world-picture. *Language in Use* and Penguin primers like *Lost for Words* and *Language, the Learner and the School*[21] would, I think, see much of their ground as common. All propose the close descriptive scrutiny of everyday verbal transactions; all see the understanding of appropriate use and role as necessary to learning. In these cursorily

---

[19] *Studies in Classic American Literature* (1923), p. 112.
[20] Unit C4 contains the only brief exception to this acquisitive rule.
[21] J. W. P. Creber *Lost for Words: Language and Educational Failure* (Penguin 1972); D. Barnes, J. Britton, H. Rosen, *Language, the Learner and the School* (Penguin 1969).

summarised circumstances I want to turn to James Britton's book, *Language and Learning*.[22]

I take his book at this point because I believe it will be a critical force in encouraging language study of many different kinds. The book marks a sharp break with the radical tradition of English teaching. It is also the product of a courteous, finely bred and intelligent mind. Its author is both gentle and gentlemanly. I assimilate him to the language study movement in general in spite of the obvious discrepancies and his far greater civilisation, because *Language and Learning* also empties language of morality and its history. It only gestures towards the difficulties involved in understanding an art and its culture. When he quotes Susanne Langer as affirming the manifold and symbolic forms of art-speech, Britton is surely re-entering that arid tournament between mind and feeling, reason and imagination, body and soul, perpetuation of which simply serves to underline the defeats that art has suffered since the Romantic poets initiated the tradition of cultural dissidence. That is, he votes for the forms of language which define the liberal and law-abiding self. There is something almost madly irresponsible about such a choice at this time of day. Not only has the cultivation of the sensibility done nothing for the many children who could not learn to speak its language from many kindly instructors; it is also helpless in the world of power. It has no authority over public places. Art-speech of this sort – on this *pedagogic* definition, not what is there in great poems – is private capital. It has no social purchase. Britton has seen that the radical promise has failed; children have not won themselves for themselves by poetry. But he does not know why it has failed. He cannot tell us what else to do with speech.

> History may be servitude,
> History may be freedom. See, now they vanish,
> The faces and places, with the self which, as it could, loved
> them,
> To become renewed, transfigured, in another pattern.[23]

The pattern is the problem. Think of a few experiences of written language : Adam Smith's letter on the death of Hume, Fielding's *Diary of a Journey to Lisbon*, Keats' letter to Wodehouse on 22 September 1819, Mill's last letter to Stirling. Or in different accents,

[22] Allen Lane, The Penguin Press 1970; Penguin 1972.
[23] T. S. Eliot, 'Little Gidding', in *Four Quartets* (Faber & Faber 1943).

think of Chapter 1 in Milovan Djilas' *The Unperfect Society*, of Lenin's pamphlet *What is to be Done?*, Sartre's letter from the Resistance in Paris in early 1945, of Guevara's last letter to his ten-year-old daughter. These are all great poems. They fill one's mind to the brim. They alter the mind. They are profound and civilised in all their details. They become a part of one's life. But Britton cannot tell us what to do with such experiences. He provides the old ideology in a new dark suit. Left to themselves, children and students hear such voices on their own, the listener's terms. They do not hear that the voices tell them across time and geography of the freedom and the goodness which they could make for themselves. And the good liberal will not tell them either.

For someone of his orientation it is astonishing at this time of day that his chapter 'Language and Thought' can stop short at the lucid psychological model out of Vygotsky and early Bruner which Britton describes. I am bothered not simply by his failure to mention the efforts of the philosophers since Wittgenstein and Austin, particularly in Stuart Hampshire's (for Britton) indispensable *Thought and Action*, but his critical omission of the major conceptual revisions, especially in the difficult relations between language, society and behaviour, which Britton is attempting to integrate. What is it to act independently? What speech is due to yourself, and what to your culture? What is art for, if you are bombed-out and starving? Britton takes too little care of this. His developmental graph is innocently linear and chronological; his images of self are still peopling an Eden without genetics or international mass murder.

Just as crippling is his failure to see right through the argument about the *identity* of language and thought – the classically English epistemology (though born of Wittgenstein) that language alone makes reality knowable, and that its manifold, dark, electric mobility renders impossible the antique classifications of the well-tempered Piagetian. To say this is not to go in for Nietzschean or vacant interstellar spaces. Imagination will create more difficulties than it solves. As Bernard Williams writes in an essay much to our point, 'with regard to the self, the imagination is too tricky a thing to provide a reliable road to the comprehension of what is logically possible'.[24]

[24] 'Imagination and the Self', *Studies in the Philosophy of Thought and Action*, P. F. Strawson (ed.) (Oxford 1968), p. 213. Reprinted in *Problems of the Self* (Cambridge 1973), and quoted below, p. 216.

What is needed is a much more delicate and varied (one might have said, literary-critical) account of what it is to say that to understand a communication 'is to know under what conditions one who utters it says something true'.[25] The curricular imperative which follows looks simple and traditional: that children should learn to tell the truth. What Britton gives us instead is a version of a now familiar ideology which complements much of *Language in Use* and serves to close the circles of thought to history and to social movement.

> We can add, of course, that protest or reform or revolution always draws into its train individuals who are working out their own private grievance, their own sicknesses: with the consequent danger that, as Yeats puts it in a similar situation:
>
> > Mere anarchy is loosed upon the world,
> > The blood-dimmed tide is loosed, and everywhere
> > The ceremony of innocence is drowned.
>
> To distinguish the healing tide from the blood that muddies it, to discern what must be trusted and what must be cured – this remains the problem.
>
> Putting that problem aside, and thinking of the rising generations more generally, we have to trust them for their own sakes: there is in the long run no viable alternative. For teachers whose concern does not go beyond the ordered framework in which a class may work, there is the alternative of so managing that situation that individuals have no power and eventually no will to break his rules. He may even hope, though forlornly in most cases, that this habit of conformity will spread to life outside the classroom. For parents, and for teachers whose concern is for the individuals themselves, the alternative to trusting them is to try to be them, to live their lives for them. And this of course is a long, anxious road into failure. It is themselves that they must become; and Carl Rogers (as we have seen) takes this to mean a positive act of committal on their part.[26]

These are the head-magisterial accents and reflexes: 'Putting that

---

25 P. F. Strawson's inaugural address, *Meaning and Truth* (Oxford 1970), p. 24.
26 *Language and Learning*, p. 270.

problem aside, and thinking of the rising generations more generally . . .' Britton gives us the liturgy of our modern and educational
neo-liberalism: the nervous decency, the generosity and helplessness, the anxious rejection of moral decision and diagnosis, the
forlorn hope that 'All shall be well, and all manner of thing shall
be well.' I do not want to talk like a colour-supplement apocalyptic
but we have passed the time when we can suppose that 'they will
become themselves' and that what we must do is leave them to it,
while giving them a tape recorder and as much room to talk in as
we can clear. I am grateful for Professor Britton's manner and
style, for his charm, his cultivated eclecticism and his strong personal sympathy; but his book has no heart or stomach. It gives us a
useful and sometimes moving summary of one girl's developing
command of literacy and of herself. Its disheartened condition, its
broken nerve can give us little else. The gradual and gentle growth
towards maturity well described in *Language and Learning* flourishes in ground held by cash. The comparable social confidence
which generalises from that individual experience is without heirs
and in ruins.

IV

Linguists say that they are trying to devise an adequate theory of
language and its contexts. This is necessarily impossible without a
theory of culture. What we need to work out is a culture-based
curriculum for English and for anything else. Acquisitiveness about
subjects ('English first and foremost') has been a chronological
accident; English teachers noticed the state of culture first. The
alleged techniques of rationalisation are pointless because affecting
someone's world-picture simply is not a subject for the flow-
diagram grid. (Critical path analysis is only slightly more fatuous
when applied to teaching than when applied to the giant corporations.)

Our aims, assumptions and short-term experiences all mix up together. What we need is a theory of culture which, in spite of gaps,
tensions and irresolvable contradictions – and to honour these has
been a main activity in literature – answers our sense of what it
means to be alive in today's world. We need a sequence of quite
simple, short-term intentions – let's discuss poverty, let's finish this
poem, let's read this play – related to an adequate cultural map.

Knowledge as power

For we are all of us figures in a living politics. The great poets of childhood of the past – Blake, Rousseau, Dickens, Emerson, Wordsworth, Froebel, Freud, Lawrence – have always known this. Certainly Chomsky, Fromm, Erikson, Polanyi, Bruner, have declared that they have learned it, hard and sharp all over again. If we don't learn the same contingent truths, language won't have a use; it will merely become another of the working instruments handed out by our masters.

86

4

Social immobility and the examination system

One of the breaking points of the liberal teacher's faith which I described in the first chapter is the examination system. It is there that the fit between liberal education and the bureaucratic function of schools as selector for the job-market is particularly clear. At that point a wedge can be inserted and the two prised apart. But the incorrigibly Fabian nature of teachers' consciousness leads them to suppose that a changed examination system to fit new interdisciplinary and team-taught curricula will guarantee liberation. I think this idea is a fallacy, though it is absolutely right to see exams as the critical point of change and the focus of arguments about ideology and education. To lay claim, as many teachers in Britain do, to the exemption of educational matters from ideological adherence, is simply to convict oneself of blindness. To allege freedom from ideology is itself an ideological act, and to argue that examinations as a centrepiece in educational structures have strictly educational significance is to fall into the same error of supposing that a very local set of affairs is not contingent and alterable. For the lifetime of modern education – let us say, since the 1902 Education Act – the national examination system has acted as an increasingly refined filtering system for the requirements of a society at a given stage in its development.

We now know that the tests which Cyril Burt and others began to devise in the 1920s and which purported for the first time to assign educational places on the basis of innate intelligence and not the privileges of birth, marked out the ground along the same tracks already deeply scored in the land by cash and class. These tests, as they were developed, served to underpin the unbreakable divisions of the School Certificate with the intelligence quotient. The notorious assertions on the part of the Norwood Committee's report (1943) on school curricula in turn defined three universal types of human ability in order to fill the three types of schools available — types of school which provided the manpower (intellectual, practical, manual) for a changing technology. These assertions, so simply reflecting the distributions of power, wealth and privilege in Britain, held through, and hold still in many places. Their rhetoric may be read in the system of 'banding' in many modern comprehensives and in the extremely elaborate examination structure which is both cause, effect, and legitimation of that heaven-sent system. We have 'A' level, 'O' level, and CSE; we have universities, polytechnics and colleges of further or teacher education; we have HNC, ONC and City and Guilds. Within this relentlessly tripartite structure we also find another, latent ideology, and it is one which is radically challenged and in part subverted by the present movement towards the integrated curriculum and the examinations of this form which will inevitably follow. I doubt very much whether many devout apologists for the well-integrated curriculum and its timetable have identified its socially transforming nature.

Now what we see in the traditional structures of educational knowledge is a powerful system of insulated and exclusive 'frames'.[1] Within each insulation rests a highly specific 'classification' of contents, the sequences, transmission and evaluation of which are widely known and accepted. Thus, learning traditional mathematics via Euclidean geometry and seventeenth-century algebra was and is an elaborately graded and paced sequence of exercises and theorems explained, practised and assessed by a controlling teacher: the tightly bonded system of controlled instruction assumed not only that certain concepts depended on the satisfactory prior acquisition of other concepts, but that certain forms of knowledge, certain skills and techniques necessarily followed by a developmental order. Logarithms came *after* long division; meteorology after rivers. What one finds, therefore, acting as manifest legitimation for much of the secondary school curriculum, is a vulgar developmental graph written by a *lumpen*-Piagetian. What, however, serves more latently to justify things-as-they-are is a confused and inflexible allocation

---

[1] Much of the terminology and subsequent analysis here I take again from Basil Bernstein, 'On the Classification and Framing of Educational Knowledge', in *Class, Codes, Control* (Routledge & Kegan Paul 1971). I also owe much to discussions with Ioan Davies, and to his paper 'The Management of Knowledge: A Critique of the Use of Typologies in Educational Sociology', *Sociology* 4, 1, January 1970.

of knowledge according to the existing lines of a country's politics and the hidden rituals and superstitions which secure that political order. Mary Douglas describes the process:

> Society [is] a house with rooms and corridors in which passage from one to another is dangerous. Danger lies in transitional states; simply because transition is neither one state nor the next, it is undefinable. The person who must pass from one to another is himself in danger and emanates danger to others.
>
> The danger is controlled by ritual which precisely separates him from his old status, segregates him for a time and then publicly declares his entry to his new status. Not only is transition itself dangerous, but also the rituals of segregation are the most dangerous phase of the rites. So often do we read that boys die in initiation ceremonies, or that their sisters and mothers are told to fear for their safety, or that they used in the old days to die from hardship or fright, or by supernatural punishment for their misdeeds. Then somewhat tamely come the accounts of the actual ceremonies which are so safe that the threats of danger sound like a hoax. But we can be sure that the trumped-up dangers express something important about marginality. To say that the boys risk their lives says precisely that to go out of the formal structure and to enter the margins is to be exposed to power that is enough to kill them or make their manhood. The theme of death and rebirth, of course, has other symbolic functions: the initiates die to their old life and are reborn to the new. The whole repertoires of ideas concerning pollution and purification are used to mark the gravity of the event and the power of ritual to remake a man – this is straightforward.[2]

Notions of purity in the transmission and withholding of educational knowledge complicate themselves with notions of suitability and compatibility. Thus, the long, rancorous quarrel at the University of Cambridge as to whether the upstart discipline sociology could merit an examination of its own, let alone a professor; thus, too, the difficulty of allying 'impure' combinations of 'A' level subjects, say, English, Biology, Politics (a subject almost impossible

---

[2] Mary Douglas, *Purity and Danger* (Routledge & Kegan Paul 1966), pp. 116–17.

to take at 'A' level in any case); thus, finally, the strong rules of subordination implicit in the discrepancies between the 'A' and 'D' stream syllabuses. 'I am bright; I shall study Italian: you are middling; you shall learn Geography; he/she is dim; he/she shall do Metalwork/Domestic Science.' They are all, however, servants to a power-elite; the verb of educational declension proceeds largely to deny secondary school pronouns any access whatever to anthropology, psychology, prehistory, to the economics of modern capitalism, to the history of Asia, or to post-Heisenberg physics. The structure of subjects generated by strong insulation is confirmed by other boundaries: those drawn between what is held to be suitable educational knowledge and what it is improper to bring into the classroom. This extra-curricular knowledge comprises almost all the social and moral knowledge and experience which the child takes from his immediate community. Folklore, TV programmes, sport, local recipes, Trade Unions, gynaecology, sexuality are counted outside the permitted ambits of educational knowledge *unless* the child falls below the line[3] marking off those who are considered educable by the educational system. Then, in sympathetic but largely uncomprehending response to the visible alienation of half our future, and the irretrievable injury done to their intellectual identity by the complex cruelties of initiation into national knowledge, we have drawn up a new curriculum for that well-known spectre, the less able child.

It is not, however, the structure of knowledge which alone generates the atomised and individualist treatment of knowledge which we see pictured and magnified in the education system. This structure necessarily confirms itself by the transmission of its classifications and boundaries by the specialists whose intellectual identity often depends on that continued and successful transmission. Thus the specialist teaches his subject, and controls the speed, sequence, and occasions at and on which the pupils shall acquire the hierarchies and knowledge and body of concepts of that subject.

II

Thus far, I have described the structure of knowledge and the means of its transmission as exemplified by the national examination system; within this structure most British teachers have grown up

[3] Drawn of course by the Newsom Committee in *Half Our Future* (1963).

and acquired their professional identity. That structure is faithfully maintained by examinations which allocate power, privilege, status and income. It is this situation which any call for integrated examinations must understand. Consequently *any* movement towards an 'integrated' pattern of examining must recognise its own deeply subversive potentialities. For a system of examinations which was based on an integrated curriculum would rest upon the following changed conditions:

1. The collective acquisition of knowledge and skills.

2. A non-hierarchical and very much more loose-textured classification of that knowledge.

3. The informal storage and retrieval of that knowledge.

4. The necessarily softened and altered boundaries between subjects and, much more importantly, between educational and extramural knowledge and experience, which in turn mean that the knowledge is informally transmitted.

These changed conditions would enforce certain consequences. From the first condition, it follows that the traditional testing of the individual's acquisitive prowess (the pupil as *rentier*) is no longer possible. If the work has been performed collectively, it must be tested collectively, or we violate a main premise of liberalism, fairness. It would seem intellectually indelicate to teach collective, integrated and group work and then to assess it individually. (The indelicacy doesn't alter the fact that this is what will happen.) From the second condition it follows that there can be no simple testing of recalled information, but rather the attempt to assess ways of knowing and inquiring. Not only that. It also follows that with different criteria for the assembly and sequence of the curriculum, conventions of order, difficulty and autonomy become soluble and interchangeable. In these circumstances not only must new ways of knowing (e.g. psychological or political ways) appear in the curriculum, but also a good deal of extramural knowledge and experience will become relevant inside the walls of the school.

From the third condition it follows that an examination can no longer be a timed affair in which candidates are required to write out answers in formal, more or less official prose. Because the modes of working enforce different ways of perceiving and learning, students will store what they learn in a variety of ways: in notes, on tape, in brief talks, in tables of figures, in articles, creative work, photography, film, and so on. It would clearly be unreasonable to expect them to retrieve this in a uniform and generalised disquisition. Indeed the nature of much material (for example, palaeography; ecological inquiry; demographic movement) would by definition make this form of retrieval impossible. Finally, from the last condition it follows that the informal transmission of knowledge and the greatly enlarged areas of choice opened to pupils and teachers which would result, also mean that assessment becomes much less specific. The criteria rest not upon a recognised body of knowledge, nor upon recognised modes of exposition; they can only rest upon general agreement about the purposes and intentions of learning. I shall later argue that such agreement is impossible and that consequently integrated curricula, whose outlines are seen most nakedly in public examinations, will serve to emphasise the profound contradictions of our educational intentions, and the moral crisis which, in turn, lies behind these contradictions.

For the present, however, let us consider the implications of the four changed conditions and the consequences which I argue will necessarily follow them. For they involve a wholesale upheaval in the way teachers have seen their own authority, and that authority as embodied in the secure systems of a particular subject. They must see themselves as challenged by the novel need to teach with their colleagues watching and to share what they know with them. Such a challenge may lead not to an authentic community of inquirers, but on the contrary to an embarrassed restriction of method and material, to a deep-seated conformism. The examining which results may then assess only the lowest common multiple of such dismal collaboration. In our culture there is no inevitable salvation to be found by the wholesale abandonment of atomised theories of knowledge, for the examinations which confirm and strengthen those theories will only reflect the social forms and intentions which are there. Now these theories, I have said, when they are so altered as to require the new forms symbolised in an integrated curriculum, will further alter the way a teacher sees his authority, and will profoundly affect that part of his intellectual identity and self-respect which is bound up with a particular discipline. With these changes there may go a loss of confidence which will issue in banal formlessness. I think one can see this in much allegedly 'integrated' teaching in schools. If this happens, then the consequent examination system will depend, certainly, on a changed map of knowledge and the bearings by which to reach it. But it does not at all follow that this will lead to more flexible, independent and audacious powers of self-discovery on the part of those who learn how to read the map. Deprived of the zeal and self-confidence which a single discipline can provide, especially when it has the powerful historical sanctions which give the structure of a subject objective reality, teachers may resort to assessing the LCM of their methods.

What we shall then find will be an increase in conformism and in the shared informality of the teaching styles. The significance of charisma in a teacher is likely to diminish. Fear – a sometimes irresistible source of energy in learning – which a student may feel before a teacher of force and complexity in full stride, will disappear. Instead the student will maintain much more friendly and casual links with the teacher, and his important reference is likely to be made to the group with whom he is working. It will then become difficult for any examination system to express the vigour and idiosyncrasy of individual teachers or ways of teaching. Instead the system will ask for evidence that the candidates are competent in the techniques of inquiry across certain topics or themes. In the uncertainty as to what constitutes the subject and without a sanctioned system of evaluation, the examinations which teachers devise may seek only to identify the efficiency of a candidate's information system. Can we apply the techniques of inquiry and storage which he has practised? It will be hard, unless we are prepared for a much greater degree of intellectual disturbance and clarification than has shown up so far, for a pupil to attach significance and meaning to what he finds. Examinations will therefore remain the assessment of competence as to means, and will as before deny the presence of ends. They will, however, require very different methods of validation. Since they will depend on very much more varied materials and upon modes of thought and perception rather than bodies of knowledge, the pupil or candidate needs to put very different kinds of material on display to those which have traditionally represented his examination answers Not only will a candidate display his work much more informally, but that work will involve revealing many more personal aspects of behaviour than traditionally go on record.

This process has been particularly evident in the systems of course assessment already devised on some CSE boards. In English, for example, it has become normative in CSE and in several 'O' level boards for candidates to submit course work which will contain a good deal of personal and creative writing. There is extensive oral examining, the criteria for which must finally render down to an assessment of a candidate's moral and social adequacy in an extremedly peculiar situation, the implicit message of which is, 'Now let's see whether you can carry off a conversation like a decent, well-set-up, decorously subordinate social class 3(2) kind of person?' Insofar as this examining is carried out by the same teacher whom the pupils see day-by-day, the informal penetration of each sensibility by the systems of late capitalist technology nears completion. For the same man or woman who is called upon to examine, and therefore to allocate pupils to a particular social and economic position, is also required, by the terms of teaching an ingrated curriculum, to be informal guide, casual encyclopaedia, manager, tipster, confidant and friend to the pupils. Thus, the teachers who know the behaviour of the pupils in very varied and sociable ways will then be responsible to a central authority for correct reports on the competencies of the children. There are deep paradoxes and contradictions here. On the one hand if, as I have suggested is possible, integrated work diffuses and weakens the intimacies of teachers and pupils so that the collaborative teaching becomes the supervision of committees and the transmission of skills, then the pupils have no means of assigning value and significance to what they do. If, however, integrated work leads to the far deeper penetration of a pupil's personal feelings and ideas than we have seen so far, then to that extent the control of his or her education has been vastly extended over areas of the self which ought to remain private. We have already seen this happen when teachers bring extramural experience into the classroom in order to interest the fifth-year April leavers and further to exert controls over their bloodymindedness which the *absence* of formal examinations[4] has liberated for intermittently extravagant shows of truculence. But the contradiction in *assessment* which I have argued comes out neatly in this quotation from a story written for me by a thirteen-year-old boy, solitary, reticent, and withdrawn.

> The old man sat all over the tiny, sturdy fishing stool, his
> bottom spread across the canvas in his vast trousers, wrinkled

---

[4] I have not atempted to analyse here the function of examinations as a form of social control. The cant word is 'incentive'.

and loose and flabby looking like the behind of an elephant.
    The little boy turned up a white eager face and watched
him lean hugely back and the rod bend a little and flip up.
The small fish flew through the air, and glittered as it flew,
glittered like a scrap of rainbow. The little boy caught it.
    'We've got a fish, we've got a fish.' He jigged about.
    The old man leaned forward. He creaked in his throat.
    'Nahr' its only a fuckin tiddler. Frow the fuckin thing back.
We'll get plenty biggern' im, ah tellz yuh.'
    And the youngster had to throw it back, and look pale and
strained.

This is obviously a remarkable piece of writing for a boy – showing off here and there, anxious to please (and to shock) the teacher,
but with a real ear for cadence and rhythm, and with a gift for
catching something of authentic speech. The minor, pointless
obscenities are dead right for the old man. This is writing which
evidences a spirit looking for and finding meaning in created experience. Very well, submit it to the examiner. And he too will
recognise these qualities and surely give the passage a high grade.
Yet the award then is given for certain temperamental and creative
energies on the part of the candidate. The basis for allocation to a
profitable place in the filter is his human sympathy rendered in his
creative prose. Yet such sympathy is scarcely what is required of
him by many of the jobs he gains in this way. In his later roles therefore he has to learn to eradicate it : to substitute for his quick, vivid
powers of evaluation that homogenised, vague humanitarianism
which passes with our society for the milk of human kindness. The
function of the examination and the ideology of the teacher who
examines do not begin to square with each other. It is to this crux
that I now return.

III

One undoubtedly beneficial consequence of the upheaval in curricula and examinations is that the debate about substantive ends in
education may be reopened. In the very fluid state of many curricula and the inevitable uncertainty about evaluation, sequence
and contents, there is clear need for the extensive public discussion
which could stay silent as long as educational knowledge remained

within the tradition. This discussion will involve all teachers and, in some cases, students and pupils as well. And this will provide one of the first points of open conflict. Not, I mean, between teachers and students, though obviously this occurs; but between two sorts of social tendency. For the movement towards integrated curricula is in part the product of technological change and changed economic requirements; in part it is also the product of changed theories of knowledge and learning, and of the redistribution of power and prestige which has followed the altered status of education in the West. There is a central, mutual resistance to identify. On one hand the demand of late industrial technology is for a very much more technically flexible manpower, able to retrain itself rapidly and adapt to altered frames of information without at the same time inquiring beyond the strictly technical culture about the ideological structure which contains it. On the other hand, there are signs within the educational systems of the West of a spasmodic but distinctive movement towards a break with the consensus. I do not simply mean May 1968 in France, or the English student sit-ins, though these are symptomatic. I am trying rather to isolate minority misgivings about the directions of industrial culture which transpire in a constellation of signs as varied as courses at new universities, the Schools Council Humanities Project,[5] the proposed changes in teacher training, the Society for Social Responsibility in Science, English teachers' lessons about the evils of advertising, students' councils instead of prefects in comprehensive schools, right through to primary children pinning up histograms of their traffic count outside the school gates. These contrary pulls – towards a criticism of industrial culture and away towards a mobilisation of education in order to meet the demands of productivity – are most visibly in opposition in public examinations. For the examinations, as I have argued, have been the rite of passage which initiates the pupils into the knowledge appropriate to their station and abilities. Yet in devising new examinations it is necessary to define what the criteria of judgement are: what shall be said to constitute adequate realisation (i.e. making real) of what has been learned? This necessity in turn throws the discussers back to defining what the ends of education are.

---

[5] I feel that this scheme takes deeply mistaken conceptual bearings. All the same, with unmistakably official backing, it puts into circulation no less unmistakably dissident forms of knowledge.

There is however no possible agreement in this discussion. There are those who would be happy to see education culminate, as it always has, in the examination rites which confer sufficient wealth, power and prestige according to the ancient social forms of the country. In changed technological circumstances these apologists acknowledge that although the rites themselves alter, and the specific distributions, their essential function remains the same. Hence the concept of the meritocrat which usefully deflects attention from the realities of inherited wealth and property and focusses upon the Protestant ideal of cash return for individual effort: works as the visible signs of grace. As in most versions of liberalism, the world is as it is, and radical change is either impossible or so uncomfortable as not to be worth the effort ('look at Russia/China/Cuba!'). Since we must assign everybody to a place in a fixed social order; since, indeed, they assign themselves inherently and all we need is an examination system which reads these coded assignations correctly – why then, A-streamers shall go to university and learn how best to run the new technology;[6] the B-streamers shall be subdivided amongst the Polytechnics and Further Education colleges and become more or less skilled archivists and maintenance men; the less able or C-streamers who are ready to leave and need no more education will do as they're told on the production lines and in the labour gangs of demolition crews or chainstores. Those who argue like this want only functional and never ideological change in examinations. Against them are ranged those who, while accepting that – in the interests of 'standards' – examinations are a necessity, see them as a scrupulous and searching exposure of a pupil's capacity to think, to feel, to respond articulately and to show himself his own man. Between the two, coloured deeply by versions of both ideologies, stand most teachers. So far as my reading extends, there is no decently argued presentation of the (very strong) case for the abandonment of examination assessment altogether in the interests of an image of education, the point of which may not be the classification of persons by their real or their alleged abilities nor by their putative contribution to the GNP.[7] It is perhaps enough in defence

---

6 The cant term is 'structure-innovate' (v.). The good liberal-technocrat's handbook is Donald Schon's Reith lectures in 1970, *The Stable State* (Penguin 1973).

7 I by-pass the now abundant statistical evidence that there is no observable relation between national economic behaviour and educational investment.

of this belief to say that it cannot be ultimately justifiable to deny any man who claims his right to attend it, education at any level, since that education is a matter of possessing his own. You may only say that there isn't enough to go round at the moment (which does *not* mean that you can't decide who is good and who is bad at education). In the absence of widespread opinion to this effect, most teachers, split within themselves by allegiance to the conflicting ideologies, will continue to suppose that examinations are inevitable.

Now it has been unforgettably said that 'this is an age when no one is blessed and reasonable and most are mad and unhappy. The task is to be unhappy but reasonable'.[8] It seems to me that any schoolteacher who is teaching an integrated curriculum towards an examination is unusually well-placed to understand reasonably the moral basis of his unhappiness. (If he thinks he is happy, then he has not noticed the incoherence amounting to madness of what he does.) Such a teacher has to live the central contradiction I have tried to identify: between his belief in a liberal, humanising, morally decent education and his function as taxonomist for industrial society. But he must go beyond this. In the exceptionally fluid conditions created by the chances of integrated work there is a necessity to make all the educational assumptions visible and explicit. To say this is to utter a tautology; there clearly cannot be an integrated curriculum unless teachers sort out what is being integrated. Thus (to say it again) to discuss an integrated curriculum, and specifically an integrated examination, is to discuss the ends of education.

But we are in a state of such moral confusion that agreement about these ends is impossible. There is only agreement of any kind that the ends of education should be roughly congruent with liberalism. And that liberalism even in its heyday largely defined itself in terms of a handful of moral imperatives of such generality that individual agents could not guide themselves by these imperatives. Indeed, for liberalism and the education which it has created the central act and paradigm of morality *is* the act of personal, unimpeded, rational choice. What you choose, is your business. Liberal education, then, amounts to clearing as large a space as possible for autonomous moral choice. In a morality which is hollow by programme it can-

[8] Alasdair MacIntyre, *Against the Self-Images of the Age* (Duckworth 1971), p. 87, following Pascal.

not really come as a surprise if the forces of a stronger ideology – the ethics of conspicuous consumption – rush in to occupy the vacuum. All the teachers are likely to agree upon is the need for as uninterrupted an exercise of individual liberty as possible. What you then do with that liberty, apart from helping others to gain it in your free (*sic*) time, it is a moral precept of liberalism not to be able to say. It follows that there can be no shared vision or ideal to confer significance on educational action. In these circumstances it is a comfortable quirk of liberalism born of the astonishingly successful compromises between classes which we find in English history since the 1912 strikes to suppose that what is, is pretty well what ought to be. This compromise is now perhaps beginning to break up. One agent in this slow fracture is the change of consciousness within education which I have tried to name.

The worst that can be said of integrated examinations is that they may lead, in the absence of agreed ends, to the public assessment of as many of the skills as are readily measured both by the psychometrician and by the job-market. This seems to me the most likely consequence. For where ends are in dispute, it follows that someone must be autocratic. The least offensive form of autocratic control will be the assessment of skills and competences. But in some areas of the curriculum, particularly those dealing with the human and social studies – even more markedly where, as in much contemporary English teaching, the line between educational and community knowledge is moved back – we may find an examination of personalities, of those dispositions and traits and moral characteristics which square with liberalism.[9] Neither kind of examination could be a reasonable resolution of educational confusion. The best that can be expected of integrated curricula-with-examinations is that, along with the unhappiness, they will force as many teachers as possible to make explicit and acknowledge the more insane contingencies of their work.

---

[9] I hope I don't need to emphasise that such personalities would include many who are not conformist or docile.

Part 3

Private identity and public culture

5

Rolling up the map of knowledge: Teacher training and inter-disciplinary study

The study of culture and the study of education meet in the training of teachers. It has been argued right through these pages that teachers need to find and are trying to shape a frame of mind, a state of consciousness which is better able to cope with the world as they find it. Under the impact of vague but irresistible historical forces – technology, economics, moral change – the lines of educational knowledge have altered drastically. I have tried to show something of the way in which states of knowledge create consciousness, in Parts 1 and 2. But as these processes go forward, the political and educational system tries to mediate them. It turns technology and moral change into work in the classroom and into the intellectual experience of students and children.

One well-known and inevitable version of this mediation has been the discovery that new social reality has come to distort the old lines of knowledge. The boundaries between the subjects become fluid and uncertain. But a 'subject' is itself only social-experience-become-intellectual-discipline and to see this is to understand that a hand in that 'becoming', a hand in making a discipline, is a unique source of social power.

As soon as a discipline is made, it tends to become fixed. When, in the present circumstances, people try to redraw their boundaries, they commonly stay within the area of what they know, but invite the participation of another specialist. Thence the strained politeness of those seminars under the heading literature-with-sociology or history-and-philosophy. The old discipline proceeds much in the old way and absorbs minor modifications as it goes along. It fails to bring itself into any relation with a whole scheme of knowledge. It further fails to consider its own structural and ideological nature. In teacher training, to come back to the form of higher education in which theory and practice are bound most intimately

together, the present inclination for innovatory studies has addition-
ally failed to set itself the important questions about moral ends
in education (either for the teachers or their pupils in school),
without which the training lapses into narrow technicality, academicism, and pointlessness.

It is just these charges from its students that a teacher-training
curriculum has to meet. And facing the charges is a matter, as I said
in Part I, of working out an ideology which meets present-day
conditions. This chapter, therefore, attempts two sorts of project.
The first is a matter of looking for success where I have named
failure: success in finding a curriculum which unites theory and
practice for a future teacher; success in understanding whereabouts
a certain kind of knowledge stands in its relations with other kinds;
and then, within that understanding, success in seeing at least some
of the constraints which make that kind of knowledge the thing it
is.

The second project of this chapter is a matter of using various
disciplines in such a way as not only to provide a consistent curriculum, but also a curriculum with a human face. That is, the discussion of what to do now should go forward with the questions
always in mind, 'what is our culture good for?', 'where is it
alive?', 'where is it excellent?', 'what is its *point*? Its human
point?'

Any answer to these questions needs to justify itself. If we ask,
'What shall we do to be saved?' we must learn to return rational
and not superstitious answers. So when someone says 'this part of
our culture is as dead as a doornail', we have learned to expect the
sceptic's reply, 'Who are you to say so?'. When a man says 'that
war is a wicked war' or 'this is a great painting' he will be asked,
'what grounds have you for supposing that you are doing anything
other than expressing your own feelings as your opinion?'[1] And
the power of the liberal faith in a man's right to his own point of
view is such that any opinion comes to have value, irrespective of its
reasonableness. Judgements of the sort commended here – judgements about what our culture is worth – depend for their truthful-
ness on an uncomputable form of reason. And they further depend
– as I said in 'Ideology and the Curriculum' – on the necessary connection between what it is to be reasonable and the standards of

---

[1] The position classically expounded by A. J. Ayer in *Language, Truth
and Logic* (1936).

morally admirable actions which a reasonable man invokes. The inspection of rationality is at the same time the study of values,[2] and to consider rationality on these terms is to refer to the reasonableness of sentiments, intuitions, and natural instincts. The difficulty of getting any agreement about what shall count as 'natural' in no way exonerates us from the pressures of these grounds towards reason and goodness.

A first point of this essay, therefore, is to suggest how to restore objective reasonableness to the discussions of value *without* equating 'objective' with 'computable'. In short, questions about the values of our culture and the worth of a life within it, must be made to turn on reasonable grounds. The discussion of values (*sc.* ideologies) as being reasonable or not *is* philosophy; this truth supplies the first justification of interdisciplinary studies. The discussion of values as living or dead social institutions *is* sociology; this truth is the second justification of the studies.

These links are more than liaisons; they are an identity of interests. But there is a lot to do,[3] and one student can hardly learn to do it all. The studies I have in mind depend upon a *community*[4] of interest in the common questions – 'what is our culture good for?' and so on. I shall now try to show how a student of the humanities who also wants to be a teacher might work in order to pull together theory and practice; how, further, this student might see where the study of the arts comes in relation to other studies; how, finally, this student might see that to use other disciplines when he could, would give him a better sense of his own approach. Thence he might learn the contingency of the alleged 'disciplines', the way in which to do something as simple as read a novel is itself the product of a whole set of anterior assumptions.

The main concern of the chapter is to show how these activities compose the essential centre for academic study by anyone (particularly a teacher) working for the transmission and the creative

2 A debate with a long twentieth century history. I offer justifications in the last chapter of this book. I am also very much aware that on this showing I am trying, so to speak, to put Hume's 'Civil Affections' back into ethics.

3 Kant said it first. See *The Metaphysic of Ethics*, Abbott's edition (Longman), p. 3.

4 Finely described and emphasised in Seymour Betsky's splendid work, much of it unpublished. But see his 'Concepts of Excellence: Universities in an Industrial Culture', *Universities Quarterly*, Winter 1969.

renewal of our civilisation. (The following chapter gives an example of how to do the work in question.)

II

To start, then, where we must start: with the inescapable difficulty of knowing what judgements we can make about values. I take it that we all agree that it is at least theoretically possible to feel that certain evaluations of action may be wrong, may be mistaken. Clearly it's possible to feel that certain descriptions of the formal properties of a work of art may be wrong: we should find it very hard to agree with anyone who thinks that, say, Mozart's clarinet concerto K622 is a miserable piece of work or that Berlioz' great *Damnation of Faust* is a faint and pleasing tinkle. It's not enough (is it?) to say that such judgements are unapt; we clearly feel that some mistake is involved in such an account and (it's a familiar teaching experience) we should start making explanations and excuses to ourselves on behalf of the person who made the remark in the first place. We say they're inexperienced or insensitive or listening carelessly.[5] The point is that we feel that it is possible to believe in a correct view, or a view which tends more towards correctness, whose status is of more than private significance. Of course this assumption is something we all share and yet it seems to me vital to restate the epistemology – the grounds upon which we know this to be so – because there is increasing confusion about the status of our judgements as to value. The extraordinary difficulty about coming at any satisfactory moral or critical judgements (and I take it as a truism that the two intersect and overlap constantly), especially at a time of widespread moral confusion, has meant that those people whose business it is to study the values of

---

[5] Most of my argument at this state is straightforwardly summarised from the symposium 'Objectivity and Aesthetics' given by F. N. Sibley and Michael Tanner and published in *The Aristotelian Society: Supplementary Volume XLII* 1968, pp. 37–73. Their discussion is extremely plain and quite untechnical. It is a measure of the distance travelled from Ayer's division of all statements into analytic, synthetic and meaningless which he set out in *Language, Truth and Logic* that Sir Alfred Ayer isn't mentioned by Sibley or Tanner. See also Stuart Hampshire, *Freedom of Mind* (Chatto & Windus 1972), on 'Sincerity'.

our culture have come either to feel a radical loss of self-respect or a compensating self-assertion against a world which increasingly isolates and insulates such a study. For it is also plainly true that our culture does not much care whether its guardians and trans- mitters of culture live or die.

The provisional and uncertain quest for significance and living value is not among the honoured modes of thought, even though Britain is still a country where it is possible to raise substantive questions of human value for public debate. But the thought which carries the point of its own conviction and validity is the product of three hundred years of moral and economic individualism, of a three-hundred-year preference for practical action. It is this thought which dominates the sort of social engineering and economic plan- ning we all find acceptable.

This is latter-day utilitarianism. But there can be no question of our accounting for the study of values in literature or any other art in terms which will satisfy the scientific models. A quotation from Karl Mannheim makes all the necessary points very firmly.

> On this point, too, those who accept the degree of precision attained in exact natural science as their standard will insist upon complete conceptualisation of the object, i.e. the complete explication of the object in terms of theoretical concepts. They will not admit that we have 'knowledge' of anything unless this condition is satisfied. The categories which permit the fullest explication in terms of theory are form, relation and law. But we should be compelled to disclaim the possibility of knowledge in vast areas of exploration, if we took such a rigid standard literally, instead of calling to mind that each area, as it were, lays down the requirements, the limits, and the nature of possible theoretical analysis, so that criteria of exactness cannot be transferred from one field into another. There are data which can be treated mathematically; others may be described in terms of different but still uniform regularities; still others are uniquely individual but nevertheless display an inner law of their unique structure, an inner consistency which can be described conceptually; and finally, there are some in respect of which all theory must limit itself to an 'indication', 'approximation', or 'profiling' of certain correspondences, because their

substantive characterisation has already been accomplished in pre-theoretical experience.[6]

If we hope to establish an 'objective' codification of the understanding of values we shall be humiliated. Yet we can make appeals to the presence of properties which in some sense are 'out there' in the work discussed. There are important logical distinctions between our perceptions of values and our perceptions of colour, but the *proof* of colour perception provides a useful analogue in trying to describe our procedure in weighing the moral value of art, or indeed of any kind of social action. The sceptic who asks, 'how do you know that this poem is moving, or graceful or eloquent, and who says so?' rarely asks 'how do you know that this patch of colour is red?', but if he does he would have to be satisfied[7] with the sorts of proof we offer in reply to the first question. We would demonstrate redness by pointing and comparing and by referring to past experience of colour, and we would probably go on to refine the perception by discriminating between kinds of redness: between magenta and crimson, carmine and scarlet, and so on. This very elaborate system of dialogue, testing and maturing and pondering, is the best we can do, and the sceptic cannot reasonably ask for more.

This brief argument by no means cancels all difficulties. The debate is very old, and everyone is a great deal less agreed about values now than when it began. There is still the whole problem by which we are faced when two people see the same work of art – let's say, *Rigoletto* – and one finds it lush and sentimental and the other passionate and moving.

At this point, we move from the roughly philosophical to the sociological stage of the enquiry. The student of culture or of education might hitch such a philosophic lift as I have described in order to give his ideology point and purchase on social reality. He would need to proceed to ask something about the social context and history of the values he established in this process of comparison and pondering. The status of value-judgements needs epistemological grip; that is the point of the philosophy. It also needs a sociological grip, and the ideology will attain this only if it scru-

---

[6] Karl Mannheim, *Essays on the Sociology of Knowledge* (Routledge & Kegan Paul 1952), p. 71.
[7] Setting aside the use of spectroscopes, which don't affect the substance of this argument.

tinises its history with a view to deciding what values that history permits. Such a grip is also the basis for a restoration of teachers' self-confidence.

III

The history of the present confusion in moral values is brilliantly summarised in Alasdair MacIntyre's *Secularisation and Moral Change*.[8] He writes:

> If you read any book produced from the late nineteenth
> century onwards about English life written by an Englishman
> from an English point of view, the virtues which are said to be
> characteristic of the English are a pragmatic approach to
> problems, co-operativeness, fair-play, tolerance, a gift for
> compromise and fairness. I call these secondary virtues for
> this reason, that their existence in a moral scheme of things
> as virtues is secondary to, if you like parasitic upon, the
> notion of another primary set of virtues which are directly
> related to the goals which men pursue as the ends of their
> life. The secondary virtues do not assist us in identifying
> which ends we should pursue. The assumption made when
> they are commended is that men are already pursuing certain
> ends, and that they have to be told to modify their pursuit
> of these ends in certain ways. The secondary virtues concern
> the way in which we should go about our projects; their
> cultivation will not assist us in discovering upon which
> projects we ought to be engaged . . .
>
> The religion of English society prior to the Industrial
> Revolution provided a framework within which the
> metaphysical questions could be asked and answered, even if
> different and rival answers were given. Who am I? Whence
> did I come? Whither shall I go? Is there a meaning to my
> life other than any meaning I choose to give it? What powers
> govern my fate?
>
> The dissolution of the moral unity of English society and
> the rise of new class divisions led to a situation where within
> different classes there appear different aspirations, and
> different attempts to express and to legitimate these in

[8] Oxford 1967, pp. 25–32

religious forms. But the compromises and abdications consequent upon the class co-operation of English life produced a situation where it was impossible for any one group plausibly to absolutise its own claims and invoke some kind of cosmic sanction for them – hence, in part at least, the failure of the Labour churches and of Marxism. Yet it was equally impossible to re-establish coherent social unity – hence the failure of Green's social philosophy. The consequence of this is that there remains no framework within which the religious questions can be systematically asked. For different classes the loss of a religious framework proceeds in different ways at different rates and in different periods, but for all there are left at last only fragments of a vocabulary in which to ask or answer these questions. And this is especially true of the working class. Moreover, secularist views of the world provide answers to the same questions as do religious views. A consistent and systematic secularism, if it is the doctrine of a social group, depends upon the possession of a vocabulary by that group in which these questions can be asked and answered. Hence the loss of a framework and vocabulary by the English working class is itself perhaps the major inhibiting force which prevented secular views dominating them. It is not surprising that instead there remains with them a strong vestigial Christianity, manifested whenever at times of birth, marriage, and death questions about meaning, purpose, and survival become inescapable . . .

'What our children are left with is on the one hand a vestigial Christian vocabulary of a muddled kind and on the other an absence of any alternative vocabulary in which to raise the kind of issues which it is necessary to raise if there is to be not mere assessment of means, but some kind of explicit agreement or disagreement about social and moral ends. This is of course not merely the fate of the English working class. It is the product of the history of the whole of our society, and the whole of society shares the same fate.'

The way we do our looking at society is itself the product of the same history. In the absence of a strong indigenous tradition of moral philosophy, the centre of moral hortation, for better and worse, shifted for a key period in this century to departments of English literature. But they, who began by providing a theory of moral and social change and who carried their studies into the heart of their history, ended by asserting claims to centrality in an over-acquisitive way. English studies came to dominate serious intellectual discussion partly because of the way the other subjects were understood, and partly because of the brilliantly creative restatement of the subject at Cambridge in the 1930s which I mentioned in Chapter 3. The founders of *Scrutiny* routed the simple-minded Marxism of their contemporaries and put into circulation a total theory of society and its relation to the popular and expressive arts – in short a theory of culture and being. In the end only Leavis and Denys Harding stayed on to break through to an idea of liaison. By now English studies have lapsed either into academicism, or that vulgar association of culture with being which damns the twentieth century out of hand, just because pulp fiction and TV are so awful. Once again, English has retired to the stand of one subject among many.

We learned from the Victorians and earlier the power of the individualist tradition – in ethics, in economics, in intellectual affairs. Alongside this individualism and powerfully linked with it stand the doctrines of scientific positivism. These affirm that the controlling principle of science is 'classify and count' and *assume* that the phenomena you observe are separable atomic entities which accumulate until deductions are possible. Facts are seen as atomic objects, and given in themselves (data) as opposed to their being selected through a tight-meshed conceptual filter. The atomistic view of knowledge is confirmed by the specialist tradition. You study your facts, and he studies his, and their contingencies are ignored or supposed to be an accident of essential knowledge. The whole configuration of attitudes tends, for what Marxists would diagnose as economic causes, to make objects of all names, and to acknowledge reality only in those phenomena which may be reified, i.e. made into objects. Thus a fact is an object and a value is too elusive to study.

The reifying habit of mind has tended always to work against the serious study of our values and our society. It has emasculated grand social theories, and even in the day of the integrated day we barely glimpse the subtle relations between language and institutions, language and roles, language and facts. It isn't enough to talk of 'arbitrary barriers between subjects'. The barriers are of very varied sorts and some of them are real enough. They may derive from the nature of logic, or from history, or from the body of material studied, or from the limitations of the language we have available. No one way of talking, no academic discipline, can *possess* the central ground on which we know ourselves and understand our values. But the many kinds of speech – those of literature, social anthropology, history, psychology, economics, politics – constantly intersect and change their limits.

The main preoccupation of all these forms of study has been these past forty years the nature of language, the study of the meanings and significances of language. To study the changing meanings carried and assigned by language is to get much closer to that understanding of ourselves without which we can hardly hope to build an adequate moral vocabulary. Such a study has been the main inquiry of the two great poets T. S. Eliot and Wallace Stevens; one of the facts that made the restatement of English studies possible was that Eliot was writing at the time. Language as theme, as here in Stevens' 'The Idea of Order at Key West' : [9]

> The sea was not a mask. No more was she.
> The song and water were not medleyed sound
> Even if what she sang was what she heard,
> Since what she sang was uttered word by word.
> It may be that in all her phrases stirred
> The grinding water and the gasping wind;
> But it was she and not the sea we heard.
>
> For she was the maker of the song she sang.
> The ever-hooded, tragic-gestured sea
> Was merely a place by which she walked to sing.
> Whose spirit is this? we said, because we knew
> It was the spirit that we sought and knew
> That we should ask this often as she sang.
>
> . . .
>
> It was her voice that made
> The sky acutest at its vanishing.
> She measured to the hour its solitude.
> She was the single artificer of the world

[9] In *Collected Poems* (Faber & Faber 1955).

In which she sang. And when she sang, the sea,
Whatever self it had, became the self
That was her song, for she was the maker. Then we,
As we beheld her striding there alone,
Knew that there never was a world for her
Except the one she sang and, singing, made.

Ramon Fernandez, tell me, if you know,
Why, when the singing ended and we turned
Toward the town, tell when the glassy lights,
The lights in the fishing boats at anchor there,
As the night descended, tilting in the air,
Mastered the night and portioned out the sea,
Fixing emblazoned zones and fiery poles,
Arranging, deepening, enchanting night.

Oh ! Blessed rage for order, pale Ramon,
The maker's rage to order words of the sea,
Words of the fragrant portals, dimly-starred,
And of ourselves and of our origins,
In ghostlier demarcations, keener sounds.

Even in such eloquence there is a touch of two-sided simplification, which renders this opulent world a chaos of particulars, and language the means of making sense. What happens is less heroic. We take the insights to which we have access – psychological, political, literary, and so on – and we direct them towards a common understanding. We should take part in a common pursuit, though quite without that being taken to imply any normative reduction of the teeming variety of human responses. Understanding then where we are will at least prevent us from supposing either that we are trapped by history or that history may be ransacked for any meaning we care to assign to it. Most important of all, such understanding will prevent us from imagining that the past is spatialised, and that the point of history is to have created now.

The problem of the past is always there. One contemporary answer to the problem is to treat the past as though it were all contemporaneous and arranged to hand all about us, i.e. 'spatialised'. In these convenient circumstances the modern mind thinks it may dip into what is there for whatever interests it, and may consider its catch wholly on modern terms. It forces the past to provide materials for the self-congratulation of the present. The reverse process leads in a curious way to the same end. In this, the experience of the past is held to be so completely submerged in the contexts of the past that it is barely retrievable, and that what we must do as far as possible is keep ourselves and our ideas completely out of the way in attempting any retrieval. Yet this alleged respect for context denies precisely what is over-asserted in the first process – that modern minds come to the past in order to shed light on the present. There is nowhere else to learn from. To deny the bearing of past on present – and in the sense of this argument, all students are historians – is to leave history as a museum. Once more, the habit of reification comes into play. The past becomes a random set of objects dug up for our acquisition.

'Acquisitive' has (rightly) become a political word. Both the mistaken approaches to the past outlined here deny the complicated interaction of the present with the past, such that we go to the lost, alien past because we would pluck out the heart of the mystery of the present.[10] The past is irretrievable. What can be found must be taken on its own, intransigent terms. Yet we have such terms of our own. To study the relation between the two – the living conversation of that dead author and this live intelligence – is to study the meaning of social action. It is to ask, how can I understand myself in relation to this alien voice? Myself not as an autonomous individual, but as a figure in this present history.

Then the question becomes: How do I change the way I think in order to overpower the obstacle between me and this other man's way of thinking?[11] And this line leads on to asking: How is society changing while I do this? Changing me, and the conditions in which I read? Then, finally: What bearings can I find by which it is possible to steer a moral course? (How shall a man live well, and study well, when the eye of God is no longer upon him?)

I V

These are political questions and this a chapter in the politics of education. Marx has taught us to accept the commonplace that our

---

[10] Chapter 10, 'Human Studies and the Social Crisis', returns to this issue.
[11] Cf. Stuart Hampshire, 'The Anology of Feeling', *Mind* LXI, 241, January 1952.

society places unrecognised constraints upon our imagination.[12] To perceive where the constraints press hardest is to alter their pressure and move the limits within which intellectual action is possible. Now I take politics to mean the distributions of power, prestige and wealth, and the relations between these. A permanent exercise of any ruling class is to spend a lot of its time legitimating the ideology of its own power, prestige and wealth. The dominant ideology obviously affects in profound ways the manner of conducting education.

Thus, to apply the two forms of spatialising the past which I have sketched out, to the study of literature: literature has been and sometimes still is justified on the one hand as the possession of beautiful historical objects – literature as a museum – and on the other as the possession of an immediate experience – literature for existentialism.[13] Either way the relation of past to present is distorted for acquisitive purposes. I could chronicle a long list of such misappropriations performed in departments of literature. There is stocktaking an inventory of approved qualities – rhythm, imagery, plot-diagrams and so forth: art become commodity. There is quarrying literature for 'relevance', 'universal morality', and 'timeless human nature': art for the today people. There is, especially in the former university colleges and the colleges of education, literature for the historicist, the attempt to get round as many of the monuments as possible in the time available, which generally turns out to mean a glance at Chaucer, Shakespeare and the metaphysicals, a dash round Augustan London, a short stop in the Lake District, and breathless arrival amongst a heap of the Victorians, all topped off by Lawrence and the First World War.

Finally, there is the kind of English study which dominates so

---

12 Here and following I owe a good deal to Quentin Skinner's paper 'Meaning and Understanding in the History of Ideas', *History and Theory* VIII, 1, 1969. What Skinner says about narrowly practical criticism of 'the words on the page' and the plundering of the past for 'dateless wisdom' is very much to the point in discussion of literary study, and even more in discussing courses in 'philosophy of education', or 'By seven-league Boots from Athens to the London Institute'. His further criticism of exclusively *contextual* approaches to the past, in which society is seen as the *determinant* of the text, is no less to the point when one sees the arid historicism of so much University English study. Text v context, and neither can win.

13 I owe this insight to Mr John Goode of the University of Reading and his exceedingly original essay 'Character and Henry James', *New Left Review* 40, 1967.

much school work, as much the product of the sociology of mass communications as anything, controlled as it is by the need to hold the largest possible number of people docile for the largest possible amount of time. The model for such directionless time-killing is the television programmes like *Talkback*, where rows of people are lined up and instructed to react to the available alternatives. It is our degraded notion of democratic debate in a society in which choice is predominantly limited to different forms of mass consumption. Seen in these terms, the political striations of school textbooks become pretty obvious. Each of the forms of English I have outlined takes submarine and deep-seatedly political bearings. To render this politics visible is, once again, to make our understanding of values more searching, and to suppose that this is not so is to take an exaggeratedly static or competitive view of English studies.

Nonetheless, change is taking place. Social change signifies that there will be change in social notions of what students will study. The very term 'social change' suggests forces beyond the control of man. But it would be bad faith to suppose that the people most directly concerned about the cultural life of society are not in a position so to study that life that they work for its replenishment and extension. There is a historical opportunity to take. For teachers not to take it, is to betray themselves. In the present fluid state of things, they are in a position to name the direction of their studies. Very well, then. Which way? The opportunity will not remain open for good.

The lead seems to me, in his undramatic, searching, utterly ingenuous and serious way, to be given throughout Leavis' remarkable call to action (it has passed largely unremarked), *English Literature in Our Time and the University*,[14] from which this is a representative quotation :

> The evoking in *Four Quartets* of what we ordinarily call
> reality as unreal, the astonishing resource with which the
> ways in which it is unreal are brought home to us, is part of
> the total process by which our need to recognise values and
> apprehensions not allowed for by the technologico-
> Benthamite ethos is enforced. And the enforcing takes a

14 Chatto & Windus 1970, pp. 131–2. (These were the Clark Lectures in Cambridge in 1969.)

form that compels a close attention to the subtleties of
linguistic expression – to the ways in which the conceptual
currency may affect the problem of how and what one
believes and what believing is, and in which linguistic
conventions and habits partly determine experience. That
the creative battle to vindicate spiritual values should be
associated, as it is in *Four Quartets*, with the subtlest kind
of analytic interest in language seems to me a piece of good
fortune that we, who are concerned for humane education
at a time when linguistic science, or scientific linguistics, is
making its victorious advances, have a duty to exploit. For
they have, those advances, menacing possibilities for the
matters of our concern.

Here we have the kind of lead we are looking for. In proposing
T. S. Eliot, with all his genius and his many shortcomings, as the
supreme type of the modern poet – and the poet as the point of
growth in his civilisation – Leavis is sketching out the *kind* of study,
immensely arduous and intense, apparently formless but profoundly
disciplined both by relevance and by local possibility, which I would
want to recommend.

I proposed earlier three conditions for a successful teacher-training course which had the humanities in mind. First, that it know
where one kind of knowledge stands in relation to other kinds. The
study of art or music or literature comes at critical points up
against philosophic or psychological or other difficulties. What we
need at those points is not territorial dispute but a community of
interest allied to a theory of knowledge which leaves each party
knowing what help he can look for and what he may borrow from
the other in order to push on past the difficulty he finds.

The requirement is that a student in teacher training should possess a map of knowledge. It follows from this that he also needs a
theory of how knowledge changes. He needs a politics of knowledge. Students of literature, for example, have drawn on such a
thing in describing the Rise of the Novel,[5] or the change from rural
to industrial literature, from the classical to the romantic frame
of mind.[16] But their politics has often looked narrow and arbitrary.

[15] Cf. Ian Watt's excellent book of that name (Chatto & Windus 1957).
[16] Leavis' theories have been easily the most influential here. See, e.g.
the essays on Bunyan in *The Common Pursuit* (1952) and '*Anna
Karenina*' *and Other Essays* (1967), both published by Chatto & Windus.

A richer politics would also be a contradictory one – Marxist as well as Freudian, classical sociologist as well as English Whig. But the amplitude looked for is not in the interests of a genial pluralism; it is rather to rescue intellectual life from a vision of itself as timeless. The venality of English human studies is their omission of history embodied as class consciousness.

The third condition was that a student understand (from Wallace Stevens' poem *The Idea of Order at Key West*, among other places) at least in part that his approach to his material – his concepts and frames of mind – is the product of a temporary and malleable state of social and intellectual affairs. It is not fixed and it is hardly a procedure. But he must know what he is looking for. The student of culture is looking for answers to his question, what is the life of our society worth? The question, in a utopian university, would bind together students of all disciplines. The student of literature goes on to ask *his* distinctive questions in the effort to get at the substance of the human values which animate his subject.

> The literary student asks first : 'what is the thing in itself?' Thereafter, although some of the questions he goes on to ask may be at bottom quite close to those of the social scientist, he doesn't put them in quite the same way; and this is important. He asks not so much : 'what do people do with the object?' but 'what relationship does this thing in itself, this complex thing, have to the imaginative life of the individuals who make up its readers or audiences?' Then whole new sets of questions begin to appear. Does it reinforce an accepted pattern of life? Or does it seem like a form of play? Or is it oblique, drawing upon deep psychic needs, perhaps running counter to the assumptions of its society? Or does it celebrate, stand in awe before, what one might call fundamental mysteries about human life? These questions have to be asked if one is to understand a work of art 'in itself' and so its relationship to its society; however they are answered, they will tell us something about that society, not just about the work of art.

This is Richard Hoggart's version[17] of the inquiry. He goes on,

---

[17] In *Contemporary Cultural Studies: An Approach to the Study of Literature and Society*, CCS occasional papers 6 (University of Birmingham 1969), pp. 18–19.

literary contribution lies, when it succeeds, in its integrity
and sensitivity of response to the objects studied (again, one
thinks of a phrase of Weber's : 'emphatic understanding').
It is concerned always with reading for value. Works of
literature at all levels are shot through with – irradiated with
– values ordered and values acted out. What literature does
all the time and what, therefore, the handmaid of literature,
literary criticism, must do is insist and demonstrate that,
in Coleridge's words, 'Men ought to be weighed, not
counted'. Societies most interact with the value-heavy,
psychic life of individuals – at these points an expressive
culture is born . . .

Such work has its meaning in collaborative inquiry. The literary
student has his particular body of knowledge, his techniques and his
main preoccupations. The anthropologist has his, the economist
his. And so on. But if inquiry marched towards the constantly implicit questions: where does the essential life of a society flow?
where is a full life in the present maintained, and by what sort of
culture? how does a culture transmit and renew itself? what has
humanity meant in the past or in alien societies?, then our intellectual life, and our training of teachers, would recover its lost
community.

More simply, the question might go, what is the truth about
ourselves? It is a question which can only be answered compara-
tively. And it is clear, if also it is commonplace, that the nature of
any attempted reply to these questions makes it unthinkable that
such study is ever either 'practical' or 'theoretic'. 'Participation',
they have cried. Such study is profoundly participatory. Work within these terms might for all the human and social studies take
Victorian Industry as a common theme. The nineteenth century saw
the decisive beginnings of modern democratic ideology; its imagination decisively formed itself in collision with the first ravages and
triumphs of industrialism. We are its heirs, and any teacher who
would understand his situation in the classroom of the 1970s could
begin with Wordsworth, Cobbett, the Reform Bill, Cobden, and
1848 all over Europe.

According to the liaisons suggested here the literary student would
have his reading of George Eliot's *Felix Holt* and Dickens' *Dombey
and Son* constantly checked on the one hand by social psycho-

logists who could point to George Eliot's powerfully Victorian view
of class psychology and behaviour, on the other by such 'history
from below' as E. P. Thompson's, and on the third and fourth hand
by Mannheim's[18] kind of close reading and an acquaintance with
the fiction Louis James reports in *Fiction for the Working Man
1830–1850* or Steven Marcus in *The Other Victorians*.[19] A sketch like
this is by now familiar. It is thematic in that it addresses itself to
substantive movements in history, but it defines its own identity
and point. Changing the boundaries in this way makes for no
accompanying loss of bearings. It unites theory and practice. Felix
Holt, Radical, and Florence's redemption of Mr Dombey have a
keen relevance in the classroom alongside E. P. Thompson's and
Royden Harrison's account of the rise of English socialism and the
Freudian explanations of Victorian sexuality in Steven Marcus'
book.

In the next two chapters I shall take a more directly educational
topic – children's literature – and show how this specifically literary
study can go forward, taking its tips from psychology, sociology,
and so forth. A full study might isolate two points of history : say,
the 1890s and the present day, and go on to explore these two areas
in as full detail as the documentary evidence and the available
specialists would allow. Such a study must include the penny dreadful and bloods, the horror and girlie comics, as well as R. L. Stevenson or Philippa Pearce. (In Raymond Chandler's words, 'down these
mean streets a man must go'.) This work, too, is familiarly literary.
But the student of literature might also share a close, full inquiry
into the social meanings of punishment and responsibility, starting
out from H. L. A. Hart's great book of that name.[20] His special contribution to a literary reading of legal language, of parliamentary
debate and newspaper report (as well as various plays and TV
serials) would go alongside the anthropologist's and historian's reports on sanctions in other societies. The whole debate would clearly
be an essential part of working out what human relations can and
should be like in a school in our society. It might empty of some of
its bitter pointlessness and rancour the familiar accusation that

---

[18] Exemplified in *Essays on the Sociology of Knowledge* (1952), esp.
pp. 33–83.
[19] Oxford 1963; Weidenfeld & Nicolson 1966, Corgi 1969.
[20] *Punishment and Responsibility: Essays in the Philosophy of Law*
(Oxford 1968).

training courses tell you nothing about discipline. As if they could! The study of punishment and responsibility is in itself the necessary 'practical' guidebook. We say together, 'let us explore what meaning we can, as upright and intelligent citizens in 1970, assign to these words'. And of course the inquiry could not but raise questions about social justice and privilege.

I could go on to set out the lines of a cross-cultural inquiry into the social and moral significance of sport, the most widely shared cultural activity of our society. It would be very enjoyable. But it is enough to mention it in order to make clear how piercingly such an inquiry would raise the question, 'what, in and out of school, are the main ceremonies of our life today worth?'

6

Reading children's novels:
private culture and
the politics of literature

This is the case study suggested in the last chapter. In this section of the book, headed as it is, 'Identity and Culture', it will be useful to launch inquiries from each end of these two poles. Identity and the self are too shadowy and difficult a pair of concepts to sort out here. It will have to do to say that your identity is in part a 'you' which would stubbornly remain, even if you'd been born a different person at a different time, and in part your identity *is* the total set of your responses to the dominant culture. This part of your identity is then defined as a more or less patterned and regular sequence of actions, and beliefs manifest in action, made in response to your culture's demands and expectations. Culture, on this definition, is the total and mobile system of demands and expectations, issuing from common values, expressions, arts, and institutions. Later chapters – on townscape, on the mass communications network – examine culture as this tidal movement. This chapter considers a part of conscious identity as it transpires in writing novels: the shaping spirit, perhaps.

'Conscious identity' is a deliberate phrase. We are not entering the realms of psychoanalysis. 'Conscious identity', or again, 'consciousness', has its meaning in relation to a system of values and an ideology. That system takes its shape in a social context; in interaction, as the psychologists say; in everyday life, we might better say. It follows from this that to read novels at all is to enter a social institution – the institution of socially permissible fantasy. To read or to write a novel is to deploy a social, sociable, heavily conventional means of exploring and defining our private fantasies and their relation to our realities. Even though we tend to read our novels (or write them) in a rather isolated, often absorbed way, reading the novel is inescapably a social and a cultural transaction. We transact with the author both his and our own social meanings.

It follows, in turn, from this truth, that to study fiction is to stand where the boundaries of various ways of seeing intersect. Those ways of seeing – the subtle interplay of perception and cognition – gradually harden into a distinctive and official form of study. Social experience becomes a discipline in the academies. But if we return to the examples of the novel and ignore the traditional claims of the discipline of letters (right enough, by its own lights), the beams of those perspectives cross and play upon one another in exhilaratingly uncertain ways.

Traditional literary study captures the novel for a proper but necessarily limited kind of inquiry, yielding similarly limited conclusions about society. If we recall the questions repeatedly posed in this book against the times we live in, then the literary-critical answers come clearly enough. 'Where does the essential life of society flow?' 'Whereabouts does our culture renew and transmit itself?' For the literary critic capturing the novel presupposes the answers; his account of the novel springs from the great tradition of English liberalism. The novel itself derives from that rich and creative tradition, and its sturdy, indomitable spokesmen in the nineteenth century. The novel, that is, speaks up for the continuing experience of individual lives. The individual in the liberal novel, as in its parent ideology, liberalism, is the realm and the fount of all value. The individual life is the moral measure of the worth of life, and this is how, in this country, the students and critics of literature teach us to see novels.

It has been an honourable and is still a very powerful picture of the world. I have argued elsewhere in these pages that it is no longer a possible picture to believe in without brutally distorting the reality of that world. But for the purposes of this argument, what matters is the explanatory weakness of such a scheme. Having learned that the individual – as teller of the tale, as content of the tale, *and* as reader of the tale – is the central factor in our accounts of why the novel matters, then students of fiction, and of fiction as the official fantasy of a whole culture, have cut themselves off from other, more various accounts. The disciplines I propose to invoke – for this chapter represents an example of interdisciplinary inquiry – are social psychology and politics. Thus it should work out that ideology and the imagination move into the closest and most fruitful relation.

II

The great strength of English literary studies has been and in part remains the building of a vocabulary in whose key terms it is possible to speak of matters of life and death. One can speak of them in this way with dignity and conviction. The seriousness and truth of this speech must be retained in any new forms of academic or further educational study, if we are to recover some living community in intellectual life. There is no knowing whether the area of life which we choose for our study will reward us. But even if we return with a bleak and desolate report – 'no life there' – we know to that extent where the valley of the shadow lies.

The area of life I propose for inspection is not simply fiction; it is modern children's fiction. The subject has an obviously topical relevance to courses in the training of teachers; present-day fiction for children is in any case widely held to be enjoying a renaissance it has not known since the days of the great Edwardians; it is, finally, a key product of the social fantasies which embody some of the main values of a culture. To study a segment of this vast area of production is to study the interplay of mythology and ideas.

The language of literary criticism, whatever may justly be said against it, has permitted its students to draw connections between the individual work and its genesis in a society. The connections, by and large, have been made in the terms of individualism, but they have been made. The conceptual credit has repaid a lot of interest. But the historical genesis of the studies themselves has equipped students with a number of very reach-me-down stereotypes about reading fiction and the ways in which fiction gets written – the systems of production. The stereotypes – about the role of fantasy, about escapism, about 'flight from reality' and sentimentality – are crabbed and ungenerous. Fiction and that part of the reading public which is made up of children offer a useful occasion for revisionism. While any teacher or parent would agree that we must at some stage get our value-judgements right about children's fiction, getting them right is acknowledged, in a muddled way, to be a harder business than it is in adult fiction.

Teachers, novelists, parents, come to read children's fiction with an eye on our specifically literary notions of a communicable tradition. At the same time they keep at the back of their minds vague notions of psychology and linguistic development. And even more vaguely, sociological echoes of stratification theory and class bias in literature drift somewhere across their imaginations. Each of these preoccupations rises at times to the top of consciousness. Half of their feelings, tangled in psychology, in conscientiously anxious clichés about class differences and sub-cultures, and in that half-baked, soft-middled, low-keyed humanitarianism which acts as a value-system amongst so many teachers, pushes us towards saying 'let the child find and choose his books in his own good time; my books aren't necessarily his books'. The other half, under the impulse of the great tradition and the moralism which as an index of the strength of English studies so widely penetrates school, university and college teaching, pushes us on to say 'here are fine books; read them; they'll do you good'. The tension, between a vivid sense of social justice and individual values, and a no less keen response to a continuing tradition and a common destiny, is the source of our moral (and teaching) energy, as it is of many contradictions and confusions. To see this is to abandon the arid dichotomy between 'child- and subject-centred teaching', which in turn gives rise (on the Left, as it were) to a lot of rather canting rhetoric about the privacy of the child, and on the other side (the Right) to the stiff-lipped defence of set-readers, *explications de texte* and salutary hard work on the notes.

These complex forces come into irresistible play when we, as teachers and students, decide to read children's fiction. We are then reporting from a segment of our culture – children's experience – to which the present day gives a quite unprecedented attention. We are now at the high point of enthusiasm in the study of children's experience, a point which would have looked absurd to its earliest instigators, Blake, say, or Rousseau. To understand and to judge this state of affairs is to say something of final importance about ourselves and the meanings we give our lives. It is to face a question of which the political resonance is as deep-seated as it is inescapable: what is the life of an individual child worth? Or, to put the same question in another way: what is the life of an individual children's novel worth?

This question serves as point of departure. It leads naturally to those more general ones which might serve as the focus for an intellectual community, the centre of reference by which different concerns align their perspectives. Questions, again, such as: how does our culture renew itself? where is it alive or dead? what religious or political direction has it? Study of this sort, having a positive centre and a positive intent in the sustenance and replenishment of a common culture, provides for children, students, or teachers, the conviction which our work must have if it is to mean anything more than the degraded images of self-interest conventionally available in late capitalist society.

III

We are making an effort to describe the total context within which a fiction has its genesis and is read. We need therefore a sociology of knowledge. That is to say, we want in what will be an inevitably patchy way to understand the interplay between the elements of our study: between reader and author, reader and his social experience, author and *his* social experience. We try to see how they know (or read) what they know (and read). Sociology has meant many dreadful things, but the least it can mean is that it help us in a small way to become what we are, and know what we may do to change that state of affairs.

The first stage of inquiry is to define a particular context for the birth of the fiction – the public fantasy. The second stage of adequate cultural inquiry is to relate what we study to our ideas of social and moral change. If the first stage concentrates (in reading fiction) on the mutual expectations of authors and readers towards each other, the second stage may roughtly be said to apply itself to the experience shared and what each contributor makes of it. Here we raise political questions about the relation of the shared experience to its society, and about the discrepancy between what the author makes of his experience and what the readers make of it. A further effort at detachment is needed in order to throw into relief that we are adults appraising the significance of these forms of cultural life – these children's novels – partly on our own terms but partly on children's. That is, we must know in as searching a way as possible what it means to us to invite children (as children or as incipient adults?) to read these books, and not others. And as we become conscious of the need for this knowledge, our intention must then be 'to make fully conscious and articulate the sense of value which "places" the book',[1] to bring to an unusually developed intensity the specific gravity of the work, its moral weight. This is the final stage of a continuous process and of course it penetrates the whole enterprise. Not that the value-judgement is itself anything to settle for finally; like any judgement worth having it is subject to 'testing and re-testing and wider experience'. Nor is it, as by this stage of my argument should be clear, a matter of simply deciding whether the book is any good. What we hope to have done instead is to provide as rich an account as possible of the context within which the work occurs and within which our act of valuing must also take place. We cannot, at this time of day, ascribe a timeless value to a work or see it with the eyes of God. The work and our judgement of it exist within co-ordinates of time and space. This is not to say that acts of valuation lose themselves in a jumble of relativist signals, any more than it is to say we can make arbitrary contemporary meanings out of past works. Because present value is a part of the present day and could not have meant the same in another place does not mean the value is random and pointless; its point is in its times. By the same token, we cannot take that point to alien times, and make the past into the present.[2] But we find in literature what we need. We take from literature what we are looking for. The integrity rests in being sure that what we are looking for is there.

The study of literature written specially for children is more obviously the study of the present. Given the subject of these novelists, it also happens to raise again the question, what shall we do with the past?, but this is not at first the problem. Children's novels stand, like the mass media, like the home we live in, exactly where ideology and the imagination cross. Like the study of bestsellers, they should tell us about a powerful area of social mythology: writers', teachers', or children's? I shall take one successful writer. In order to generalise adequately from the one example, I shall begin with the social psychology of fiction. What are the many uses of literacy?

[1] The phrases are Leavis' in *The Common Pursuit* (Chatto & Windus 1948), p. 213.
[2] Cf. chapter 10, 'Human Studies and the Social Crisis'.

IV[3]

Reading a novel is an inescapably *social* action. Our response (and children's) to situations in a novel is instantly evaluative, though the value-judgement may change with time. For the novel, perhaps more than any other artistic form, makes nonsense of the distinction between literature and life. Novels cannot be said, as it were, to lie along a scale at one end of which is raw, day-to-day living, and at the other heavily stylised and diagrammatic novels like Ivy Compton-Burnett's, or semantic jokes, like *Tristram Shandy*. If we are faithful to our experience, we surely recognise that novels occur to us in the same way as gossip, anecdotes, large areas of conversation, even larger areas of experience in which we take part as onlookers. Think how readily we watch a couple of people, or a group, in some kind of conflict with one another. As we watch them we come to a complex evaluation of what happened, guessing at what some people feel while others make their feelings explicit in words or gesture. Similarly, when a colleague or friend tells us some piece of school or college gossip, we instantly range ourselves sympathetically with various sides in a dispute, not only feeling *with* our friends but also *against* other factions, yet at the same time trying to imagine one's opponents' feelings and in our sympathy feeling *for* our friends as well as with them, feeling protective, irritated, surprised. Thus we are socially involved in such events, even in gossip over a cup of coffee. The nature of this involvement is not just analogous to the involvement we feel with the characters in a novel, it is at many points the same. In either situation we are never 'mere' or passive listeners or spectators; our range of interests may extend or modify itself as a result of what we watch. We never see only a reflection of that range thrown back at us. Our psychology is endlessly busy, moving swiftly from reality to memory to fantasy

---

[3] This following argument summarises and departs from a group of splendid essays by D. W. Harding, see: D. W. Harding, 'Reader and Author', in *Experience into Words* (Chatto & Windus 1963), pp. 163–74; 'Considered Experience: the Invitation of the Novel', *English in Education*, 2, 1, Summer 1967, pp. 7–15; 'The Notion of Escape in Fiction and Entertainment', *Oxford Review* 4, Hilary 1967, pp. 23–32; 'The Bond with the Author', *Use of English* 22, May 1971. The first notes towards these lucid, commonsense essays may be found in 'Psychological Processes in the Reading of Fiction', *British Journal of Aesthetics*, 2, 1962, pp. 133–47.

and back to supposition. We constantly imagine, evaluate, and discard possibilities other than those in front of us, and we perform this astonishingly rapid filtering and sorting operation during a dialogue with our interlocutor and the rest of his audience. If he is really there in front of us relating what the prefect said to the Head, the dialogue is spoken aloud, and our reactions to the story, our appeals to the other listeners and our interjections into the story become part of the total experience which we recollect and weigh up.

A very similar dialogue is going on when we listen to an author, even a dead one. We hold a silently evaluative conversation with him and make it clear by our appeals to other readers in discussion that we are looking for endorsement of our responses ('This is so, isn't it?' 'Yes, but . . .'). Even if we never attend a formal discussion, we still make appeals to a shared and social context of experience, as we read. At the same time, therefore, as we respond to, sympathise with, like or dislike characters in narration, we see them alongside the author, as *his* voice selects and distorts and renders. Even very small children are sometimes aware of this refracted relationship with the people in the story. They ask 'was it really true?' ('or are you having me on?') or 'why does it say that?' Quite often, for example, Beatrix Potter or A. A. Milne break the story-telling convention, or give it a double-focus within the tale itself. Even a four- or five-year-old can be quite clear that fiction is 'a convention for enlarging the scope of the discussions we have with each other about what may befall' (Harding's words). So a four-year-old knows that Peter Rabbit is naughty in ways that she or he may be naughty, but is in danger of much more drastic reprisals – becoming a rabbit pie for Mr McGregor. The four-year-old, like the adult, discusses with the author his imaginary and offered judgements, and may well reject them, either out of an intense sympathy, or by being bored. The discussion with the author, and the subsequent discrimination, will be according to the limits of more or less advanced criteria.

These processes are immediately recognisable. It is important to remember that they are not truistic. Literary students and teachers at all levels have for so long made such confident play with very different models of the psychology of reading, that there needs to be an explicit challenge made. Conventional teaching accounts of reading behaviour deploy as their essential concepts 'vicarious experience', 'identification', 'escape', 'light entertainment', 'wish-fulfilment', 'fantasy'. But a novel is *not* vicarious experience, it is reported and (perhaps) imaginary experience; we do not 'identify' with the characters, we respond in complex ways with, to, and for them out of the framework of all our prior experience, literary or not. No reader imagines that his alleged desires are gaining actual satisfaction. Rather, what is happening is that his desire for affection or romantic love, for adventure, prestige, or cheerfulness, defines itself in a new context. The reader discusses with the novelist the possibilities of giving his desires statement in a social setting. This is not to say that the level of such discussion may not be embarrassingly low, nor that the desires themselves may not be horrifying. But this is not at all the same as saying that the reader 'identifies with' a character and 'lives through' vicarious experience. We are not satisfying our desires, in any fiction (obviously including TV); we are defining them, and it is worth remarking that to relinquish one's desires, fantasies and aspirations is to give up hopes for oneself as a free man and in a profound sense to release one's grasp upon life.

As a function of our humanity, then, we constantly imagine entry into other people's lives and derive from these excursions an extension of what we imagine to be possible in life. We do this with snippets of overheard conversation or glimpses through half-curtained windows, with three-line paragraphs in *Titbits* or the evening paper, with fragments of news on TV or radio. These scraps alert us to human possibilities, trivial or important, which have occurred to other people but knowledge of which develops, refines *or* coarsens our personal maps of humanity and our own significance upon them. To an expanding degree as we experiment with more and more adult intelligent literature we live through the same process.

Our study of the cultural life which flows through a novel must therefore include our imaginative estimate of what the novel means to the life of its various readers. If the novel is 'institutionalised fantasy', what do we learn of that society which at the first hand generates the fantasy in an individual writer, and at the second takes the new work back to itself and makes it part of present social experience? Perhaps I can go over this social psychology again before laying another scanning grid across the inquiry.

    1. Reading a novel is a social transaction.

2. Novels or any fiction are a continuous part of social experience.

3. Reading a novel is very similar to being an onlooker of human actions.

4. We do not 'identify' with characters in a novel nor live through wish-fulfilment; we respond to a total situation which may clarify or confuse our wishes.

5. Reading novels, like any other experience, is evaluative.

6. In our rapid and elaborate processes of evaluation, we understand ourselves to be considering new human potentials in the company of the author.

Lastly, a further note on the idea of 'escape'. The idea of escape is often too happily used in the condemnation of what are obviously poor works of literature. A reader may 'escape' from our world into a much darker and more horrifying one; 'escape' may be narcotic or reassuring. When we escape with the most intense relief into a novel, it may be that the novel is a relief because it is much more intelligent and rewarding than the tedious staff-meeting from which we have 'escaped'. We regularly need respite when repairs (or repression and evasion) can go on. Thus we cannot say any work is necessarily a form of 'escape', though we can say a great deal about its quality. We can speak censoriously of escape as regression only when the activity is self-deceiving, a deliberate manipulation of our humanity in order to 'alter feelings without altering conditions' (Harding, again), a pursuit of a fraudulent solace in which we purposely retreat from our usual level of cultural interest and stamina.

V

These last remarks may too often be fired point-blank at teachers and parents reading children's literature. For it is necessarily true that the present flowering of children's literature is, in its genesis and sociology, an adult product : the conditions of production, distribution and consumption are created by adults. It seems to me further true that the enthusiasm amongst many adult readers for such writers as Alan Garner, Henry Treese, William Mayne, Phillippa Pearce, Rosemary Sutcliff and others is often a disguised taste for *Kitsch*, for the thoroughgoing, rank, tasty meat-and-gravy of an old-fashioned best-seller. For reasons which are surely part of our study a number of intelligent adults, in their wholesale enthusiasm for some children's novelists, may be said to be reading well below their proper standards. (Maybe this is best exemplified in the extraordinary popularity of J. R. R. Tolkien, most of all when he writes allegedly *for* adults.) The list I have named (it could be much longer) is very varied in its members' gifts. I propose to consider only Rosemary Sutcliff, a writer in this mode of genuine distinction and cultivation. It is because she is among the best English novelists for children now at work that she can stand as exemplifying as precisely as possible the ideology and system of myths scattered less intelligently and less boldly through the works of her contemporaries.

Let us begin where the good literary student has always begun; with the quality of the prose. Open any of her novels at random, and one finds at once these late Gothic resonances, the misty accents and landscapes of an iambic rhetoric which wrings the solar plexus of all of us brought up on Rider Haggard, Kipling, Stevenson, Scott and Sir Henry Newbolt :

> They looked back when they had gone a few paces, and saw
> him standing as they had left him, already dimmed with mist,
> and outlined against the drifting mist beyond. A half-naked,
> wild-haired tribesman, with a savage dog against his knee;
> but the wide, well-drilled movement of his arm as he raised
> it in greeting and farewell was all Rome. It was the parade-
> ground and the clipped voice of trumpets, the iron discipline
> and the pride. In that instant Marcus seemed to see, not the
> barbarian hunter, but the young centurion, proud in his first
> command, before ever the shadow of the doomed legion fell
> on him. It was to that centurion that he saluted in reply.
> Then the drifting mist came between them.[4]

Listen to her fatal mastery of plangent cadences :

> The murmur of prayers in the Latin tongue reached him in
> the quiet. It was the first time that he had known a Christian
> place of worship since the summer when his world had fallen
> to ruins. He remembered all at once the grey stone preaching
> cross in the hills, and behind all the silence of the service the
> deep contented drone of bees in the bell heather; he
> remembered as he had not remembered them for years,

---

4 *The Eagle of the Ninth* (Oxford 1954), p. 203.

Priscus and Priscilla, who would have shared their cloak with
him . . . Slowly the sore hot places of his heart grew quiet
within him.[5]

Her villains are masterfully drawn from the dynasties of Sapper's
Carl Peterson, Buchan's Dominic Medina, Baroness Orczy's silkily
impassive French inquisitor.

'Ah yes, I had forgotten that you both contrived to come
alive, together, out of that fight.' Vadir's light eyes flicked
him, like the careless flick of a whiplash, and came to rest
on the long white spear-scar that ran out of his torn sleeve.
'I have never seen you stripped. How many scars the like to
that one are there on your back?' he asked softly. 'Or can you
perhaps fly faster than a spear?'[6]

Or the dog-like subordinates, taciturn, resourceful Men Friday,
Chingachgook, to the hero's Natty Bumppo (a part of Rosemary
Sutcliff's development is the story of the subordinate-become-hero,
in *The Lantern Bearers*):

Esca tossed the slender papyrus roll onto the cot, and set his
own hands over Marcus's. 'I have not served the Centurion
because I was his slave,' he said, dropping unconsciously into
the speech of his own people. 'I have served Marcus, and it
was not slave-service . . . My stomach will be glad when we
start on this hunting trail.'[7]

One remembers the commanding simplicity of the dramatic cli-
maxes in her novels: Aquila's lighting the symbolic beacon on
Richborough tower in *The Lantern Bearers*; the death of the villain
Vadir on the God's horse in *Dawn Wind*; the return of the Eagle in
the middle of the initiation rites in *The Eagle of the Ninth*. Behind
these moments stand Kipling's memorable tableaux (the late Imperial subalterns of the Wall, the powerful evocation of Sussex in
July, right through *Puck of Pook's Hill*) and before him the great
nineteenth-century melodramatists – Walter Scott, Maria Edge-
worth, Charlotte Brontë, the early George Eliot – the cackling of the
crazy Mrs Rochester, the scaffold scene in *Adam Bede*, the flood
in *The Mill on the Floss*; supremely, the master of such moments,

[5] *Dawn Wind* (Oxford 1961), p. 201.
[6] *Ibid.* p. 117.
[7] *The Eagle of the Ninth*, p. 107.

Dickens: the death of Bill Sykes; the house split down the middle in *Little Dorrit*; Lady Dedlock in Tom-all-alone's; Sidney Carton's execution; Magwitch recaptured; on and on, an incomparable roll-call.

In her smaller way, Rosemary Sutcliff stands in this line. Now there is no doubt that a great novelist commands as part of his qualifying equipment a popular rhetoric – Lawrence is the great example of this century. But Rosemary Sutcliff's muted trumpets do not have the orchestration of an authentic popular voice: one can hear in most of the examples the prose ring with a certain wistfulness, a faded, regretful glimmer plays over its surfaces and rhythms, and her popularity amongst school-teachers seems marked more by a need to hear these antique harmonies again rather than by a fully mature response to a great gust of elemental feeling – the kind we respond to in Mrs Dombey's death, that astonishing combination of horror, prurience, pathos and magnificence:

> 'Mama!' said the child.
> The little voice, familiar and dearly loved, awakened some show of consciousness, even at that ebb. For a moment, the closed eyelids trembled and the nostrils quivered, and the faintest shadow of a smile was seen. 'Mamma!' the child cried, sobbing aloud, 'Oh dear Mamma! Oh dear Mamma!'
> The doctor gently brushed the scattered ringlets of the child aside from the face and mouth of the mother. Alas, how calm they lay there: how little breath there was to stir them!
> Thus, clinging fast to that slight spar within her arms, the mother drifted out upon the dark and unknown sea that rolls round all the world.

The collusion of writer and audience which we need to study in the case of a children's novelist[8] is perhaps explicable by comparison with Dickens, but only in a very much more local way. Yet this is where we might start: by comparing Rosemary Sutcliff to best-sellers of the past, and by defining her relationship with a certain social group, a group which contains but goes beyond her audience. For the explanatory relationships between society and culture are not *only* a matter of content. We shall of course learn a great

[8] According to the lines suggested in *The Sociology of Literature*, R. Escarpit, E. Pick transl. (Ohio 1965), pp. 77 ff.

deal by drawing up a system of the typical features of best-selling or popular literature[9] or of the characteristics of a social system. But we shall learn more about the life of a society (and its unnoticed deaths) by trying to see the non-conscious structures which shape a writer's work and are the inescapable product of his having written within the framework of a particular social group. When I say 'non-conscious' this does not mean 'subconscious'. The English mode of criticism tends to overestimate the individual in understanding the significance of a work of literature. Thus we undertake the fruitless business of charting the influences of one writer upon another. Such studies see meaning as linked only to biography and psychology.

In addition, however, we must scrutinise the contexts of a novel for a more pervasive structure, the shape of which fixes the arc of a writer's gesture, much as it determines the inflections of everyday speech. To understand the situation of a present-day, liberal-spirited teacher with a training in the humanities and a struggling sense of history is to understand the genesis of Rosemary Sutcliff's novels. It is also to draw in the heavily political overtones of any literary study. For such an imaginary teacher finds in these novels the grander chords which seem to have been extinguished in the universe of adult novels – to have been absent, indeed, in modern literature since the death of Yeats. It's more than the grand style, of course, which is missing. It's a combination of courage, manliness, candour, patriotism, too. Such writing is as much a matter of having a subject as anything – of being able to speak from a living situation and having the strength to stand up to jeering and dislike. There are queer links between a nation's rhetoric and its sense of itself.

I do not doubt that there is a need to hear those notes struck which have gone mute in the rest of literature, to find a prose which moves with ceremony and amplitude, with a portly courtesy and forgotten grace. I can't help it if this analysis comes near the complaints of letters to *The Daily Telegraph* – 'The age of chivalry is dead'; Rosemary Sutcliff is the best of a disparate group of writers who register objection to a gaunt and toneless language, inept as to rhetoric, graceless as to manner. These writers have no academy

---

[9] As witness Leo Lowenthal's classic studies of *Collier's Magazine*, which traced the supercession of the 'producer' hero (captains of industry, entrepreneurs, pioneers) by the 'consumer' hero (filmstars, fashion designers, socialites) between 1900 and 1939. See his contribution to *American Social Patterns* (Doubleday 1951), W. F. Peterson (ed.).

to sustain them, and their only set of beliefs is that pale, anxious and rinsed-out humaneness which is the best most of us can do by way of a contemporary world-picture. What, therefore, comes through as the strongest impulse to feeling is often an intensity of loss and regret, not bitter but intensely nostalgic for the sweetness of a youth and a landscape intolerably vanished.

Rosemary Sutcliff invokes time and again the great images of an organic literature – pure water, oak, ash, may, blackthorn, a cleansed and abundant landscape; sorrel, heart's ease, eglantine, laurel; wren, nightingale, lark; honey bees, fresh milk, woodsmoke. At moments her over-full prose begins to sound like a catalogue of Habitat living – the scrubbed tables, the sheepskin rugs, the scoured flags. But this country-lore is another symptom of a disinherited present. She appeals to a symbolism which is largely destroyed and she does so because she needs to deny the reality of that destruction. The appeal is one detail of the 'significant structure' of her novels.[10] It signals that relation in which she stands as the most telling representative of children's novelists to a certain body of ideas – the ideas of an amorphous *lumpen*-intelligentsia with a strained notion of social function, a confused but tenacious responsibility towards a theory of social justice and national high culture. The only fixed point of reference for this social group is certain principles of personal relations and individual privacy best expressed in the way they treat their children.

Rosemary Sutcliff's novels define the response of such a group to the loss of the English landscape both in itself and as a symbol of one version of Englishness; they further define a powerful and unfulfilled longing for a richer moral vocabulary and an ampler, more graceful and courteous style of living such as at the present time can only be embodied in a stylised past. The novels go on to sort and clarify an absent centre in the lives of so many of the social group whose structure of beliefs, economics, aspirations, moral rhythms and intellectual effort she embodies. The novels reconstruct a moral authority carried by the idea of the metropolis (Rome) and become ritual in the archaic and beautiful system of allegiance, fealty, gesture and rite which characterises the tales. To uphold the authority gives meaning to men's lives, and this meaning

---

[10] I take this rather awkward phrase from Lucien Goldman, 'The Sociology of Literature : Status and Problems of Method', *International Social Science Journal* XIX, 4, 1967.

is conveniently discoverable in epic battle. It is a tautology to say that the tribal ceremonies and ritual battles appeal to adolescent readers. That is my whole point. She writes of these experiences because they express for her (and her social group) in the only available way and in the only available language an adequate response to the times.

For her main sequence of Roman-British novel *is* in the end an adequate response. The attitudes I have summarised add up to a powerfully conservative and elegiac view of history. But there is much more to be said for the courage and moral stamina of liberal ideology. The history of the twentieth century has not left it unmarked. Rosemary Sutcliff's novels are also stained deeply by a profound sense of the possibilities of change, of an unknown future, not finite or apocalyptic, but with a subtle, palpitating play of alternatives deriving from its past. Even though in the early *Eagle of the Ninth* and *The Silver Branch* the young heroes take it for granted that loyalty is unquestioning and *any* usurper morally outrageous, the heroes themselves suffer and change. In *The Lantern Bearers* the presence of violent change is the theme of the book, and the bitter suffering of the hero is the rendering of a writer who knows the refuge experience of post-1933 Europe. This novel makes Rosemary Sutcliff's gradual search explicit in its title. Aquila is much less confident, much more morally adrift than the earlier heroes. He registers a strong sense of historical dialectic: of forces in shifting conflict and collision, the new direction of which is the necessary result of social contradictions.

> 'I sometimes think that we stand at sunset,' Eugenus said
> after a pause. 'It may be that the night will close over us in
> the end, but I believe that morning will come again. Morning
> always grows again out of the darkness, though maybe not
> for the people who saw the sun go down. We are the Lantern
> Bearers, my friend; for us to keep something burning, to carry
> what light we can forward into the darkness and the wind.'
> Aquila was silent a moment, and then he said an odd thing.
> 'I wonder if they will remember us at all, those people on the
> other side of the darkness.'[11]

This note is the prelude to *Dawn Wind* in which we see the politics of change clear their lines a little. For the second time the hero

---

[11] *The Lantern Bearers* (Oxford 1959), p. 250.

is forced into slavery, and the subjugation and cruelty of the twentieth century get on to the page. This hero does not escape brutality
in order to fight against it from the other side; he lives through it to
win a new sort of identity, a balance of uneasy forces meeting yet
another new interruption from an unknown ideology. What he
emerges with, in its slight, stoical, bruised way, is a positive response
to the new dawn, the determination to make a life, of sorts, more
or less where he is. This compromised, sufficient victory marks
the end of the sequence. *The Mark of the Horse Lord* (1965), bolder
in conception and in the identity of its base-born hero, loses itself
in (for our purposes) *coups de théâtre*, though the general structure
remains, as it must for any writer, the same.

V I

This argument suggests that to account for a politics of literature we
have to go further than immanent study of the work. By politics I
have meant not just the obvious clash of generals and rulers, and
sanctions and punishments, the conflict of freedom and slavery,
the wars and parleys which we already are familiar with in folk-
tale. (To make my point, I would say that Tolkien's novels are not
about politics at the explicit level at all : they represent an exercise
in the politics of an amnesiac nostalgia.) The political structure of
Rosemary Sutcliff's novels, or of any novels, is provided by the
system of responses to a given historical situation at the time they
are written. According to Georg Lukacs,[12] the historical novel is, in
the way he uses the term, the major form born in response to the
dialectic of modern industrial history. The authenticity of the historical novel reposes in the successful expression and diagnosis of
this movement. Rosemary Sutcliff is an honourable representative
of her tradition struggling with the idea of change in our time. The
decency and range of her politics mean that in some ways she speaks
up for a largish and not unimportant group of people. The fact that
she writes for children and is widely read by teachers further means
that her politics are those in circulation among people who mediate
political experience and mythology for several million children at
their most impressionable ages.

   This is why the study of a single writer in a smallish mode can

---

[12] In *The Historical Novel* (Merlin Press 1962, Penguin 1969).

tell us so much. The good *Guardian*-reading teachers and parents meet in these pages in order to speak seriously to their children. The books vividly exemplify the formation of a certain consciousness which, its authors intend, shall be urged upon their children in the most proper and pressing way. For this end, it is all to the good that Rosemary Sutcliff, and the lesser but very similar writers in her wake, write so straighforwardly. For sure, she cannot, as Leavis tells us Dickens does, 'see how the diverse interplaying currents of life flow strongly and gather force here, dwindle there from importance to relative unimportance, settle there into something oppressively stagnant, reassert themselves elsewhere as strong new promise'.[13] She is writing too simply to maintain tension between multiplicity and organisation. She doesn't allow sufficient life to the characters she condemns, and there is therefore no radical criticism within her own work of what she affirms. Nor is there any such criticism in the social group which is her genesis. There is little occasion to study the meanings – moral and political – of antagonisms within her novels, which is what gives range and tragedy to a larger work. Her group lacks a tragic vision of the world, a lack which robs their politics of stature. But her position as a children's writer makes her a figure peculiarly worth our attention in the accurate understanding and evaluation of private culture. And, having read her, we find that she has spoken up in the present-day accents of an unkillable member of our society since 1800, the liberal intellectual woman.

[13] F. R. and Q. D. Leavis, *Lectures in America* (Chatto & Windus 1969), p. 8.

7

The awkward ages; or, what shall we tell the children?

Social scientists count the memory as quite one of the lesser instruments of their trade. On the contrary, the formation of memory and its action in the present seems to me the central study for a human sociology. Consciousness in this chapter may be defined as the action of memory in the present. Memory is then not anything in the nature of revisitable snapshots, but a living tissue whose network of perceptions and associations so relates to the forms of cognition and to the symbols of language as to permit particular responses (and not others), certain actions, in the present.

This is no doubt a loose way to talk about brain processes. Psychology with a heart would aim to plot some of these connections, much more precisely. A less loose way of describing the operation of memory in an individual consciousness is indeed to study the subtle interaction of imaginative life and a system of beliefs; or ideology and the imagination. This essay attempts such a study in brief and in one individual; the next two chapters suggest the study of ideology and imagination as they take on and express a more general, cultural shape. Another way of putting it – one which suggests the kind of inquiry this chapter intends – is to say that I would like to set out some notes towards what could be unkindly described as a middle-class, liberal-minded, short-haired *Uses of Literacy*. In that patchy, homespun, earnest and intermittently dazzling book, Richard Hoggart not only tells us what Hunslet read and said in the 1930s and 1940s. He also relates this account to a rather loose-limbed but tenable theory of social and moral change.

Now it is no light business returning in high seriousness to your memory, especially to memories of childhood when we learned, hard and sharp and day after day, where the boundaries of our beings lay, or where at least our society set them and with what intransigence it would resist our childish efforts to redraw them. For our memories, which together make up the many voices of our history, none are more powerful than those we learned in child-hood. Much of what we learned, we learned because our elders told it to us. To think about our childhood is to review those feel-ings, beliefs, events and mythologies which compose our history. That history is in continuous transaction with the present; we con-stantly remake it. T. S. Eliot gives us that remaking, our remaking of the past, and the past remaking our present identities, in these awe-inspiring words, from *Gerontion* :

> After such knowledge, what forgiveness? Think now
> History has many cunning passages, contrived corridors
> And issues, deceives with whispering ambitions,
> Guides us by vanities. Think now
> She gives when our attention is distracted
> And what she gives, gives with such supple confusions
> That the giving famishes the craving. Gives too late
> What's not believed in, or if still believed,
> In memory only, reconsidered passion. Gives too soon
> Into weak hands, what's thought can be dispensed with
> Till the refusal propagates a fear. Think
> Neither fear nor courage saves us. Unnatural vices
> Are fathered by our heroism. Virtues
> Are forced upon us by our impudent crimes.
> These tears are shaken from the wrath-bearing tree.

It is, in a much more prosaic and lengthy way, this process to be considered when reading *and* writing literature for children.

One of the best things that has ever been written on the topic – the effects of the transmission of a history and an ideology to child-ren – is D. H. Lawrence's essay 'Hymns in a Man's Life'.[1]

> Nothing is more difficult than to determine what a child
> takes in, and does not take in, of its environment and its
> teaching. This fact is brought home to me by the hymns
> which I learnt as a child, and never forgot. They mean to me
> almost more than the finest poetry, and they have for me a
> more permanent value, somehow or other.
>
> It is almost shameful to confess that the poems which have
> meant most to me, like Wordsworth's *Ode to Immortality* and
> Keats' *Odes*, and pieces of *Macbeth* or *As You Like It* or

[1] *Evening News* 13 October 1928. Reprinted in *Selected Literary Criticism*, Anthony Beal (ed.) (Heinemann 1955), pp. 6–11.

Midsummer Night's Dream and Goethe's lyrics such as *Uber allen Gipfeln ist Ruh*, and Verlaine's *Ayant poussé la porte qui chancelle* – all these lovely poems which after all give the ultimate shape to one's life; all these lovely poems woven deep into a man's consciousness, are still not woven so deep in me as the rather banal Nonconformist hymns that penetrated through and through my childhood.

Each gentle dove
And sighing bough
That makes the eve
So fair to me
Has something far
Diviner now
To draw me back
To Galilee.
O Galilee, sweet Galilee,
Where Jesus loved so much to be,
O Galilee, sweet Galilee,
Come sing thy songs again to me !

To me the word Galilee has a wonderful sound. The Lake of Galilee ! I don't want to know where it is. I never want to go to Palestine. Galilee is one of those lovely, glamourous, worlds, not places, that exist in the golden haze of a child's half-formed imagination. And in my man's imagination it is just the same. It has been left untouched. With regard to the hymns which had such a profound influence on my childish consciousness, there has been no crystallising out, no dwindling into actuality, no hardening into the commonplace. They are the same to my man's experience as they were to me nearly forty years ago . . .

Now we come back to the hymns. They live and glisten in the depths of the man's consciousness in undimmed wonder, so that the miracle of the loaves and fishes is just as good to me now as when I was a child. I don't care whether it is historically a fact or not. What does it matter? It is part of the genuine wonder. The same with all the religious teaching I had as a child, *apart* from the didacticism and sentimentalism. I am eternally grateful for the wonder with which it filled my childhood.

Sun of my soul, thou Saviour dear,
It is not night if Thou be near –

That was the last hymn at the board school. It did not
mean to me any Christian dogma or any salvation. Just the
words 'Sun of my soul, thou Saviour dear', penetrated me
with wonder and the mystery of twilight.

Fewer and fewer people can call on a culture as thick-textured
and passionately alive as Lawrence's. And yet it is not enough to
shout names at the decline of culture and have done with it. *The
Uses of Literacy* was important for so many teachers precisely because of a clear sense of gratitude and astonishment when they
heard this decent, friendly, rather flat voice which was taking
straight the vivid experiences of a generation, and was weighing
and sorting them gradually and truthfully, and not prejudging them.
For better or worse our culture was *Itma*, *Much-Binding-in-the-
Marsh*, 'Monopoly', Bulldog Drummond and Richard Hannay,
Rita Hayworth and Tommy Lawton. These ghosts drift up from a
densely populated Hades, as in that lovely poem of Thomas Cam-
pion's:

When thou must home to shades of underground,
And there arrived a new admired guest,
The beauteous spirits do engirt thee round,
White Iope, blithe Helen, and the rest . . .

Each of us would stop different shades and ask them if the corpse
planted in the garden last year had sprouted yet. In an inevitably
autobiographical way, therefore, I shall cite some of the passages
which penetrated one reader deep with their wonder – prose whose
rhythms are still resonant in my man's experience. These remain
touchstones of a certain high seriousness for children; they are not
so much a self-indulgent anthology (though there must be a touch of
that) as measures of moral meaning which have deeply penetrated
one man's consciousness and sensibility. If the choices are the right
ones, it should at least be possible to see that they do act as measures
– that is, they provide a moral and comparative scale within which
to place one's memories and experiences.

I I

I take four examples. The first is recognisable at a glance.

The floor was well-worn red brick, and on the wide hearth
burnt a fire of logs, between two attractive chimney-corners
tucked away in the wall, well out of any suspicion of draught.
A couple of high-backed settles, facing each other on either
side of the fire, gave further sitting accommodation for the
sociably disposed. In the middle of the room stood a long
table of plain boards placed on trestles, with benches down
each side. At one end of it, where an arm-chair stood pushed
back, were spread the remains of the Badger's plain but ample
supper. Rows of spotless plates winked from the shelves of
the dresser at the far end of the room, and from the rafters
overhead hung hams, bundles of dried herbs, nets of onions,
and baskets of eggs. It seemed a place where heroes could
fitly feast after victory, where weary harvesters could line
up in scores along the table and keep their Harvest Home
with mirth and song, or where two or three friends of simple
tastes could sit about as they pleased and eat and smoke
and talk in comfort and contentment. The ruddy brick floor
smiled up at the smoky ceiling; the oaken settles, shiny with
long wear, exchanged cheerful glances with each other; plates
on the dresser grinned at pots on the shelf, and the merry
firelight flickered and played over everything without
distinction.
    In the embracing light and warmth, warm and dry at last,
with weary legs propped up in front of them, and a suggestive
clink of plates being arranged on the table behind, it seemed
to the storm-driven animals, now in safe anchorage, that the
cold and trackless Wild Wood just left outside was miles and
miles away, and all that they had suffered in it a half-forgotten
dream.
    When at last they were thoroughly toasted, the Badger
summoned them to the table, where he had been busy laying
a repast. They had felt pretty hungry before, but when they
actually saw at last the supper that was spread for them,
really it seemed only a question of what they should attack

first where all was so attractive, and whether the other
things would obligingly wait for them till they had time to give
them attention.[2]

Kenneth Grahame embodies here a central image of our literature, and consequently of our morality. The images of safety and
security, warmth, known and fondled comforts, of ample food and
paternal affection, are all caught up and released in the magic re-
verberance of the word 'home', and the rich play which the novelist
gives it in his description. And of course this is more than a single
ikon. 'Home' in this memorable novel is part of a whole view of the
world, a structure of feeling and of moral organisation which beautifully defines for us what well-off Edwardian England wished to
make of the consciousness of their children.

This makes two main points to the argument. First, that it is an
extremely rare children's novel – only a novel of genius like *Huckle-
berry Finn* – which registers an authentic change of consciousness.
What lesser novels will do at their best is define a certain view of
the world in the most coherent and memorable way possible to
it. Without seeing that the demands of history require them to
become a different sort of social group, to register a different consciousness, they will express the old consciousness as well as it can
be done. My second point is the platitude that consciousness often
changes very slowly indeed – long after its concrete and specific
condition has gone. It is for example obvious that 'home' in Kenneth Grahame's sense has gone. The known familiarity of its objects,
the worn, rubbed continuity of furniture, the rich culture of a
national gastronomy, even the likelihood of deep and lasting friendships, all of which Grahame celebrates, have all been weakened
profoundly in the past seventy years, and our consciousness is
bewildered by the change. (Which is perhaps why this reader and
other readers still respond so intensely to the novel.)

Now to the second touchstone.

> Meanwhile the dark ring crept on, while all that great
> assembly fixed their eyes upon the sky and stared and stared
> in fascinated silence. Strange and unholy shadows encroached
> upon the moonlight; an ominous quiet filled the place.
> Everything grew still as death. Slowly and in the midst of
> this most solemn silence the minutes sped away, and while

[2] Kenneth Grahame, *The Wind in the Willows*, 1908, Chapter 4.

they sped the full moon passed deeper and deeper into the shadow of the earth, as the only segment of its circle slid in awful majesty across the lunar craters. The great pale orb seemed to draw near and to grow in size. She turned a coppery hue, then that portion of her surface which was unobscured as yet, grew grey and ashen, and at length, as totality approached, her mountains and her plains were to be seen glowing luridly through a crimson gloom.

On, yet on, crept the ring of darkness; it was now more than half across the blood-red orb. The air grew thick, and still more deeply tinged with dusky crimson. On, yet on, till we could scarcely see the fierce faces of the group before us. No sound rose now from the spectators, and at last Good stopped swearing.

'The moon is dying – the white wizards have killed the moon,' yelled the prince Scragga at last. 'We shall perish in the dark.' Then animated by fear or fury, or by both, he lifted his spear and drove it with all his force at Sir Henry's breast. But he forgot the mail shirts that the king had given us, which we wore beneath our clothing. The steel rebounded harmless, and before he could repeat the blow Curtis had snatched the spear from his hand and sent it straight through him.

Scragga dropped dead.

At the sight, and driven mad with fear of the gathering darkness, and of the unholy shadow which, as they believed, was swallowing the moon, the companies of girls broke up in wild confusion, and ran screeching for the gateways. Nor did the panic stop there. The king himself, followed by his guards, some of the chiefs, and Gagool, who hobbled away after them with marvellous alacrity, fled for the huts,

'Come,' said Infadoos, turning to go, an example which was followed by the awed captains, ourselves, and the girl Foulata, whom Good took by the arm.

Before we reached the gate of the kraal the moon went out utterly, and from every quarter of the firmament stars rushed forth into the inky sky.

Holding each other by the hand we stumbled on through the darkness.[3]

---

[3] Rider Haggard, *King Solomon's Mines* (1885), Chapter 11.

What view of the world and structure of feeling is in expression here? Most simply, there is the adventure tradition – not a long-lived one at all; perhaps a product of eighteenth- and nineteenth-century imperial expansion. But the positive and life-enhancing possibility of high adventure is a strong moral charge in the English novel from (say) Walter Scott onwards.[4] In *King Solomon's Mines* adventure is inevitably accompanied by a highly specific form of courage – understated, amused, canonised for ever by the English war film industry – together with a no less specific and traditional acquisitiveness. The treasure of the mines is there for imperialist plunder, and even great cosmic events – like the eclipse – are proper instruments for exploitation. But there is another rhythm to this consciousness, which marks all four of these examples. The rhythm of this eloquent prose, the confidence with which the lurid colours of the melodrama appear, is itself the product of a given world-view. It is a view which cannot comprehend the *idea* of any loss of identity. There is no conceivable threat to the self, or at any rate the European self, and there is a splendid arrogance in the idea that not only do the heroes, those supremely confident realisations of nineteenth-century English industrialism – aristocrat (Sir Henry), entrepreneur (Good), and technocrat (Allen Quartermain) – command themselves and their own times, they even command causality. They move the heavens to their own (humanitarian) ends.

Rider Haggard is the most audacious example of this conscious-ness, and it is to the point that he thought he was writing for adults. The change in values which has made him and other writers into authors for children is itself worth study, as part of the most im-portant relations between a body of fiction and its reading public.

The difference of the present from the structure of values in this third quotation is more obvious.

> Rudolf made no answer. When Sapt had first uttered the
> Queen's name, he had drawn near and let his hand fall over
> the back of her chair. She put hers up to meet it, and so they
> remained. But I saw that Rudolf's face had gone very pale.
>   'And we, your friends?' pursued Sapt. 'For we've stood by
> you as we've stood by the Queen, by God we have: Fritz and

---

[4] It is interesting that *Robinson Crusoe* was quickly remade as an adventure story. That is hardly how the main character sees it. He is *homme moyen économique*.

young Bernenstein here, and I. If this truth's told, who'll believe that we were loyal to the King, that we didn't know, that we weren't accomplices in the tricking of the King – maybe in his murder? Ah, Rudolf Rassendyll, God preserve me from a conscience that won't let me be true to the woman I love or to the friends who love me !'

I had never seen the old fellow so moved; he carried me with him, as he carried Bernenstein. I know now that we were too ready to be convinced; rather that, borne along by our passionate desire, we needed no convincing at all. His excited appeal seemed to us an argument. At least the danger to the Queen on which he dwelt was real and true and great.

Then a sudden change came over him. He caught Rudolf's hand and spoke to him again in a low broken voice, an unwonted softness transforming his harsh tones.

'Lad,' he said, 'don't say "No!" Here's the finest lady alive sick for her lover, and the finest country in the world sick for its true King, and the best friends – aye, by Heaven, the best friends – man ever had, sick to call you master. I know nothing about your conscience, but this I know : the King's dead, and the place is empty; and I don't see what Almighty God sent you here for unless it was to fill it. Come, lad – for love and her honour ! While he was alive I'd have killed you sooner than let you take it. He's dead. Now – for our love and her honour, lad !'

I do not know what thoughts passed in Mr Rassendyll's mind. His face was set and rigid. He made no sign when Sapt finished, but stood as he was, motionless, for a long while. Then he slowly bent his head and looked down into the Queen's eyes. For a while she sat looking back into his. Then carried away by the wild hope of immediate joy, and by her love for him, and her pride in the place he was offered, she sprang up and threw herself at his feet crying :

'Yes, yes! For my sake, Rudolf, for my sake !'

'Are you too against me, my Queen?' he murmured, caressing her ruddy hair.[5]

This too is a novel originally written for adults which is now in various school editions. Once more, the rhythms of this rhetorical

---

[5] Anthony Hope, *Rupert of Hentzau* (1896), Chapter 21.

prose rest upon a confidence of consciousness which has since, if not dissipated, then altered drastically. But without seeing it, Anthony Hope renders a deep fracture within that frame of mind: the appeal to duty is incompatible with the appeal to an adulterous true love. In spite of arranging a *coup de théâtre* to fix things up happily, Hope endorses in the end the nobility of renounced love, the primacy of caste and class, of duty and loyalty. To do this he has to discard Edwardian capitalism, and reinvent the courtly love and feudal perfection of Ruritania. He then inserts into this idyll the code of an Edwardian English gentleman, his honour and his suppressed sexuality. Now there seems to me much to be said for this system of values. Without some notion of the irrevocability of love and duty and goodness, one cannot have a morality at all. But there is no need to emphasise how far our present images of love and honour have travelled from Anthony Hope's.

The last example is, like *The Wind in the Willows*, specifically a book for children. I have found and still find its force unforgettable. This, for many children, was a rite of passage: entry into a masculine world of irony, stoic duty, withheld meanings and, above all, of the deployment and clash of power. Every page in this astonishing book breathes out an air heavy with political intrigue and calculation, of victory won by deviousness and cunning and quick wits.

> In three days came seven chiefs and elders of the Winged Hats.
> Among them was that tall young man, Amal, whom I had
> met on the beach, and he smiled when he saw my necklace.
> We made them welcome, for they were ambassadors. We
> showed them Allo, alive but bound. They thought we had
> killed him, and I saw it would not have vexed them if we had.
> Allo saw it too, and it vexed him. Then in our quarters at
> Hunno we came to council.
>
> They said that Rome was falling, and that we must join
> them. They offered me all South Britain to govern after they
> had taken a tribute out of it.
>
> I answered, 'Patience. This Wall is not weighed off like
> plunder. Give me proof that my General is dead.'
>
> 'Nay,' said one elder, 'you prove to us that he lives'; and
> another said cunningly, 'What will you give us if we read
> you his last words?'

'We are not merchants to bargain,' cried Amal. 'Moreover, I owe this man my life. He shall have his proof.' He threw across to me a letter (well I knew the seal) from Maximus. 'We took this out of the ship we sank,' he cried. 'I cannot read, but I know one sign, at least, which makes me believe.' He showed me a dark stain on the outer roll that my heavy heart perceived was the valiant blood of Maximus.

'Read!' said Amal. 'Read, and then let us hear whose servants you are!'

Said Pertinax, very softly, after he had looked through it: 'I will read it all. Listen, barbarians!' He read that which I have carried next my heart ever since.

'To Parnesius and Pertinax, the not unworthy Captains of the Wall, from Maximus, once Emperor of Gaul and Britain, now prisoner waiting death by the sea in the camp of Theo-dosius – Greeting and Good-bye!'

'Enough,' said young Amal; 'there is your proof! You must join us now!'

Pertinax looked long and silently at him, till that fair man blushed like a girl. Then read Pertinax:

'I have joyfully done much evil in my life to those who have wished me evil, but if ever I did any evil to you two I repent, and I ask your forgiveness. The three mules which I strove to drive have torn me in pieces as your Father prophesied. The naked swords wait at the tent door to give me the death I gave to Gratian. Therefore I, your General and your Emperor, send you free and honourable dismissal from my service, which you entered, not for money or office, but, as it makes me warm to believe, because you loved me!'

'By the Light of the Sun,' Amal broke in. 'This was in some sort a Man! We may have been mistaken in his servants!'

And Pertinax read on: 'You gave me the time for which I asked. If I have failed to use it, do not lament. We have gambled very splendidly against the Gods, but they hold weighted dice, and I must pay the forfeit. Remember, I have been; but Rome is; and Rome will be. Tell Pertinax his Mother is in safety at Nicaea, and her monies are in charge of the Prefect at Antipolis. Make my remembrances to your Father and to your Mother, whose friendship was great gain to me. Give also to my little Picts and to the Winged Hats

such messages as their thick heads can understand. I would
have sent you three Legions this very day if all had gone
aright. Do not forget me. We have worked together. Farewell!
Farewell! Farewell!'

'Now, that was my Emperor's last letter.' (The children
heard the parchment crackle as Parnesius returned it to its
place.)

'I was mistaken,' said Amal. 'The servants of such a man
will sell nothing except over the sword. I am glad of it.' He
held out his hand to me.

'But Maximus has given you your dismissal,' said an elder.
'You are certainly free to serve – or to rule – whom you please.
Join – do not follow – join us!'

'We thank you,' said Pertinax. 'But Maximus tells us to
give you such messages as – pardon me, but I use his words –
your thick heads can understand.' He pointed through the
door to the foot of a catapult wound up.

'We understand,' said an elder. 'The Wall must be won
at a price?'

'It grieves me,' said Pertinax, laughing, 'but so it must be
won,' and he gave them of our best Southern wine.

They drank, and wiped their yellow beards in silence till
they rose to go.[6]

There's initiation into the mysteries of power! – and Kipling's
wonderfully tactful reminder that the children are listening takes
the tension out of the scene a little. Even as a child I remember perceiving dimly that there was something desolate in this splendid
loyalty. The young subalterns served a master because they loved
him – they loved this dazzling jauntiness, the display of humane
bureaucracy, the bluff, rueful courage – but beyond that they served
(like Conrad's seamen) a conception of duty with no ultimate
purpose. A man and a soldier saluted the Eagle (or the Union Jack)
because it was all that could give inevitable death any dignity. But
it had no meaning beyond itself, for by this stage Kipling could
see that the point of the British Empire was to perpetuate itself.
The code of service and duty ensured that you pulled your questions up short of the moral and economic bases of your work. The

[6] Rudyard Kipling, *Puck of Pook's Hill*, 'Prefects of the Wall'.

next step along *that* line was to be Orwell's *Burmese Days* and *A Passage to India*.

And yet what child could but feel chokey after that letter in *Puck of Pook's Hill?* The language promises such secrets – such manly clarity of purpose, such resolution, and such dark unmentionables – 'I have done much evil' – such gay, unfettered courage, 'it grieves me . . . but so it must be won' and, with this, such grace and quaint nobility; Tacitus crossed with Disraeli.

III

These four novelists have been part of a long living tradition, but almost everything they embody with such conviction in their prose is now incredible. You say, 'Why not? I can believe it; so could you.' And clearly men can hold beliefs which it appears are contradicted every day within their own experience; they do so all around us. But the ideals of duty and service – necessary as they are – turn upon acceptance of either purpose or authority if they are to be vindicated at some level beyond the institution. Otherwise you are loyal (i.e. serve and do your duty) *simply* to your ship or your regiment or your political party because you are a member of it. There is no more ultimate *telos* or point to your loyalty. This attitude is what comes through strongly from Kipling's soldiers and Conrad's sailors: your duty is to do your job. But since they wrote the idea of authority has undergone very severe alteration. So have the ideas of heroism, of adventuring, and of love and friendship, too. The images we have of these things are much more cloudy and obscure than they were. It is much less clear what it is to use these virtues as moral references. You have to recreate them from within.

At this point ideology and the imagination intersect. To see where they cross, we must turn to the concepts of the late Lucien Goldmann in describing the 'non-conscious structures' of novels. By this he means not only the value-systems of a writer, but the hidden lines of community which a reader recognises when he hears Kipling or Stevenson or, indeed, Dickens, and says 'that sounds very Victorian'.

A non-conscious structure is not a vulgar way of saying subconscious. The English tradition in the study of literature has valuably stressed the importance of the individual – his psychology and biography and ethics – in the understanding of a work. The tradition has overspent itself. The non-conscious structures of the four novels I have quoted also determine the limits of the work, just as our power of colour perception and our innate capacity to generate sentences with a particular syntax set the conditions for how we see the world. The same structure is present when Titian paints a naked woman, and the picture looks nothing like the same anatomy at much the same poundage when painted by Goya. In the novels quoted the non-conscious structure fixes the rhythm of the story; for example, its dilation towards excitement and its contraction towards a safe home; the way each story pulsates between the strong moral poles – love and duty (Hope, Kipling), manly courage and the adventure (Rider Haggard, Kenneth Graham) – which help to hold the characters upright. And in these novels, as indeed in the great tradition of Victorian novels, the characters all have a substantial self, an identity which so to speak precedes immediate experience. Things happen in a given sequence; the movement of time is straightforwardly linear; the agents in the stories are uninterruptedly free; events are caused and not arbitrary. *This* structure – what we may call 'the syntax of experience', with its main parts of speech being Time, Freedom, Identity (the self)[7] – is what most people in England were taught and learned as children. And since the novelists and poets and fiction-builders are the most potent myth-makers of a society, they are the people who decisively vindicate the beliefs, morality and value-system of that society. Not that they do this alone. All art has its genesis within a certain social group. Every work, even of the solitary outlaw-genius, is a conversation with that group about its assumptions. In the conversation between teachers and novelists the forces of both ideology and the imagination become unusually explicit. What is more, there is an unusually close fit between the moral syntax of our best children's novelists and of our best children's teachers. What is it that they tell the children? Is it indeed both suitable for them to hear, *and* true?

To ask this is to look at contemporary ideology. It is to look at the system of values which binds together the social group which interests us, and their spokesmen, the writers. (It is interesting that so many of the best novelists for children are women, given that

[7] The 'syntax' proposed by John Harvey in *Character and the Novel* (Chatto & Windus 1963).

the majority of teachers of the age-group mostly intended as audience for the novels are women, and women of course have far less *direct* political connections and far more connections with young children than men. These facts are reflected in the novels.) Such a system of values is embodied in certain data about the way the world *is*, and *therefore* about how you ought to act, and it is embodied in social institutions which express both data and precepts. In this case the institution is the novel and the novels express data and precepts. A key datum for the novelists who (I am saying) speak for so many teachers is that the individual is the fount and realm of all value. The defining characteristic of an individual is his freedom, and this is realised in his freedom of choice of action. What you do is less important than that you choose to do it.

But it is the most familiar truth of the modern world that this freedom is progressively harder to exercise. In order to maintain this doctrine we have steadily, though unofficially, had to give ground to the enemies of freedom, the demands of the bureaucracies, of the police, of economic or military forces, depending on where you live. People rightly reserve the exercise of tolerance and sincerity and freedom for their private lives because out there, in the public arena, they have seen so much freedom melt away. They have watched, all over the world and at the back door, the scene Auden describes so relentlessly :

> The mass and majesty of this world, all
> that carries weight and always weighs the same
> Lay in the hands of others; they were small
> And could not hope for help and no help came :
> What their foes liked to do was done, their shame
> Was all the worst could wish; they lost their pride
> And died as men before their bodies died.

One understandable reaction has been to pull back into their homes and bolt the kitchen door and hold on to what is there in private. Two consequences have followed. One, an intolerable imprisonment within an over-personalised private life; two, the relinquishing of public and political life to giant, anti-human forces whom we all have to resist for the sake, literally, of ourselves and our children.

In a bitty way we find this reaction expressed, judged, and very occasionally transcended in the best novels now written for children. These books reflect the drastic retrenchment which individual liberty has undertaken since January 1933. In a way impossible to Mark Twain, R. L. Stevenson, Mrs Hodgson Burnett or even Ballantyne and Henty, they have quit history and society. And they have by their lights been right to do so . Society is what we see glimmering on the shield of Achilles.

> Out of the air a voice without a face
> Proved by statistics that some cause was just
> In tones as dry and level as the place :
> No one was cheered and nothing was discussed;
> Column by column in a cloud of dust
> They marched away enduring a belief
> Whose logic brought them, somewhere else, to grief.

As I said in the last chapter, when Rosemary Sutcliff has the courage to return to political history she takes two forms of evasive action. First, she stylises her past so that the ceremony and fealty can command a real love and duty; secondly, she continues to locate all ultimate value in the single relationship : the hero and heroine of *Dawn Wind*[8] hold grimly through the refugee exile they suffer, the bondage and wounding, and then they go back to find each other. But she never lets go of her sense that the individuals are what count, and all other elements are destructive. When similarly Jill Paton Walsh wants to invoke adventurous courage as a public master-symbol in *The Dolphin Crossing*,[9] she has to go back to Dunkirk, the last possible chance in recent history for the children, in Wilfred Owen's words, who are 'ardent for some desperate glory' to be told 'dulce et decorum est pro patria mori'. When Katherine Peyton[10] makes *her* historical choice between the old, rich, smelly world of Flambards and the new technocrats she votes first for progress and then, realising what progress meant – from Orville Wright to the B-52 bomber – cleaned up Flambards for a safe return. And when Philippa Pearce does try to juggle with time, she has to give up, and fudge the end for Tom, in *Tom's Midnight Garden*;[11] genuinely to pursue her insights would mean discarding the stable self, the freely choosing individual.

---

[8] *Dawn Wind* (Oxford 1967).
[9] *The Dolphin Crossing* (Puffin 1968).
[10] *Flambards in Summer* (Oxford 1969).
[11] *Tom's Midnight Garden* (Oxford 1958).

These few examples show how strong is the hold of their structure of feeling. The paradox is that at a time of moral conflict, this value-system is so settled and uniform. Its structure of feeling is deeply coloured by an intense and nostalgic longing for things as they might once have been, but now emphatically are not. Nostalgia, it must be clear, is not a swear-word. It can be a positive, strong current of feeling.[12] But a great arc of writers, formidable and intelligent men and women, ranging from (so to speak) William Mayne or Mary Norton on the right to Helen Cresswell and Mrs Peyton on the left, are in full retreat from their times, and behind them are the hosts of teachers with whom they speak to the children. There is a different moral highway for their exploration, given that a novelist or a teacher cannot get away from moral thought; what moral direction might do instead of liberalism?

IV

The one exhilarating aspect of literature for children today is that, unlike most novelists for adults in England and the USA, its authors have not relinquished the idea of goodness. The prime virtues of and for a modern liberal are freedom of choice, self-knowledge, sincerity and empirical common-sense. That is not, for goodness' sake, to say that these aren't real and essential virtues. Bigotry and insincerity are evils. But these virtues are not enough; they are not primary. It is a mark of those who live by them (and our education system does) that they largely do without the ideas of goodness, truth, and beauty. The self-conscious figure who lives by these canons shares with his culture the conviction that nothing can be shown to be true which is not defended by a regular system of computation. Outside these principles of empirical verification, all statements tend to be opinions, expressions of personal judgement which though always to be tolerated cannot readily be refuted as false or hateful. What does such a figure lack?

For a start, progressive and liberal man (as novelist or teacher) needs some criteria of public right and wrong. This is not to say that every good children's novelist cancels her subscription to the colour supplement and goes on a demonstration. It is to say that the novels, to be adequate to the word, need to move the old fixed

[12] See D. W. Harding, 'A Note on Nostalgia', in *Scrutiny* I, 1932.

points and live in tension with the uncertainties of modern reality. I would say that Mrs Peyton's *Flambards in Summer* and Philippa Pearce's *The Children of the House* make the first showings at such an account. Beyond this, beyond the urgent need for resistance to the headlong destruction of the world by industrialised nations, we shall have to find some account of ourselves which permits a different idea of the self. And at this point it is simply not true to say 'but children wouldn't understand a different self'; Marx himself was the first to point out as the notorious mark of liberalism that it supposes human nature to be fixed and unalterable and timelessly liberal-minded. As it is, children take in and make their own a bewildering, very complicated, and deeply confused version of the self. The confusion is most easily seen, though not at all isolated, in the question of religious belief. Most children move comfortably and unnoticingly between belief and secularism, and let the contradictions go hang. In this they simply reflect the adults of their society who disregard religion until it is forced upon them by the great events of their life, birth, marriage, and death. Then they return to ceremonies and liturgy in which they do not believe.

Comparable confusions declare themselves at every turn of the children's and their parents' moral lives. They are taught to believe in a self which is free, spontaneous, and self-determining. They also learn that they must be docile and obedient to their superiors. The response of some children to these contradictions is an anxious eagerness to please, and that of others is cynicism. These points are not simply intended to score off educational ideology, but to show that from the pushchair onwards children take in from their elders a picture of themselves.

Just how various human ideas of freedom and causality can be (to children as well as adults), comes out when we turn up any of the great fairy stories retrieved from an alien culture by the Romantics. The noise and ferocity of giants (*Jack and the Beanstalk*), the arbitrary malice of witches (*Snow White*), the randomness of events, especially under the control of magic (*Rumpelstiltskin, Sleeping Beauty*), the precariousness of most human situations (*Childe Roland, Knight Wynd*), all these familiar aspects of life arise constantly in fairy stories and hardly at all in the present-day children's novels. In the face of random and destructive events, the fairy stories oppose only the absolute moral quality, goodness: the goodness of pauper girls, of deformed dwarves, of beasts and metamorphosed princes. The ideas of time, causality and the self canvassed by these stories are self-evidently intelligible to children; they are sometimes – at least if you are a beggared or starving or bombed-out refugee – more faithful to our times than many novels.

So it is surely nonsense to say that different propositions about the psyche and society would be beyond children – about, if you like, politics and morality. Insofar as they are accurate, they would help us find a more satisfactory morality, one in which we may learn to be good in spite of innate or irresistible tendencies towards selfishness, cowardice, and cruelty, both singly and in classes. But how, chaos and old night now being the prime mover of things, how shall this morality direct itself with any purpose? The moral centre of one's life being according to liberalism one's own business, it follows that liberalism cannot tell us what to do. Indeed, not only 'cannot'; it is a principle of liberalism that it *must* not. 'Consequently', I suppose, 'I rejoice, having to construct something upon which to rejoice.'

V

It is a peculiar truth that anyone should need to remind novelists – and poets and artists in general – that it is the main point of their work that they should find out what it means to be good. In Iris Murdoch's remarkable trio of essays *The Sovereignty of Good*[13] she writes,

> I think there is a place both inside and outside religion for
> a sort of contemplation of the good, not just by dedicated
> experts but by ordinary people: an attention which is not
> just the planning of particular good actions but an attempt
> to look right away from self towards a distant transcendent
> perfection, a source of uncontaminated energy, a source
> of *new* and quite undreamt of virtue [Miss Murdoch's italics].

This is in no sense a consolatory pursuit. As she says elsewhere,

> What does seem to make perfect sense in the platonic myth
> is the idea of the Good as the source of light which reveals
> to us all things as they really are . . . The Good has nothing
> to do with purpose, indeed it excludes the idea of purpose.

[13] Routledge & Kegan Paul 1970, p. 95.

'All is vanity' is the beginning and the end of ethics. The
only genuine way to be good is to be good 'for nothing' . . .

Miss Murdoch makes it utterly clear that she holds this distinctly
unfashionable (and, no doubt, voluntarist) view in full recognition
of how it will be refuted by an empiricist and natural-psychological
ethics. And a secular doctrine of the good will have to write itself
in accordance with a realistic map of human psychology. What
is also clear – and clear as a matter of empirical appeal – is that
empirical psychology is disastrously not enough of a basis for an
ethic which insistently refers to a conception outside the range
of that psychology. (This is not the old error of supposing that what
is metaphysical is necessarily so; twentieth-century physics has
taken over too much once metaphysical space to be confident on
that score.) The limits of empirical psychology are by definition
individual – either the literal individual, or the individual in accu-
mulation. Such a psychology can describe but cannot account for
the frightfulness of modern mass slaughter; indeed there is no
modern ideology which can account for it, let alone rescue some
decent moral reference. The sceptic can make mincemeat of any
feeling that such a lack may ever be redeemed. He will tell us that
all we can salvage is some rather piecemeal utilitarianism – the
reduction of famine, equality of opportunity, social welfare, free
speech, low-grade existentialism – and that metaphysical goodness is
neither provable nor usable. The argument Miss Murdoch returns is
from art : 'great art is evidence of [the] reality [of goodness]. Art
indeed, so far from being a playful diversion of the human race, is
the place of its most fundamental insight, and the centre to which
the more uncertain steps of metaphysics must constantly return.'
(p. 73) What might it mean to say that a great work of art is the
most promising access to goodness? What shall we rejoin to the
utilitarian and the sceptic?

A reply to both questions perhaps rests in the experience of such
a work of art. Take a supreme piece of chamber music – Schubert's
C Major Quintet (incomparable and supreme in the second and
third movements at least). In music the argument about its moral
meaning is sometimes clearer than in literature because it has no
referential language It can't be said to be 'about' an experience in
quite the same way that *Othello* is 'about' Othello, Iago and Des-
demona. This quintet represents more than the *experience* of

beauty – goodness cannot be experienced in the sense that beauty can, or indeed in any sense at all. So that the alleged supremacy of the quintet is not a function (as the sceptre puts it) of its producing a nice feeling'. For while there are in the music unmistakable correlates of human experience such that the heartbreakingly sweet cadences which form the second statement of the second movement, echo in their chromatic progression through a series of minor fourths a specifically religious liturgy, the central meanings of the music are not just a *reminder* of that tradition. They are necessarily bound in a culture. At the same time they provide a metaphor for that specifically human behaviour the effort of which is so to attend to the forms of experience, so to eradicate merely self-ish claims, and so to tense the unblinkable facts of human wretchedness against a larger, utterly impersonal peace which does pass understanding but the possibility of which is necessary to any morality which falls neither into commonsense vulgarity nor into despair, that one perceives the significance of goodness to be itself. The return to the tonic in the Schubert movement, compounded as it is of a recapitulation and the haunting counter-claims insisted upon by the minor is, in the most literal sense, a metaphor for goodness, for that convergence of selfless moral behaviour upon 'the image of the Good as a transcendent magnetic centre [which] seems to me the least corruptible and most realistic picture for us to use in our reflections upon the moral life'.

The musical metaphor for goodness (and that phrase is itself a metaphor) does *not* represent an abstraction from day-to-day living. Hard and exact thought about morality is a main preoccupation of our lives. It gives point to our lives. We are unlikely to find another point. And yet the harsh austerities exacted by the effort – and such an effort is more than the product of the spirit of capitalism – also commit us to learning an altogether more refined and rich, passionate and vivid language of moral description than is yielded up by owner-occupied England. This richer language and this vision of goodness will need new kinds of moral attention (Miss Murdoch's word). This language requires a discipline, an attention to what men have found good at other times and places; the result will be the product of a shared and identifiable experience, and of metaphor, of new names and ideas invented in order to give meaning to moral features we can see for the first time. Such an enterprise, as Chomsky has pointed out, should long ago have provided the purpose and direction of a decent-spirited sociology and psychology. But it is not narrowly the domain of the expert. The artist, the composer, and particularly the gifted novelist (however rare a bird) speaks for every day. In his and her hands the task rests for providing such metaphors – such *images* – of good behaviour. (What is a poet if he is not a maker of images?)

If it is an anomaly (it is) that so much good novel writing is specifically for children, there cannot be too much grumbling. We need what allies we can find. The good progressive notwithstanding, children's novelists could find a language which transcends the vacant principles of liberalism, 'sincerity' and 'self-knowledge'. These latter principles when they become their own teleological end can lead to the obsessive inspection of personal moral machinery, particularly when it is in bad repair. In the effort towards artistic creation we find the only lasting proof that human beings can attain a sacred and loving perception of reality free from consolatory superstition and fantasy, and can make it an instrument of moral purification and freedom. In literature at the present time the children's novelists keep alive some vision of their community and of their task as writers. They find a set of drained-out moral concepts; their task is to revive them. Morality is more than social welfare, freedom more than domestic self-assertion, love more than domestic kindness. 'Whatsoever things are true, whatsoever things are honest, whatsoever things are just, whatsoever things are pure, whatsoever things are lovely, whatsoever things are of good report; if there be any virtue and if there be any praise, think on these things.'

Any sufficient ideology carried by a group of writers who know their obligation might turn back to these imperatives. The state of international politics being what it is, it is clear that to think on these things and to write about them must now be to think and write novels politically. Cultures are not so alien but that men of many races know that they lack in their lives places of justice, purity, loveliness and good report.

8
Public townscape and popular culture

Any argument about culture in this large sense must imply, or make explicit, a powerful political content. Culture reposes within the circuits of a living politics, and it is that politics which may explain how our culture may move and change. For our culture is our way of life – its whole busy action, its values, its arts and symbols, structures and institutions. More than that, or rather, penetrating every corner of this giant and intricate organism, culture is the total, mobile body of feelings and beliefs, intentions and reasons (terms none of which is in the least synonymous) which inform that ceaseless action. When we talk about our culture we have learned to lift traditionally sanctioned areas out of the living totality and treat them separately. Culture then is literature – and within literature, novels, plays or poems – or it is music, painting, or individual buildings. In the unbroken reproductions of a technological culture it is harder to make the act of separation – to lift out TV or electronically stored music and to look at it hard. But whenever we do, it is vital to remember that we distort the body of beliefs and feelings carried by the form – TV or films or poems or whatever – and that we study an experience drawn out of the living substance which gives it meaning.

This warning is perhaps most needed when we report on the meanings and values carried by our townscape. For we can talk about an individual building: it is a traditional and precious activity. Besides, we know who designed it, and generally for what purpose. We can walk round it and give it a date; we may place it in the continuity of a given style or a certain architect's work. But to read and understand the whole texture of a landscape is not only a much more recent endeavour, it is bafflingly complex. Such reading requires not only a careful defence against vulgar-minded generalisation, either about the damnable decline of industrial culture or about its neon excitements, it also needs a readiness to launch upon generalisations which without being blank or cruel to the human experience summarised nonetheless grasp its central meanings. Such a readiness can only take off from 'an intelligent saturation' in the life which is to be analysed. Judgements about popular culture will yield no truth if they are made out of any doctrinaire framework – either about the awfulness of pop, or about its *sacralisation*.

An adequate reporter from an area of culture will need to work through three stages. He will first need to recognise not only what traditions his materials derive from, but something about the source of his own criteria and judgement. He will need, in the case of townscape, to know how he has learned to look at his environment. Secondly, he will need some theories to explain what has happened, why changes occurred and what order they may have. Again, in the case of townscape, he will need to construct some explanation, however reach-me-down, of why industry has arrived and what it has done. It is a measure of English queasiness about the word that one needs to point out at this stage that as a matter of logical necessity his explanation will have political bearings. Third and last, deriving from the first two stages as well as all such previous analytic experience, he will bring to bear his vivid sense of the human and moral meaning of what he sees – his sense of its deathliness or vitality, of its significance both for him and for the people who made it and use it, its religious power maybe, or its playfulness, its coarseness or its reassuring homeliness. At this stage too the painful strictures may have to be passed on to other people and their culture. A man who studies his culture cannot ever break off his human connection with what is there in front of him, however intolerable he finds it. The final insult would be to soften any criticism for the sake of keeping in touch; to do that would (paradoxically) involve a drastic foreshortening of human possibility. As who should say 'I will tolerate your unspeakable Japanese garden, stained-glass leaded lights and Cotswold-stone-cottage slab chimney because (poor chap) you and I are both men'. There is something rank in both the pitying kindliness or the high euphoria with which some people patronise either pop or subtopian cultures. But then there is a no less disagreeable iciness breathed out by the disdain and weariness of the disapproving.

163

There is a poise, there is a resistance, which can speak cuttingly to its audience, both for it and with it; which can speak with warmth and largeness of temper, without conceit or mock modesty. To write like this would be indeed to create a sociology with authentic powers. Such a sociology – one should instead say a politics – would make of our culture a place in which it would be possible to find oneself. It would supply routes to the individual without sacrificing an independent authority, larger than individuals but containing them all. Of its nature it would sacrifice preposterous (in the exact sense of the word) claims to 'value freedom'.

Here are some notes towards such an inquiry, based on the landscape which affects the lives and understanding of everyone of us profoundly. Here is 'public culture' as contrasted with the last chapter's 'private identity'. (The approach I suggest could be taken up in part or in whole by groups of students in primary school or extramural class or university. I know at first hand of examples of all three.) The judgements made are certainly intended to have a more than narrowly personal relevance; at the same time, like any idea of politics, they imply the chronicle of an autobiography, they grow from one man's life at a point where the roads cross: these books, on one side, a life and a history, on the other.

I I

The warning shots against the onslaught of industry upon the English landscape were first fired with some telling power at the beginning of the nineteenth century. It was then that forward spirits began to notice the evils of industrialism. For we find, in the works of the great Romantic revolutionaries, in Blake, Wordsworth, Byron, Cobbett, Shelley, Beethoven, Delacroix, Courbet, Victor Hugo, a central contradiction. These men speak as the voices of the new populism; for the first time poets gave a voice to the whole inarticulate crowd of men and women who entered European history for the first time. At the same time, in the magnificent works of the Romantic movement, in *The Prelude*, or the *Pastoral Symphony*, these same men damned the city, and got out of it. The history of nineteenth-century art, literature, and music and much of the past seventy years as well has been the history of a national imagination trying to keep faith with its rural memories and at the same time to make cities it can believe in. The experience of the city is a central source of energy in Dickens, in the Impressionists, in Proust, in the Cubists, in Stravinsky. Lawrence's novel *The Rainbow* is the great threnody in our language upon the ruin of the lovely English landscape; it closes with a vision of the hateful rash of little red houses creeping across the Nottinghamshire hills. In Eliot's poem *The Waste Land*, the city is the place of desolation, of restless, isolated strangers hurrying about their business.

> Unreal City,
> Under the brown fog of a winter dawn,
> A crowd flowed over London Bridge, so many,
> I had not thought death had undone so many.
> Sighs, short and infrequent, were exhaled,
> And each man fixed his eyes before his feet.
> Flowed up the hill and down King William Street,
> To where Saint Mary Woolnoth kept the hours
> With a dead sound on the final stroke of nine.

This is the imagery which a great many English people have absorbed. From dozens of reports, from diaries and letters and novels and bits of sociology early and late, there breathes out the sweet, musty and penetrating odour of a nostalgia which longs for the lost beauty of the English garden.

Nostalgia for the countryside even in Dickens is intolerably sweet and strong. At the end of *Our Mutual Friend*, of *Bleak House*, of *Martin Chuzzlewit*, as refuge in any of his other great books, the poet of the city invoked the great images of the English garden, the man-made landscape which at its best probably held the loveliest balance between climate, topography, agriculture and human repose in European history. Those images penetrate our whole consciousness and our national imagination. From Spenser's *Prothalamion*

> Against the bridal day, which was not long,
> Sweet Thames! run softly, till I end my song . . .

to Keats' *Ode to a Nightingale* the antique images are called up tirelessly to dance to new measures. From Spenser to Keats and on to Yeats those images drift in plaintive cadences into the mythology of a nation.

> I cannot see what flowers are at my feet,
> Nor what soft incense hangs upon the boughs,
> But, in embalmed darkness, guess each sweet
> Wherewith the seasonable month endows
> The grass, the thicket, and the fruit-tree wild;
> White hawthorn, and the pastoral eglantine . . .

The landscape of these poets was man made, slowly and as matter of quite conscious vision for the future. The gardens left London for the country during the great boom of late Tudor and Elizabethan England. The castles turned their moats into ornamental water and became country houses. The infinitely shrewd and aesthetically faultless plunder of the New World and of the East began. The buccaneers did not only bring back the hauls of El Dorado; they planted the great gardens of Audley End, Wilton, Burghley and Hardwick with cedars from Lebanon; they brought back fig-trees, grape-vines, apricots, peaches; they planted new flowers – clematis. wistaria, Dutch bulbs – to join the traditional dog-roses, speedwell and may of the madrigals. As the country houses became mansions and palaces, the gardens became parks. The enormous increase in flocks of sheep, deer and cattle cleared vast tracts of forest, and the eighteenth century set to, to make the picturesque landscape. The cultural contribution of this century is still robustly alive in a million Ideal Home gardens. For the eighteenth-century landowners, the country gentlemen farmers, the landscape gardeners, painters and architects colluded to produce the main concepts of the exquisite landscape which today we see in our imagination as typically English, which crops out in miniature versions in front of picture windows and spec. builders' neo-ranch-houses all over Britain, and which is kept alive in the offices of the British Tourist Association and shipped abroad, in the teeth of the truth, to the dollar-spending and hard currency nations. In the eighteenth century, the gentlemen devised the nooks, bowers, surprises and sudden prospects to which the small, changeable scale of English topography lends itself so easily, and at the same time they turned the common people off their own land and enclosed it. Now it is never easy weighing the suffering of the past in the scales of the present. There can be little doubt that the enclosures caused a great deal of immediate human misery; there is equally no doubt that they were a part of a revolution in agricultural methods which transformed production and made across the years up to the Corn Laws for an enormously larger quantity of food to become available, if only grudgingly. But the relevance of the Enclosures Act for our purposes is that it completed the colonisation of the English landscape from the bleak, ungiving heath we find today in North Yorkshire or Cornwall into the subtle, rhythmic patterns of wall, copse, hedge, wagon ways, small fields and the connecting farmsteads and market towns, which we have learned by heart from the nineteenth-century novelists, poets, and painters. The enclosure confirmed the *scale* of the English country; the size of the fields, the generous placing of chestnut, ash, elm and oak, the permanence of the low hedges which gave both privacy and neighbourliness to the landscape; all this rich orchestration formed a style which still dominates much of our imagining about the communities we live in and try to plan for. The Englishness of the English landscape (and, necessarily, townscape) is one of the richest achievements of a popular culture.[1]

No doubt the argument will be advanced (again) that this manifestation of culture was hardly 'popular' in the fullest sense, and that the men who have left their mark most visibly across the map of England were grandees and seigneurs, or their landscape gardeners – the Kents, Reptons and Browns – whose office was to do their master's pleasure in consonance with their own taste; or that, again, the recorders of the masterpiece, the landscape painters from Morland and Gainsborough through Constable and Cotman to Palmer or Lear sentimentalised the life they recorded and only saw the squalor of the cottages from a long way off, the other side of Dedham Vale. Such a case makes a number of mistakes which it is important to get straight if the study of culture really is to give us some idea of what meanings to their lives men have made in the past; if we are to learn from that past, and – futurology and tealeaf-reading apart – there is nowhere else we *can* learn from, then our understanding of culture must take in many more dimensions than the reflex class-consciousness and simple-minded social determinism which, for example, characterise most educational thought today. We shall need a reading of cultural conditions in a way which does justice to the density of life which they contain. But more than a full, imaginative inwardness with the material we

---

[1] Its system of typical features has been described by Nikolaus Pevsner in *The Englishness of English Art* (Architectural Press 1956, Penguin 1963).

need a grasp on the structure of feeling which provides the explanatory key to the cultural life we are studying. What would such a key be like which would explain the version of the English landscape which came into circulation about the beginning of the nineteenth century and exerts such a pull today?

I have described in a very compressed form the making of the English landscape up to 1800. It is about then that a few writers began to notice what the industrial and agricultural upheavals were doing to the landscape. At the same time they were able to draw on a tradition as ancient as the history of their own literature to confirm the opposition of town and country. From medieval courtly love stories through *As You Like It* and *The Winter's Tale* to the Pastoral eclogues in imitation of Virgil and Horace by Ben Jonson, Dryden and Pope, the poets had ample precedent for naming the city as the centre of grime and corruption and the country as the source of innocence, cleanliness and beauty. But the vision of the English landscape was not simply the product of its literature,[2] nor indeed of a topography derived from pastoral poetry. Not only did Cobbett and Wordsworth put the people of England squarely down on their own land, but the painters brought an entirely unidyllic attention to the people at work. The great line of English watercolourists: Crome, Cotman, Girtin, Cozens, the Varleys, not only introduced and confirmed a new imagery and gave a fresh, sparkling surface to the national imagination, they also peopled this world with men and women at work – ploughing, sailing, shepherding, feeding beasts.[3]

The man who confirmed these tendencies and made them his own was Constable. The people of his pictures are building boats, drawing barges, driving wains, and all this rendered with what he himself saw as the scientific eye – the eye which had been taught by the giants of the eighteenth century that surface impressions are the source of all experience. Constable wrote: 'Painting is a Science, and should be pursued as an enquiry into the laws of nature. Why, then, may not landscape painting be considered as a branch of natural philosophy of which pictures are but the experiments.'[4]

[2] My anthology *The Scene* (Cambridge 1972) collects together some of the best-known poetic visions of the countryside since Spenser.

[3] The seminal record of their work, outside the galleries, is Martin Hardie's *Water Colour Painting in Britain*, 3 vols. (Batsford 1967).

[4] C. R. Leslie, *Memoirs of the Life of John Constable*, privately published by Peter Leslie (1931), p. 323.

The sedate, precise intention of this sorts well with his remark 'It cannot be too much to say, that the landscape is full of moral and religious feeling'. Constable gives us an insight into 'the structure of feeling' in his time, and a measure of its unity. The infinitely fine and delicate balance which then obtained between the state of technology, the systems of production and the moral perception of shape and tincture is fully realised in this part of its popular culture. Constable was a rich miller's son – as his brother said, 'When I look at a mill painted by John, I see that it will go *round*.' He knew the work at first hand, and the details of his pictures – the precise bevelling of the ancient wain, the newly planed wood just bent into shape for the boats – are the artistic equivalent of the actual wood, itself the product of what was a necessary morality of work.[5] George Eliot put it for Adam Bede at work as a carpenter in 1799, like this:[6] 'His work . . . had always been part of his religion, and from very early days he saw clearly that good carpentry was God's will – was that form of God's will that most immediately concerned him.' We can see the same values carried by the lock-gates to the canal which Constable painted, and in the thousands of lock-gates all over the country. They testify in the most eloquent way possible to the presence of an authentic and common culture, and provide a point of comparison when we wish to know whether or not we may find another such point of vitality today. A canal junction gives us a rich quarry. We may see the accuracy with which the massive gates are matched, and the niceness of balance with which gear-wheels and handles are adjusted. We may note the closeness with which hand-planed timbers have been dovetailed and morticed, braced on the outside against the great mass of water. But more than the details of an exact and efficient technology, we need to register the completeness with which a typical canal junction or a big sequence of locks is articulated. We can undoubtedly find more exquisite or more powerful forms of engineering, in ancient and modern cultures, but the canals may serve as examples of a high point in a culture of town – or landscape. The lock-keeper's cottage, the short arc of the bridge over the canal, the parallel lines of path, grass, walls and hedge ensure that such places *are* places: their parts

---

[5] In this argument I have been enormously helped by and at moments am simply paraphrasing an excellent essay, 'Workmanship and Design', by Andor Gomme, *Delta* (Cambridge) 45, March 1969.
[6] *Adam Bede*, Chapter 50.

cohere in an order and rightness which is itself satisfying and the implicit morality of which makes a stand against the smooth and impassive surface of the intense inane.

The canal junction I am thinking of (and we would each take our own examples, some obviously more telling than others) is not simply a satisfying pattern of grouped shapes. It is the difference between an abstract painting and a still-life. When all has been said about the tension generated by the painting of a Mondrian or a Ben Nicholson they are still fatally lacking in human content. Why this is so depends upon the history of the past two hundred years, and whatever it is that has driven all but the greatest painters and sculptors out of contact with the human and non-human world. A still-life possesses this advantage over Ben Nicholson: that the objects represented have absorbed something of the history of the people and the time which has worn, polished, scarred and fondled them.[7] In the same way the relation of cottage to lock to path and bridge, to coping-stones and the bricklaid platforms along the rim of whose arc the wooden beams turn, give back the meanings of the lives which made them. The laying of the rounded bricks at the edge above the water is an example not only of comeliness and soundness but also of the judgement and care needed by the workman to fasten and align bricks of slightly varied sizes. The result is a floorscape of much greater interest than a more developed technology could have shown. Its texture is more subtly varied partly because the builders only used bricks for a limited area, partly because the bricks themselves are varied. And then the floorscape takes *its* place in the tessellation of the whole place; a rhythmic, varied and living statement about the lives and work of the men who used the place, about their relations to one another, to the materials with which they had built the place, both as home and point of transit, and to those mysterious Pleistocene forces which had given them their local geography.

It is these relations whose presence or absence will make a living townscape. There are very few examples of the small corners of the English landscape made between 1758 when the Bridgewater canal opened and about 1830 when the canal system was fairly complete, which fail to be as admirable as I have described. They represent –

---

[7] D. H. Lawrence in *The Rainbow*, 'The furniture was old and familiar as old people, the whole place seemed so kin to him, as if it partook of his being ...'

if we separate them for the moment from their continuing history
– a rich point in cultural history for which the inadequate metaphor
can only be a balance, a delicate poise between the moving and
changing forces of technology, moral and labouring energy, the
landscape as a man-made and a natural presence, the relations of
domestic and industrial economy, and the stage of industrialisation.
Whatever the discrepancies in suffering and happiness in other parts
of their lives, Constable and the watercolourists, the canal-builders,
the bargees and the entrepreneurs who hired them, the landowners
who hired *them*, the landowners of Claremont, Osterley Park,
Twickenham Gardens, Chatsworth, the speculative builders of
Salisbury Cathedral Close, bear their different witness in this area
to a common culture. They knew how to make a place.

III

We are heirs to that knowledge. The upheaval in social and moral
thought on either side of 1800, the revolutions, the street fights and
rural riots, the growth of cities and the many accounts of the salvation held out by a return to nature, all this still fills our minds and
spirits with its old power. But our whole culture has moved hugely
on as well. We now need an account of that movement which will
explain at least some of the things that have happened to our town
and landscapes since the greatest period of English painting coincided with the completion of England's greatest success in making
a landscape.

There are first some obstacles to clear away. The report on the
momentum of English townscaping as it accelerated on to the
present day can only be desolate. The fine balance of reciprocal
forces tilted and smashed. Another one, in another part of people's
lives, held itself for a while. But no one with his sight and sensibility
could now say that we share a proper culture for making towns
and landscapes. Nonetheless, this does not mean that success is
impossible. A sombre view is not necessarily a passive or fatalist
one. First, no one can doubt some of our successes in, say, new
town-planning, roadscaping the motorways, rescuing old towns
from the *blitzkrieg* of the juggernaut truck or, on a much smaller
scale, in mending fences, making gardens or built-in cupboards or a
new henhouse; we can always find innumerable cases where the

job has been prettily done. The spasmodic decline of a visual culture which, like any high point in cultural triumph, could only briefly sustain itself, is not evenly downhill. And the conditions for its recovery may always be dormant in any given society. The second point is a matter of insistent emphasis. What is lost is irrecoverable on its own terms. Constable's England has gone. If we re-make a healthy visual culture it must be on our own terms. And there is nothing predetermined about this. When we regret 'ah, it couldn't last – the Florentine Renaissance, Elizabethan literature, the eighteenth-century garden', no doubt we are right. The balance of forces changes. But it changes not under the impulse of blind, non-human forces: it changes as a result of the decisions of men. The recovery of a landscape is a matter of decision, and this is true of any cultural life. When I say decision I do not mean some act of the fixed, insensate will. I mean the vital movement of men's souls to what they most need. To know what you really want is the hardest thing in the world to know. But it is knowable, if men make the creative effort. Only the knowledge is tied to a moral scale whose measurements can depend on some general recognition, and it is a truism of the present times that such recognition is impossible. We need now to consider how the disintegration came about and what the chances are for general repair and the resurreaction of a common purpose in the future.

What can we gather from history – from the irrecoverable world of John Constable, Wordsworth and Robert Owen – and put to our own purposes? And where shall we find the buds and shoots of life in the township of today? Where, too, shall we *not* find it; what in that townscape is dead and deathly?

It is a necessary piece of myth-making to say that at such-and-such a point the landscape was achieved and English towns were at their finest. The appalling jerry-built slums of Manchester had begun before Nash finished Bath. Yet we must have a point of comparison for the present, and it is certainly true that the men who built and maintained the mills of Dedham Vale, tended the oaks of the Test valley, or designed the canal village of Stoke Bruerne; who completed Marlborough, Lyme Regis, Stamford, Harrogate or Edinburgh – these men simply could not have committed some of the brutality done to the country since. It absolutely won't do to point out[8]

---

[8] Cf. the straightfaced Wellsian J. H. Plumb in *Crisis in the Humanities* (Penguin 1964).

that the landowners ripped up the parterre to get at the coal as soon as they knew it was there, and would have done every bit as horribly as Peacehaven in Sussex or the brick moonlands of Bedfordshire if they had known how. That their technology was too elementary is a constituent fact of their culture and of their frame of mind.

> The deep-rutted by-roads . . . and the winding lanes, preserve through years of neglect the traces of technique in their hedgerows . . . [and] in their ditches. On the old ruinous field gate, with its highly arched, tapering top bar rudely carved on the underside against the tenon, the grey mass cannot hide the signs of vitality more marvellous than its own – the intensified vitality of those skilled hands that shaped the timbers.[9]

This moving eloquence does not rest upon a myth. The evidence is there to check in just the places the writer names. During the hundred and fifty years (or so) since many of the gates, walls and ditches were made, that subtle combination of technology, technique, morality and working relations has utterly changed its grain.

In a very crude way the change was the result of those familiar entries in all the off-the-peg formulas of social change: industrialisation, democratisation, secularisation, and the growth of cities. Within this large grid, we can make some more particular guesses. First, it is clearer than ever today and cannot be said too often that the development of mass production systems in which the men and women ('operatives') had no interest beyond the wage they drew, drove a deep rift between a man and his work.[10] At the same time techniques of automation and assembly-line ensured that not only were more and more parts ready-made, they were produced in one place and put together in another. Across a century or so (there seems no reason why the process should take any longer; in some industries a couple of generations is enough) traditions of apprenticeship and patient indenture, of the steady and disciplined application of a learned judgement of hand and eye, gave way to an altogether different training, often pleasanter and less strenuous, but necessarily

[9] G. Sturt, *Change in the Village* (Duckworth 1912), p. 138.
[10] The history of the perception and consciousness of work remains to be written, though all diagnoses can only start from Marx and the Victorian novelists.

acquired in the abstract and in another place. The training of engineer, architect, spiderman, forester, carpenter, shepherd, teacher, became adjusted to a special programme carried through in a special place. The materials of the craft became no longer known as from one place and for a lifetime. The profound experience of the individual trees shown by the men in Hardy's novel *The Woodlanders* (one of them knows his way in the pitch-dark by feeling the trees) was no longer possible. At the same time that local inwardness is replaced by a more exact and confident knowledge of the behaviour of trees in all parts of the country. But all such knowledge became more generalised, known at a distance. Not that this alone would explain the disastrous loss of touch which our present treatment of the country betrays. We need also to invoke the distance placed between men and their work by the use of standardised and prefabricated materials. Instead of the 'workmanship of risk', in which the inherent predictability of the material ensures all sorts of working and visual interest, we find the dominance of the 'workmanship of certainty',[11] in which such interest is deliberately eradicated in order to obtain a greater efficiency. The danger then becomes that the repetition of perfect uniformity is dull and deadening.

There are two solutions. The first is to maintain within the repetition of uniformity a random variety in inessential parts of the design. In townscape, especially on the vast scale of modern construction, this is easy. You plan the variety of texture which will give you the unplannable changes you need; the surface of water, the changing reflections thrown back by glass, the dappling of light by leaves, the living variety of gardens, of drying washing, of people's movement and adaptation. (Think of the variety of places where people will sit down and picnic.) The second is deliberately to abandon the workmanship of certainty (and the likely benefits of its greater cheapness) in the interest of a more risky variety. This latter solution makes for the incredibly busy trade of the present in Heal's and Habitat iconography – the *art paysan* glazeless pots, adzed tables, rough-planed elm chairs, scrubbed pine and thick rugs of the high Hampstead style. These goods are the product of the still powerful Arts and Crafts and Garden City movements which took their energy both from the Romantics and from the

---

[11] I take this pair of distinctions from David Pye's admirable book *The Nature and Art of Workmanship* (Cambridge 1968).

picturesque tradition. I shall try to revalue that heritage in a moment. The point is this: as the technology and the systems of production changed, so did the workman's, designer's, planner's, and artist's relations with their materials. But changing technology and a consequent change in training and attitude to material do not in themselves account for the near-universal loss of touch. If a definition of idiocy is insistence on the validity of an utterly private, self-fulfilling and circular moral universe (circular because there is no point of insertion for contradiction), then we are idiots of space and shape. What caused the idiocy?

It is already clear that no one demon can be arraigned as the agent. We have looked at the creation by Romantic and picturesque landscapes of a national imagination. We have further considered the changes in technology and its culture in the situations of work. Consciousness also changed. During the nineteenth century the individualist ethic won a unique dominance. Yet at the same time the socialist ethic struck its roots and expanded at a fabulous rate. An odd, striated mixture of the two produced the first criticisms of an industrialised townscape, left and right combining in a blueprint for the future.

The first individualist was the businessman. The ethic of unregulated free enterprise without social controls and with a profound disregard for the human life which the enterprise employed produced the shocking wastes of early industrial England. There can be for us no complacent reading of this scenery. For the concentrations of capital which necessarily followed this investment programme generated a community of interests which in turn issued in the great civic building of the Victorians – in Leeds Town Hall, Bradford Exchange, Manchester Town Hall, Newcastle's Grey Street, Liverpool's St George's Hall, the Chamberlains' Birmingham – this solid, dignified, occasionally noble directory of its wealthy age.[12] The same age built the Merseyside, Tyneside, Humberside waterfronts, together with the thrilling stations and landscape of the railways. The daintiness and tiny scale of Yorkshire or Monmouthshire dale stations together with Euston, St Pancras, and the big northern terminus stations are statements of a once popular culture, the moments of confidence which that culture permitted in its own unrivalled expansion.

[12] There is a racy and excellent brief review of these places in *Britain's Changing Towns* by Ian Nairn (BBC Publications 1967).

The giant size and intermittent splendour of Victorian capitalist or industrial building begins however to become a symptom of a deep split in the consciousness. On the one hand, power, capital, organisation, the public world; on the other, individuals, domestic living, powerlessness, poverty, fragmentation, the private world. And a townscape grows up which expresses this split. The corporate state comes into being, it follows the demise of the public-spirited and philanthropic Victorian businessman. The diffusion of responsibility throughout the giant institutions, the need for capital to *increase* its surplus-values if it is to hold on to the profits, the managed perpetuation of old social forms and classes in unprecedented conditions for production and labour, all this created a townscape in which the giant agencies would place at will the cathedrals of their productivity, and individuals did what they liked with the space that was left. The unbelievable speed with which the industrial landscape covered England, the abrupt change in the materials of building, the scale of the new technology, the dominance of the free enterprise and individualist ethic and the absence of an adequate social and moral economy, combined to devastate the brief, precarious and lovely balance in the ecology discovered and held for different decades in different places between about 1750 and 1945. Capital and industry dominated the cities; beneath their vast walls crept out the long lines of private dwellings whose response to the smell, dirt, magnificence, and brute size of the city was to cherish the romantic dream of the country-side at its best. The suburban garden becomes a central symbol of English domestic living any time after 1830. Lawrence classically diagnoses a continuing condition of the whole English people – a shared and – in the imaginative sense anyway – equal culture :

> As a matter of fact, till 1800 the English people were strictly a rural people – very rural. England has had towns for centuries, but they have never been real towns, only clusters of village streets. The English character has failed to develop the urban side of a man, the civic side. Siena is a bit of a place, but it is a real city, with citizens intimately connected with the city. Nottingham is a vast place sprawling towards a million, and it is nothing more than an amorphous agglomeration. There is no Nottingham in the sense that there is Sienna. The Englishman is stupidly undeveloped, as a citizen.

And it is partly due to his 'little home' stunt, and partly to
his acceptance of hopeless paltriness in his surroundings.
The new cities of America are much more genuine cities, in
the Roman sense, than is London or Manchester. Even
Edinburgh used to be more of a true city than any town
England ever produced.

That silly little individualism of 'the Englishman's home
is his castle' and 'my own little home' is out of date. It would
work almost up to 1800, when every Englishman was still a
villager, and a cottager. But the industrial system has brought
a great change. The Englishman still likes to think of himself
as a 'cottager' – 'my home, my garden'. But it is puerile. Even
the farm labourer today is psychologically a town-bird.
The English are town-birds through and through, today, as
the inevitable result of their complete industrialisation.
Yet they don't know how to build a city, how to think of one,
or how to live in one. They are all suburban, pseudo-cottagy,
and not one of them knows how to be truly urban – the
citizen as the Romans were citizens – or the Athenians –
even the Parisians, till the war came.[13]

I am sure that this diagnosis is right, though there is more to be
said for it than Lawrence says. For (in F. R. Leavis' phrase) 'the
inevitable creativeness of everyday human life' manifests itself in
robust and admirable ways as well as in sickening sentimentality
in the English suburban townscape.

Now no one who has eyes to see can doubt that our townscape
is predominantly awful. The domestic and private ethic which
has so deeply penetrated the English spirit transpires in the revolting
details of gnome and barrowland, in sham Cotswold stone-facing
and Lego roofscapes; in fat and folksy chimneys and in the ample,
exotic rollcall of English house-names, the whimsies and the cosi-
ness of 'Silver Whispers', 'Dreamcote', 'Kosy Kottage', 'The Old
Shack', 'Rose Retreat', 'Braemar', 'Burnside', 'Thatcher's Croft',
'Meadow Memories'.

It is not enough to call them dreadful and to add new ones to
some anthropologist's bestiary. These names testify to the enduring
power of the myth of rural idylls. They pay debased tribute to that
myth, and to the assertion by the householder that here he is not be

[13] 'Nottingham and the Mining Countryside', *Phoenix* (1936), reissued by
Heinemann 1961, p. 139.

budged. In the face of the omnipotence of cash and society, he can at least see his home and garden in his own terms. This assertion is an important factor in catching for a moment the spirit of English popular culture. It is certainly alive in its horticulture and in the astonishing busyness of its domestic activities. The crude assertions that we are a nation of Bingo-players and television watchers does not square with the unquenchable flow of energy whose work is plain to see in the gardens and do-it-yourself machinery of every housing estate in England. It is a natural part of most men's education, in and out of school, that they can and do build their own cupboards, draining-boards, greenhouses and pigeon-lofts; mend and maintain their own vehicles and, by the hour, tend and shape their gardens. On any fine evening between May and September, you will find at least one person of each household out in the garden from seven till ten. The strips of land running back parallel behind the gaunt council estates of the 1940s and 1950s will turn in a wide arc of floribunda from April to the autumn; from daffodils and tulips to petunias, sweet peas, pansies, peonies, begonias and on to phlox, dahlias and chrysanthemums, commanded for almost the whole time by the multitudes of official English roses, and flanked by a crowded greenhouse. The same flowers fill the Dreamland Ideal Home estates and the show-gardens of the stately houses.

Here, I think, we find – along, say, with national sport – one of the expressive centres of our popular culture. It fulfils many conditions of a culture; it defines and expresses real moral aspirations for beauty and order; it provides a language within which friendships may be made and sustained for a lifetime, and within which a man's identity may be confirmed. It may also provide what is still rare in our culture – a meeting ground for both men and women. In their gardens Englishmen make fewer mistakes than they do in their handiwork: on the whole they do not betray the loss of touch which marks so many failures in the use of building materials, the placing of houses and the growth of townscapes, and which leaves acres of half-rural or village hillsides blitzed by selfishly placed bungalows, by the harsh angles of off-the-peg greenhouses, or the earnest obtrusiveness of the public lavatory.

The success of English gardens is not at all unmixed with sugariness and whimsicality. We have goblins, barrows, kidney ponds, stippled-pastel flags and sanipak urns to contend with. Not only that queer mixture of superstition and infantilism. There is also the

178

cloyed English taste for candy-floss blossomers at the expense of nobler trees like chestnut or elm even in city squares and in the arabesque of motorway intersections. There is unmanly preference for the dainty and pretty at the expense of boldness. There are sham rustic boarding and trellises, and coy little swoops to garden paths, instead of the sensible patterns of older gardens. But the sugar blossom and the rustic seats are (again) payment in a debased coinage to the old dream of a perfect ecology. In a fine poem, Charles Tomlinson takes the measure of the gap between dream and present reality :

Ranges
  of clinker heaps
    go orange now :
through cooler air
  an acrid drift
    seeps upwards
from the valley mills;
  the spoiled and staled
    distances invade
these closer comities
  of vegetable shade,
    glass-houses, rows
and trellises of red-
  ly flowering beans.
    This
is a paradise
  where you may smell
    the cinders
of quotidian hell beneath you;
  here grow
    their green reprieves
for those
  who labour, linger in
    their watch-chained waistcoats
rolled-back sleeves –
  the ineradicable
    peasant in the dispossessed
and half-tamed Englishman.
  By day, he makes

>   a burrow of necessity
> from which
>   at evening, he emerges
>   here.
> A thoughtful yet unthinking man,
>   John Maydew,
>   memory stagnates
> in you and breeds
>   a bitterness . . .[14]

The dream in the garden has had a larger effect than the patterns of fading allotments. Ebenezer Howard in the late 1890s, solidly at one with that vigorous, dissident conscience spoken for by Pugin, Ruskin, Morris and the much underpraised Rossetti, produced perhaps the most influential version in his *Garden Cities of Tomorrow*. Even people who have never been near Letchworth and Welwyn, Howard's two working models, know at least a rudimentary version of his ideas: that a city should have space and grass, and that it should give large, dirty, industrial plant a special place of its own; that it shouldn't be too big; that it should have ready access to the refreshments and surprises of open countryside. Howard created the image, 'green belt'. Once again, crude cultural statements do not meet the historical situation. Early in its expansion, Howard called halt to the unregulated imperialism of giant corporations. He worked steadily on through to 1939 and the stream of his influence collided with and flowed powerfully into that of the Bauhaus prophets of a new architectural environment as well as that of the acolytes of Le Corbusier, 'La Ville Radieuse' and the new machine age.

Howard's ideas and those of his often powerful disciples – men like Patrick Geddes, Raymond Unwin, William Holford, Leslie Martin,[15] and Thomas Sharp – struck strong chords in English culture. The 'green belt' appealed to that essential industrial notion, a day in the country. The provision of grass and trees and open space was a generous response to the dead-ends, the revolting shut streets and Tom-all-alones of industrial ghettoes. The idea spoke eloquently

---

[14] 'John Maydew or The Allotment', *A Peopled Landscape* (Oxford 1963).
[15] There is a useful brief history in Lewis Mumford's essay 'Old Forms for New Towns', in *The Highway and the City* (Secker & Warburg 1964), pp. 35–44.

to the eternal dream living out its time in the saccharine reproductions of *The Haywain* (Constable's blustery wind toned nicely down) in Boots and a thousand calendar photographs. But then Howard and the others, softening Le Corbusier's brutalism and the elegant forms and surfaces of the Bauhaus, reverted to their historical and cultural traditions and produced the new industrial townscape-with-grass-verges at Harlow, Hatfield, Basildon, Stevenage. The gentle liberal herbivores of the gently reforming socialist government presented the Town and Country Planning Act of 1947 and the New Towns Act of the same year. The acts spoke, as they say, to the English temperament. The town plans – and those that followed at Aycliffe, Peterlee, Hook (never built), Telford, Runcorn, Milton Keynes and a dozen others – are less the triumphs of modern rationalisation techniques and hierarchies of criteria than of the ruminant English imagination. The towns are decent, cleanly, a bit bloodless, sadly lacking in civic sense or community, in political richness; they are at their very best in local sectors, corners of towns where kids play and pram-pushers can chat. Their schools and colleges are the best things about them. The classic Hertfordshire primary schools designed by the Smithsons in the 1950s offer perhaps the most positive contribution in a single design to the national townscape. They present a world on the five-year-old's scale: she can see out of the window and she can move around as she must; classroom, working area, and corridor interpenetrate one another *and* the garden outside. The lessons of Frank Lloyd Wright come solidly home to the terrapin classroom: 'bring the outside in'. Such schools are wholesome, homely, and endlessly varied. They are both a living-room and a tiny town. Finally, they reflect a best part of a big change: the arrival of natural rights for children. However we convict our progressive selves of sentimentality, it is a happier affair being an English child these days than ever before. 'Life, liberty and the pursuit of happiness . . .' is an honourable trinity for primary schools. But once outside its educational efforts (and what I have said can be strongly applied to the plateglass and country club universities) the herbivorous planner–architect's nerve has too often wilted or borne up only feebly against the roar of the maneaters.

For the maneaters *are* winning. We pay our modest homage to the successes won under the banner (Le Corbusier's in the first place) 'Espace, Soleil, Verdure'. Perhaps even more importantly we have learned better to see what we have got. The promptings of such a man as Nikolaus Pevsner and many men after him have emphasised the dazzling variety and plenitude of native domestic architecture. Not only the masterpieces among the country houses, but also the dignity and power of Victorian industry and town-planning,[16] the charm and good manners of seaside Queen Anne, all gables and bargeboarding,[17] the energy of many modern buildings, odd structures like gasholders, steelworks, a row of shops or council offices which would not appear on conventional tourist routes.[18] The tiny few who are interested enough to think about such matters know now that the source of its distinction is the close-packed variety of the English town and landscape. There is no one perfect model, so that even as sensitive a man as Thomas Sharp[19] can sometimes sound prissy when objecting to the jostle and vulgarity of big city building. A city is not a town, and neither place is a village. In the 'man-sized' scale[20] of the English landscape the environment alters radically within a few miles: from giant cooling towers and heavy industry plant to farmland and on to the wide, birch-lined avenues of quiet suburbs. We see this landscape from the motor car and the lorry; they are now the measurers of scale for our landscape. It may be that the rapidity and insulation of travel by car has been one cause of our insensitivity. The vulgar surrender to speed implicit in the vast demolition which accompanies motorway constructions is a key symptom of a nation which does not know what to do with its own land.[21]

16 In assorted publications, e.g. Quentin Hughes, *Seaport* (Lund Humphries 1964); Andor Gomme and David Walker, *The Architecture of Glasgow* (Lund Humphries 1968); J. M. Richards, *The Functional Tradition in Early Industrial Buildings* (Architectural Press), 2nd edition 1967.
17 Mark Girouard, 'Quene Anne', *The Listener* 8, 15, 22 May 1971; Roy Worskett, *The Character of Towns* (Architectural Press 1968).
18 Sylvia Crowe, *The Landscape of Power* (Architectural Press 1958), and Gorden Cullen's classic *Townscape* (Architectural Press 1961).
19 In *English Panorama* (Architectural Press 1936), *Town and Townscape* (John Murray 1968). Compare his *Oxford Replanned* (Architectural Press 1948). Commissioned by the City Council, if it had been adopted, its brilliantly simple and inexpensive analysis would have prevented the ruin of the city thoroughfares which is now complete.
20 The metaphor is Eric Lyons', who has applied it most rewardingly to his architectural work for Span Housing. See particularly the remarkable venture of the new village at New Ash Green in Kent.
21 Lewis Mumford, *The Urban Prospect* (Secker & Warburg 1968), p. 106, 'Speed is the vulgar objective of a life devoid of any more significant kind of aesthetic interest.'

No doubt the motorways too have known their successes[22] but the primacy of the road-building programme, the huge and terrible ruin which it has already caused, and its onward thrust, are at once the symbolic and actual vivisection of the last hopes we have of making a decent modern environment. And what does that last, frail phrase portend? What homeland is thinkable for the next few decades?

First things first. It is no longer possible to plan and debate at the pace of the eighteenth-century landscapers and their patrons. We cannot, in the teeth of genocide, war, poverty and global poisoning, see our landscape as avenues and obelisks on a permanent social way. If we do – and there is every sign that is how planners *do* think – then the maneaters, the giant corporations who would rip up Snowdonia for copper, put juggernaut trucks through Bath, Chester and Canterbury, motorways in the Chilterns and airports into Buckinghamshire, will simply destroy England for returns in sterling. Arguments about the landscape turn upon our intentions now, and it is no use pretending that the orotund phrases of industrial relations will do anything to resolve the conflicts. Getting ourselves around a table, meeting each other halfway and negotiating settlements which are acceptable to both sides is flapdoodle.[23] There are hard, sharp, and bitter disagreements about which there is *no* compromise. We shall do better to see where we are. For as I have said, a popular culture is the product of human decisions. An adequate description of what we have now is necessarily a matter of choosing, of saying 'here, this is dead; there, that's what we must nourish'. Such choice is therefore a part of a continuing historical action. Now in very large areas our culture is brutal and indifferent to its landscape. Largely, the people do not care if, as is the case, one historic building per day is, against national laws, being knocked down. They see themselves as helpless to prevent a hotel being built at the head of Clifton Gorge[24] but they also see capital and private enterprise as in any case having *the greater right* over natural beauty. They accept a mindless version of 'progress' which permits the destruction of York as somehow the product of destiny when it

[22] Nan Fairbrother made some suggestions in *New Lives, New Landscapes* (Architectural Press 1970), especially 'Roads as a New Environment', pp. 271ff.
[23] Cf. *The Countryside in 1970*, Duke of Edinburgh's Commission Report.
[24] Cf. *Private Eye* no. 245; *The Guardian*, 30 May 1971.

is indeed the project of the juggernaut owners to smash down any obstacle between them and the dividend. They simply have not noticed the extinction of butterflies, the ripped-out hedges,[25] the blasted dereliction of huge areas of England and Wales, the squalid imperialism of the Army.[26] They are numb to their disinheritance: the slaughter of the nightingale, the wren, and the skylark; the dying oaks of Southern England, starved to death upon a dried-up water table punctured by hasty building; the wild flowers vanished under strychnine sprays and the tidy, tungsten-lighted mind of the county council highways department. When you have said all you may about the mobility and magnitude of an industrial landscape, you are left with the world we have lost,[27] and the smashed, littered contours of modern England.

And yet. And yet. I have said that any cultural argument is political. We are at a point in history when the evils of industrialism are seen to be declaring themselves most obviously. More people than ever before have noticed. Under the relentless onslaught of industrial expansion, we have seen the earth and sea move in outrage. It is probably essential for survival that the drive for economic growth is reversed.[28] When these changes press home upon people's immediate lives then some minorities have reacted reasonably. They have rediscovered a reasonableness which correctly rejects the criteria of the cost–benefit analysis. For it is not reasonable that ordinary human living shall become wretched and intolerable because

25 11,000 miles per year; 150,000 since 1956; the last four years have slackened off encouragingly.
26 Which now appropriates two and a half times as much land for its out-of-date and preposterous weaponry as it had during wartime. See *Hansard*, 20 March 1971; *Private Eye* no. 242.
27 I am trying to describe a change in consciousness, as much as anything. Peter Laslett's book *The World We Have Lost* (Methuen 1965) is an essential aid. 'The time was when the whole of life went forward in the family, in a circle of loved, familiar faces, known and fondled objects, all to human size. That time has gone for ever. It makes us very different from our ancestors' p. 21.
28 It is worth notice that the Labour Minister for the Environment, Antony Crosland, is still genially reproving 'middle-class defenders of their privileges' for trying to turn the tide of the motor car back from the countryside. His bluff philistinism of course (one has to keep one's eye on the electorate) is not in a position to imagine that the actions of eleven million people might still be wrong, nor indeed that they might not rather walk if anyone had built a landscape in which that was still possible. See C. A. R. Crosland, *A Social Democratic Britain*, Fabian Society 1971, reprinted in *Socialism Now* (Cape 1974).

of noise; the protesters' victories at Stansted and Cublington against the third London airport were local victories for reason. At the moment it is not clear whether the last reasonable decision – not to build an airport at all – can be taken by the helots of productivity. But the Cublington victory was a political one; it underlined what could happen to the landscape in the next thirty years, and it reminds us that in the ambit of modern technology our back garden is larger than we thought. In spite of our cedarwood fences, we cannot keep out Concorde, the M4, and the liner lorry. For it is not merely gunslinging to see the lines of the modern townscape which have become so much clearer during the past twenty-five years as battle lines. Over there, the predators of capital, the corporations, the cost–benefit analysts and system rationalisers. Their weapons: the juggernaut truck, the sales graph (especially of cars), vast and heavy plant, motorways, the wreckers' ball and chain, the unspeakable power of cash. Over here, the private life and house, the garden, the local industry, the shop, quiet, the pedestrian scale. The battlefield is no doubt too simple. Many men stand with a foot in both camps. But we shall have to choose between them on many occasions and in different places. What is now clear for the first time is that groups of local people are prepared to choose. The politics of the seventies are short term: stop the M4, resist the airport, close the bombing range, clean up the slurry, pedestrians only, mind our kids, this beach is ours, hands off our village, save the trees. Though there is no likelihood that the hundreds of amenity groups will come together for long years yet, this new, noisy crowd is the most positive point of hope for our landscape we are likely to find. The groups are minorities. Very well. We mostly live in our minorities. But (for example) the entrepreneurs and shopkeepers who turned down Lionel Brett's plan for York[29] are also a minority. They have more power than the people. They do not have more sense. They insult the people in the people's name. The sting of that insult is at last being felt by the so-called minorities. They too have their power. Their different claims – for space to play, for quiet, for room to walk, for controlling the size and speed of traffic, for trees, or simply for homes of their own – speak up for long-silent

---

[29] I would like space to treat this whole scandal as a case-history. See *York: A Study in Conservation*, by Viscount Esher (HMSO 1968), for which the York City Council has substituted a scheme of epic destructiveness.

centres in our feelings. The action groups are helping men and women to a sense of their public selves. Not in the interests of public living, but so that private living shall be tolerable again. If, in the end, we can get beyond the short-term goal and see the land as having its own, non-human life and shape, we might recover some of the dignity which goes with the knowledge that we live in a geography larger than we are ourselves.

9
Public communications and consumer culture

Sociology with a human face would mean the intense, detailed and widespread collaboration of men and women to discover how to create institutions which did not depend, as now, upon the elimination of human scale and significance. Too much, of course, is expected of education as a source not merely of problem-solving and structure-innovation (as the cant goes) but also as an agency of redemption. Without an agreed system of belief, the only source of grace our society can name is its education, which is expected to produce universal enlightenment and benign and peaceful social improvement. It is not a hope to sneer at, though counting on it for the past hundred years since the great Victorian liberals launched it, has hardly brought its consummation much nearer. But then, as *the New Yorker*'s Vietnamese war veteran dourly puts it, 'I know it's nothing to bet on, but neither is anything else I can think of'.[1]

It is surely the disgrace of the universities that there is no concerted movement within institutions which might be expected to hold in common some sense of the calling of the human mind towards collaborating in such a sociology. Not, absolutely not, in the hope of constructing some sociological faith for the salvation of the future,[2] but in the interests of finding out – in the field, both at home *and* amid alien corn – what small institutions are possible, what values conflict violently, what less piratical and ruinous economic systems could, with the intervention of small, intensive atomic plant and mass electronic communications, shake themselves clear from the great poisonous piles of rubbish dumped by the system which dominates us now.

---

[1] The *New Yorker*, 4 September 1971.
[2] A delusion sharply and correctly put down by Alasdair MacIntyre in Brian Magee (ed.), *Modern British Philosophy* (Secker & Warburg 1972), p. 200.

For a while a misplaced faith in the capacity of a critical sociology to replace a lost evangelism is the cause of many students' alienation, the chance of a human future can only rest upon the stubborn irreducibilities of human nature and society; there must be some kind of fit between planning for Utopias and the facts of life, and quite without lapsing into an expedient pragmatism; a necessary condition for academic labour was for Plato and for Erasmus, and should be again, that it direct itself towards the creative renewal of society. And if the timid advocates of knowledge for its own sake point out that renewal is what the US sociologists and planners of the Vietnamese pacifications programme supposed themselves to be working for, then the objection is the measure of our need. No university worth the name (and which of them stand up to this modest test?) could suppose that human studies should serve obviously detestable ends. The movement of the academic mind which is needed would aim to find the limits in a culture beyond which natural feelings of gentleness, goodness and delight can no longer be postponed. It would aim to sketch in the social forms within which these feelings could express themselves.

Such a movement would have to be more than an academic programme; it would indicate a whole surge in the parent culture. In the certain absence of any such concert within British society, is it any more than whistling down the wind to call for support from the academics? But yes. It is to recognise what collaboration *is* possible at the present time. There cannot be, certainly, a new sociological faith; nor could there ever be. There can be (as Hardy denied there could) a visioning of the possible within the universe, and such a visioning, if it choose its area of inquiry shrewdly, can start from what is happening now. Thus, I have named mass communications as central to the devising of small communities which it will be the only hope for mankind to create. Such communities can count on minute atomic plant and electronic circuitry to provide both the self-sufficiency and the global network of contacts with other communities which a world without superpowers or multinational corporations must have. It is not Utopian, it is simply practical to begin from Britain now, to describe the present failure of public communications to provide images of such communal contact, and to draw together the variously dissident forms of consciousness about public communications which suggest the practicability of other ways of running things. For what we have and are likely to continue with for a generation is an almost complete fragmentation of social awareness and debate. Yet the history of the twentieth century is replete with the examples of men who, no doubt misliking the cues and tableaux assigned to them, took the terms of history into their hands, and changed it. To attempt to draw together unco-ordinated groups of men and women who share similar preoccupations and grievances, but do not know it, is simply rational. It is how the first Trade Unions formed themselves; it is how any active political group forms itself. A group works with an irregular and unpredictable tide, high and tempestuous here, shallow and placid there, incorrigibly various in its constituency. But links between the different groups arise from the resolution of these constituents and not from faith in historical inevitability. Given the conditions I mention – the absence in the Britain of the 1970s and '80s of common social ends and values – given this, the contours of those groups who resist the spurious exclusions and distortions of the mass media are temporary and changeable; some of them – an official strike committee for example – come and go in a few weeks, but it is perhaps possible to discern three fairly fixed and identifiable entities who offer systematic critiques (as they say) of the mass media, and a fourth, much more elusive group, whose membership changes with the transitory issues of national politics.

The first, then, is the men in production who want to control the means of production for themselves, and not for (or, in the case of the BBC, in JICTAR[3] audience-rating competition with) advertising revenue; second, the school-teachers, especially of English, who offer techniques to their pupils for the truer judgement of the media; third, the academic researchers and students of the media whose inquiries lead necessarily to the imagination of alternative systems; fourth, and much harder to generalise about, there are the elusive, uneven, and changing bursts of noise and activity in all corners of our society which come from groups of people unable to make themselves heard, unable to speak to other people because they do not know how to make themselves heard.

'The word within a word unable to speak a word'.

[3] Joint Industry Committee for Television Advertising Research.

They want to speak up, often, on behalf of their community and its localness; what they have to say may be brave and admirable, as it was for the local citizens who fought and defeated the planners of airports, or it may be ugly and brutal, as it is for the Paki-bashers and the football supporters who demolish railway trains. Such groups are members of a people which is largely unable to speak to itself. Many of the people have no language with which to name their feelings, and so football matches and ritual window-smashing have to contain and express the inexpressible; and others of the people have no voice with which to speak to all their fellow-men of their grievance, so they strike or organise demonstrations and so, briefly, gain access to the microphone.

Such groups are all, as they say, minorities. Each man is member of many minorities. Each man is also a member of a culture whose public morality is built upon the ethic of competitive self-interest and whose public institutions give insufficient occasion for the expression of natural impulses of altruism, generosity, gentleness, and goodness. The public morality is, further, built into an alleged form of thought whose monopoly of rationality is held to consist in its ability to prove its judgements from its stock of empiric data. Such a rationality is the product of a corrupted Benthamism out of sight of the necessary aims of the earliest utilitarians, whose intentions were to repair the worst ravages of slum industrialism, but which has retained the simple-minded and indiscriminate application of a material calculus to every human situation, conceived as occupying a changeless society. That is, latter-day utilitarianism is 'all about the distribution of something called, ambitiously, happiness. Or, less ambitiously, satisfaction. And these notions of happiness and satisfaction are clearly ones which are in fact in a state of great conceptual confusion, and we can see – from very justified modern discontents of various kinds – that they are felt to be incoherent.'[4]

'Satisfaction' is construed as docility. Thus what people 'want' is what they happen to leave flickering on their TV sets in large numbers, which is about as useful as saying that the American people 'wanted' Richard Nixon to be the moral custodian of their

[4] Bernard Williams, in *Modern British Philosophy*, p. 160. See his full critique in Williams and Smart, J. J. C., *Utilitarianism–For and Against* (Cambridge 1973).

Constitution. The piecemeal and reach-me-down utilitarianism of the modern welfare state pays at the intellectual level no attention to the immaterial demands of justice and at the practical level no attention to the very material demands of the recipients to be consulted about their own welfare, freedom and reasons: it is unrelated to any larger sense of social purpose or moral identity; it is radically contradictory, generally in the interests of its controlling class (e.g. in the provision of better health services for richer and healthier people); it denies the necessity of a dignified and self-respecting morality which cannot be analysed in relation to measurable goods. All it can advocate is 'the greatest good' calculated according to the formulae of profit–loss technology. Utilitarianism is profoundly static; it can describe no principles of change nor answer demands for freedom.

Consequently, this hoped-for distribution of satisfaction is contained within an antecedent social structure and driven by an antecedent social energy. That is to say, the distribution must be paid for by a society getting richer, and must not alter the shape of things as they have always been, particularly the shape of the histogram of private capital, property, and income throughout the nation. Quite apart from the suicidal effects of such a policy upon the nearly spent resources of the globe, the policy conceals a powerful ideology, one which supposes that improvement in human conditions is synonymous with increased material comforts and is the product of more capital surplus-values all round (Percentage pay increases of course.) Social change is redefined as more pay. Social opportunity then becomes the opportunity to gain more pay. Social mobility, even in sociology, implies upward movement, and is the perfect tense of the verb: it signifies the acquisition of more pay, which is the successful use of opportunity and the embodiment of social change. These dismal transformations have to pass for the images of social hope. They represent the ideological grammar of Jeremy Bentham crossed with the protestant ethic: make every permissible effort and you will be rewarded, but the efforts must acknowledge a common weal, and your rewards must be commensurate with a lowest common multiple of social justice.

Such an ideology could perhaps get by in nineteenth-century England. At least, in a country whose structure for compromise and whose imperial wealth defused Marxism,[5] liberals were able to act upon the protestant–utilitarian calculus in a local way, and make a difference. Legislation for piecemeal reform, Victorian philanthropy and local munificence were a positive response to the physical evils – dirt, smell, sickness, poverty – of the time. That time has gone. With the fabulously increased scale of modern industrial institutions, their empire and their domain of influence, local and piecemeal response has become incomparably more difficult. It is often impossible either to fix responsibility ('here, *you* ought to rebuild these slums') or, when fixed, to impeach an agent (how do you instruct chemical manufacturers to make rivers run clear and pure again?). In the face of this faceless empire of vast and depopulated systems of bureaucracy and automated production, the response of many people in Britain and elsewhere has been to pull back into their private lives, and to abandon public life to the power élite. With no larger frame of personal vindication, deprived of Church, Party, and History, most people have to recover such significance for their lives as they can from the over-exposed details of their personal relationships, especially in the family. Not surprisingly, their personal relationships can hardly stand up to such a bright light. The individual spirit, located in a small number of normally ill-equipped personal friends, cannot be made the fountain *and* realm of all value. Not only are personal relationships strained to the limit by their ideological role as vindicators of the meanings of a man's life – a role which smashes open many a decently coping sort of marriage – but the absence of a political world beyond the interpersonal model means that people project the private range of hopes and fears upon the forces of history. However those forces may be the products of men, they are too vast to be contained within the moral psychology of the English suburb. The arid insistence with which the mass media circulate a view of politics as the rehearsal of footling office quarrels on an international scale is a main cause of the ignorant and vulgar

---

[5] i.e. the ruling class, once forced into open conflict with the working class, proved much more adaptive than for example in Russia. The Trades Unions were able to press for local reform and wages claims, and get them without being forced into the more comprehensive formation of ideology required by class warfare elsewhere in Europe (Paris 1870). Marxism never struck root; its new beginnings in 1911–12 were lost in the First War. See George Dangerfield's long-lived classic, *The Strange Death of Liberal England* (reissued by Paladin 1970).

mixture of mystification and derision in which politics is held in our folklore. Such a world picture, written deep into the national heart, deprives a man of any understanding of both his power and his insignificance in a living politics.

It is a predicament faced and variously answered in the greatest writers of this century. T. S. Eliot made his traditional court of appeal the church; Yeats made his the history of Ireland, and placed his friends on improbably heroic pedestals:

> Ireland's history, in their lineaments trace.
> Think where man's glory most begins and ends,
> And say my glory was I had such friends.

Only D. H. Lawrence successfully left the individual at the centre of the universe, and he could only do this by making his people as rare, true and free as he was himself.

In this moral confusion there remains only one shared court of appeal – the appeal to rational argument. The power of individualist ideology is such as almost in present-day debate to have secularised the last court, for the main premise of our beliefs is that we can choose what we shall believe, and this act of choice is the public vindication of our freedom, such that *what* we choose is secondary to the existential act of choice. Sometimes people seem to believe they can choose to disbelieve matters of fact. But the nature of rational debate is such that it entails an appeal to forms of rationality, moral, empirical, and logical, which are independent of personal opinion. The appeal to reasonableness entails (again) an appeal to what it is we shall admire as reasonable behaviour. This latter appeal, compounded as it is of empirical morality and political common-sense (both of which are less philistine than they sound) provides a point of leverage on the corner of that vulgar calculus I have described. The discussion of what it means to be reasonable and good must end by reversing and drastically revising the reach-me-down utilitarianism I have tried to characterise, the main premise of which is that any kind of perfectionist ethics is inapplicable in a mass society. Off and on, in one corner or another, a more dignified debate is joined which features the necessary terms, 'reasonable' and 'good'.

It is the lethal peculiarity of Western superstates that they possess the means to conduct such debate, but that they scarcely ever mounut it in public. Absence is harder to notice than presence.

But this defection is a key to a central feebleness in the hold people have upon their public lives. They feel themselves to be powerless. They cannot fix responsibility or identify political issues: they possess neither the information nor the language. More importantly, they sometimes know this and they don't care. With widespread resignation by the people from public action (speech is action) public communication systems, the means of public speech, remain in the busy service of a very few people. How does this come about, and what, in other conditions, are mass communications for?

I I

Clearly, they are not held to be 'for' the sort of debate I have mentioned. Yet such a failure of our public imagination is not seen for what it is: a drastic limit set upon the way we conceive our freedom; the sort of limit Marx had in mind in *The 18th Brumaire of Louis Napoleon*: 'Men make their own history, but they do not make it just as they please; they do not make it under circumstances chosen by themselves.' The failure to control a people's communication system in such a way as to identify and grapple with great social issues should be intolerable to a free man. It gives rise to a definition: public communications should set a people talking to itself and to other peoples. The gap between this definition and present reality measures a deadly and unspecified malaise, an indifference to political well-being which itself has deep political roots. A human sociology should respond to this 'misery of vague uneasiness' (Wright Mills' phrase), first by locating a particular social area which expresses that misery. Mass communications is an obvious choice. Second, it should uncover these deep roots in such a way as to allow men to recognise themselves – 'to know the place for the first time' – and to give themselves a position on the map and bearings by which to find it.

Nineteenth-century mass communications began to spread as the old and small communities began to break up. This is not a bucolic fantasy; when all the possible concessions are handed over to the grave-counting historians about the narrowness, conspiracy, witch-hunting and bigotry of small town and village life in old England, it remains true that the fabric of a small community

ensures that local information is universally shared, that relationships are both immediate and lasting – the idea of friendship is
nowadays exceptionally difficult to live[6] – and that the way in
which the world is seen and divided is commonly transmitted. As
this fabric dissolved, a new communication system came necessarily
into being. It reflected the multiplicity of the new capitalism.
Dozens of local newspapers appeared,[7] and as the unifying
cosmology of pre-industrial anglicanism broke up as well, the
ideology and therefore the news content of all the newspapers
spoke up for a dozen different world pictures: noncomformists,
free-thinkers, chartists, radicals, humanists[8] and the main political
parties. There was an extrordinary plurality of periodicals not,
as now, largely stratified by class and specialised into the divisions
of labour and leisure, but ranging over, identifying, and disputing
the main national and local issues of the day. Both the big reviews
and the broadsheets addressed themselves to the questions of
freedom and government. The whole network reflected, one-to-one,
the interpenetrations of ideology and systems of production in late
Empire Britain. There was, in other words, a busy market-place
for the voices of the entrepreneurs as well as for their products.
Urbanisation and the spread of the railways made the rapid distribution of news possible, but the still limited scale both of printing
technology and of the social horizons of the reading and writing
public encouraged the competitive variety and localness which was
the dynamo of capitalism. Notwithstanding the suppressions of
the unions (before the 1867 Disputes Act) and the awfulness of
some of the broadsheets and 'bloods', a host of different social
groups had separate voices in which to air their separate grievances
and consolidate their view of the world.

[6] i.e. the patterns of mobility, the break-up of the extended family
together no doubt with many more obscure causes—mean that
nowadays lasting friendships have to survive long-distance separation,
and that people substitute cronies for friends. Cf. John MacMurray,
The Self as Agent (Faber & Faber 1960).
[7] I am drawing here on chapter 3, in part II, of Raymond Williams'
The Long Revolution (Chatto & Windus 1961).
[8] For a summary of the dissolution of religious belief, see Alasdair
MacIntyre's *Secularization and Moral Change* (Oxford 1967). For
detailed reference to the proliferation of working-class publications
see Edward Thompson's *The Making of the English Working Class*
(Gollancz 1963). See also Susan Budd, 'The Loss of Faith in England
1850–1950', *Past and Present* 36, April 1967, for details of the free-
thinkers' journals.

The crisis of imperial capitalism[9] was of course also the crisis of the communication system. As the other nations caught up with Britain's uniquely early industrial progress, as the Empire itself bore rampant exploitation less patiently, as the suddenness of the war came home, the multiplicity of the classical free market economy convulsed violently towards its centres of power in a series of mergers and takeovers, and in the development of the main novelty of late technocracies, the giant international corporation.

The centralisation enforced two contradictory responses. On the first side, men and women throughout the society, separated from one another by the divisions of labour and from their work by its increasingly technical as well as repetitive nature, needed as a matter of social survival a communication system which would keep contact open with all their fellow men and women inside alien production systems. Only a national system could keep alive the social network and tell them something of where other people stood and how they felt. But on the other side, the controllers of capital, driven into increasingly open conflict with the working class by the breakdown of a shared set of beliefs, needed to direct just such a system in order to circulate a very different picture of that social reality. In either case the need was and is undeniable. Mass communications transmit the only shared and continuous body of knowledge in our community. Insofar as they overlap or constitute educational knowledge, then they colour the institutions of school, but predominantly they embody a system of knowledge of their own, incomparably more fluid, changeable and responsive than 'educational' systems of knowledge. This fluidity and changeability is a main point of access. They can and often do mean that mass communications are trivial; they also mean that they can carry an altogether different view of the world at very short notice. These truths about mass communications – and I acknowledge that I am grouping together very different media for the purposes of the argument – mean that the making of a free man's education must include an effort to understand what this system signifies in an industrial society, and how its masters may set out to control people's lives.

For there is no doubt who are the masters of the press, the radio,

9 Analysed in Eric Hobsbawm's *Industry and Empire* (Weidenfeld & Nicolson 1968).

and the television systems of the country. There needs to be no conspiracy theory nor naming of demons to learn, from the BBC and ITV *Handbooks*, from the Royal Commission on the Press, or from the pages of *Whitaker's*, that the controllers of the media are also the masters of cash and policy in the country.[10] You read the names and you know where you are. But this state of affairs is also tied to a less easily named and counted but no less certain stability of belief in the country which has been the sure foundation upon which those men walk and take for granted their power. This stability is a main part of national ideology; it registers the widely shared belief – shared also by the men whose ends it serves – that England is a single nation and 'as things have been, they remain'. That, in other words, the distributions of power, privilege, and wealth are a condition created by God and the Whig interpretation of history (also heaven-sent), and that radical dissatisfaction with this state of affairs properly confines itself to those well-known cartoon figures of the mass media, agitators, extremists and militants. The idea of change in its essential centres of power is largely extinct in Britain.

Change of this sort has obviously occurred on a fairly drastic scale elsewhere. When, however, examples from other countries are quoted, the reflex action in Britain has been to suppose that all such change, being 'violent' and 'communist inspired', is for the worse, and a more accurate perception of reality is not encouraged by the mouthings of the sectarian left. The point is this: the idea of a radical change of power in Britain has been largely anaesthetised. Consequently, when it occurs, the terms of discussion successfully localise and emasculate the idea by assigning it to the 'agitators' and 'militants', as though all political ideology and action lay at regular intervals along a timeless scale from right to left, moderate to lunatic, decent time-keeping and serving quietist to wild and hairy man. It is an explanatory system kept in being by the mass media, periodically rising to a little mild hysteria when the

---

[10] *Who's Who* lists a few of the directorates held by the major power-holders in the country. Anthony Sampson's *Anatomy of Britain Today* in a necessarily sketchy and not very searching way draws in some of the main trunk roads of power traffic. What we could do with, of course, is something like C. Wright Mills' classic *The Power Elite* which gives for the USA not only the structure of power, but an analysis of its invisible genealogies. It is much harder to do in Britain, of course.

celebrities of Television House and Whitehall launch into anodyne denunciation of scoundrelly strikers and 'politically-motivated men'. The explanation transpires from a world picture of social immobility, one in which antique social forms claim to contain and express a headlong technology to everybody's benefit.

This national ideology has, as I have said, deep social roots in the economic system produced by the new corporations. After the Victorian philanthropic barons, Firth, Chamberlain, Wills, Boot, Nuffield, there came the far vaster empires of ICI, Unilever, Portland Cement, BP, the Five Banks, the motor car oligopolies. While the world's resources held, this new capitalism created the *means* to abolish poverty. But the old institutions of those societies depended on the existence of the poor, with the degradations of 'subsistence levels' and 'minimum wage' as the base against which to measure success, possession, promotion and opportunity. Consequently there was a political need to organise the distribution of abundance in such a way as to sustain competitive inequalities. The inevitable surplus values, according to classical market theory, returned to the production system as reinvestment. But if the pace of production is allowed to slacken, then capital-intensive plant starts to depreciate faster than the formulae for return on capital can permit. There can therefore be no glutting of the market, nor stagnation, either of which leave expensive plant running half-idle. In order to maintain the high production and, further, in order to prevent the saturation of the market, the patterns of consumption must change so that people will throw things away ('consume') and buy new ones quickly enough to keep investment and returns on capital high. The controllers must therefore manipulate both abundance and innovation so that the machine keeps going.

The Indian summer of this system in Britain was the general election of 1959. Since then, its uncontrollable lurches have made the theory of its manipulation less and less credible. The attempt of the controllers, in and out of the official government, has been to balance, in a series of short rushes, rates of consumption against the delicate health of sterling and the grinding metamorphosis of old-style industries regrouping themselves in larger combinations with fewer men at work in them. The balance has held more and more uncertainly as the flow of money in the economy was poured in and drained out and poured in again, and the heart of the country's working class beat to these irregular rhythms. The moral

198

measure of such a system can be taken from the outrage expressed by the controllers when those working people whom the system *requires* to keep consuming at a steady rate demand more money in order to keep up that rate but miscalculate the sums which are considered appropriate. They are then of course holding the country to ransom because they are asking for returns from the social wealth which they have helped to accumulate in a proportion which means that the much bigger proportions taken by their superiors go down.

It is clear that what, happily, this whole system has consistently lacked and needed has been a regular instrument of public control. Advertising came into being in an effort to provide that control. Advertising is the most obviously manipulative part of a communication system which is tugged between the authentic and lived expressions of its society, and the expression of control and manipulation. It is the educational, political, and therefore moral point of studying the mass media to distinguish with confidence between expressiveness and manipulation. Between, if you like, life and death. Now advertising is deathly. For while it is clear that there is no one-to-one causal link between advertising and behaviour ('this advertisement *causes* more people to buy this car or to get drunk on this whisky or to invest more in this trust'), and while it is also clear that in many areas of their lives people are well able to reject advertising tarradiddle and to weigh up the goods on their merits, the real deathliness of advertising lies in its broadcast diffusion of an inhuman symbolism and set of values. Advertising serves the critical capitalist need for the expansion of plant and reinvestment of surplus-values, and this need, so vividly and universally symbolised in the imagery of advertising, has created a form of behaviour which will maintain the system. Men have no doubt always tended towards lust, gluttony and avarice, but these evils take a very particular form within consumer culture. The patterns of consumption within that culture are not at all innate; men and women teach and learn them from an ethic which insists on the spiritual elation and renewal to be derived from the unlicensed acquisitions of objects.

This is not simply the 'low' view of human nature. Men are always liable to behave badly; equally, independent of the forms of production and consumption, they can behave with intelligence, dignity and courage. There is no simple determinist theory of action.

(It is hard to say what it would be.) But in a society in which men are divided from men by the nature and status of the work they do and the money they have, a society in which moreover their personal relationships are loose-textured and transient, then they are particularly vulnerable to the claim that material possessions will ensure and also symbolise the competitive acquisition, mobility and opportunity for more which justify a man's life for him in the terms of his culture.

Advertising makes this claim in its most vociferous form; it is implicit in the whole structure in which competitive self-interest drives the social dynamos. It is the *obviousness* of advertising which makes it an easy subject for inquiry. The correct critique is not that the images of advertising signify an acquisitive materialism. This is the traditional mistake. Rather, they are not so much material as ethereal. Instead of being tied to specific details of housekeeping – 'washing machines work like this for this price', 'this petrol has such-and-such volatility at such-and-such a price' – the products are tied to spurious but magic images, which call up the forms of success in our society which I have listed – status, possessions, and so forth. In many cases, the manufacturer is not only selling some utterly commonplace object like a pint of beer or a bar of soap, he is selling it at prices fixed within a tight cartel of oligopolists. In an attempt, necessarily wasteful and irrational, to maintain his share of the market at whatever the cant says is the right rate of growth, he hopes to persuade his sellers to buy the magic images which the advertisement places glittering around the product. The most numinous imagery is that which plays about those areas of our feelings when many people are least confident of themselves – hence the sweet, insistent murmurings about sex, security, snobbery. Now there is no knowing whether or not a given image sells a given product, even though a huge tonnage of market research goes into the calculation of packaging, price and symbolism for the chosen sector of a social class. What seems to me irrefutable is that the whole system works to keep in perpetual motion the ideology of consumption, and that the force of this motion is such that it penetrates and suffuses whole other areas of mass media. The world taken for granted by the fashion pages of newspapers, the glossy and pop women's magazines, the car magazines, blends harmoniously with the world of the competitive quiz and panel games, TV serials glamourising the life of the rich and powerful, and with setpiece historical serials. (The whole pop and show business world is far more of a piece than *Oz* and the New Left allow.)

Perhaps this point is made by the relative *absence* of this world from the more local forms of communication. The local newspaper in format and coverage looks far more like *The Times* or *Le Monde* than like the *Daily Mirror* The national newspapers, it is well known, are purchased more or less on class lines; the local newspapers serve an area and not a class. They report, carefully if sedately, local issues genuinely defined – issues such as bad planning, callous local authorities, racial discrimination. The vigorous treatment of the Warwick University Senate by *the Birmingham Post*, the courage of the *Wolverhampton Express and Star* in speaking out against Enoch Powell from the start are well-known examples of what is often the case, especially in cities : that local papers have an admirable tradition of offering news and critical analysis of local community issues.[11] It is also the case that local papers are rarely radical, and that they are largely owned by conservative squirearchs or businessmen, especially in rural and market-town areas. But what is much more to my point is that language, style, coverage and presentation all presuppose an informed and attentive reader. These newspapers also shoulder the task of acting as the community's archivist. They are keepers of the local records. People are uncomprehending who joke about the long columns reporting school sports, WI bazaars, GCE awards, local hospital football cups, and the births, marriages and deaths in any families who have lived in the area for longer than a few years. The local newspaper provides a model of a whole community talking to itself and talking sensibly about events that matter, about social issues, and about the details of a community's life of the kind that we would all want to hear in the pub or shop from our friends. And when people go to check reports in which they figure themselves, this is not so much self-centredness as the need to confirm that they are down in the archives and have their place in the community records. The plentiful photographs confirm this analysis. They are photographs, for the record, of people whom on the whole the reader will recognise from their face and not from their photographs. This mode of recognition is wholly other than the way we have of recognising that strange product of twentieth-century

---

[11] An excellent study is *The Provincial Press and the Community* by Ian Jackson (Manchester University Press 1971).

communication, the 'celebrity'. When we see celebrities in actuality, we peer curiously to see if they're real. When we recognise local worthies in the paper, we perceive them as people whom we can seek out and consult or criticise if we want to. We can, that is, fix their name and their responsibilities in the community.

These newspapers, and the local radio stations which have developed a comparable approach to their news and community,[12] indicate in a modest way what is possible. Even at their most patrician, they maintain a respect for their readers conveyed in a careful honesty and decency of tone which was killed off by Lord Northcliffe years ago in the so-called popular press, a tone which is audibly more veering day-by-day in *The Guardian*, and elsewhere. When we turn back to the great popular success – and popular (naturally) means commercially successful – of the past few years, the *Sun*, we find a graph of contents which Lord Northcliffe put into circulation seventy years ago in the *Daily Mail*. The uniformity of this content across the *Express, Mirror, Sun, News of the World, People* emphasises the conviction that a main aim of these papers has been to combine successful manipulation with a high return on capital. Certainly they give out a strong sense of the changelessness of an England whose citizens are denied access to their public figures and have to live on a diet of gossip, scandal, and sexual intrigue as a substitute for knowledge and appraisal of the people's own politics. As Raymond Williams brilliantly pointed out,[13] it is a view of history from below stairs, a view from which we can just get a glimpse of the Prime Minister waving to us before he shuts the door of Number 10. The rest of the time we are expected to spend in a mixture of fantasies about high living, crime, imperial nostalgia, fairy story wealth and sex. The mixture appears every day in the newspapers. Its special out-of-dateness comes home in the *News of the World* treatment of sexual revelations as though whispered gossip still was a main feature of social life and radical changes in sexual mores had never taken place. These newspapers, and the TV menu insofar as it reflects the same range of subject-matter, have their ideological roots deep in 1900, and their contents help to explain the continuing of a more general social ideology which breathes the same stale air long after the more solid moral

[12] Cf. Rachel Powell's paper, *Possibilities for Local Radio*, CCS Occasional Papers 1 (University of Birmingham 1968).
[13] In *The Listener*, 15 October 1970.

positives of that time have withered away. For the profound nostalgia of England for the imagined June of 1914 when natural authority and the gold standard were in the hand of God and the Monarch (though hardly *that* Monarch) is of a piece with the immobility of its political debate on the mass media. They fit the larger ideology I have described by confining the terms of reference to those of party politics, by excluding the terms and the groups of people who voice them, which fail to fit this binary conception, and by appeal to the absolute concept of 'balance' which turns out to mean the checking of any one opinion against another. Balanced reporting is then to have one man's opinion (unions), find another who will deny it (management), and then to refract both through everyman's political mediator, the eponymous David Frost. The same habit characterises the feature and reporting pages of the dailies, each holding its own version of balance along the arc of political opinion which it calls its own: Monday Club versus Bow Group in *The Daily Telegraph*, Tribune MP versus Fabian in *The Guardian*. The model of knowledge, debate, and imaginative experience lived out in mass communications places the idea of stability at the centre of its action theory, and implies a diagram of forces which maintain that stability by taking regular and predictable moments about that centrist fulcrum. It is a model which denies the possibility of change, renewal, revolution, or conflict, and excludes history as an active presence other than as plangent, rich music from the past.

III

This is to describe a fixed and monumental edifice. Yet, to say it again, public communications are of their nature fluid and responsive to sudden change. They are too porous to occupy the edifice. It is therefore possible to make some suggestions to that small minority – and it will always be a small minority – who are ready to see the understanding of the mass media as part of education.

The main public institutions of our society are capital, production, communications, and education. They compose an interlocking structure. But each controls an uneven flow of information amongst which the educational flow is probably the most sluggish and soonest forgotten. The main instrument for the innovation of knowledge is no doubt mass communications: the consciousness they register is what controls the march of history far more than new technologies. Now there are significant connections between public communications and mass education and it seems a reasonable guess (though only a guess) that the two institutions contain enough men and women interested in reversing the dominant flows of information to have some effect.[14] Inasmuch as all change must have its expressive social institution, then education – in however novel, communal, and de-schooled a form – must remain institutionalised if rational social criticism is not to die of attrition. And this institution primarily needs now a theory of mass communications towards which this essay offers some notes. This theory can only start out from work which is feasible at the moment. Its only unassailable weapon, as the opening argument concluded, is the reasonableness of its criticisms. What work can be done?

We have only to ask this to see how empty much of the criticism and sociology of mass communications has been. Advertising criticism has stopped short of economics; sociology has concentrated on the intangibles of effects and abandoned content[15] as being, one supposes, dangerously value-laden. I would like to list a series of topics, well within the range of first-year classes at secondary school, searching and exacting for sociology students in university or extra-mural seminars. Each one grows from the analysis offered here and will be seen, I hope, to connect one with another in an elementary theory of the politics of mass communications.

1 *Newspapers.* Attempt the comparison in the way I have suggested of groups of local and national newspapers, attending with special care to the way in which social myths emerge and circulate, e.g. the myth-status of students or of businessmen, of particular events such as a strike.[16] The analysis might go on in familiar ways to appraise kinds of features, of reporting styles, story types and advertising, but pay special attention to the

---

[14] In which connection see The Free Communications Group series of pamphlets on lies and distortion on TV, *The Open Secret*, 30 Craven St, London WC2.

[15] The casebook of this timidity is J. Trenamen's and D. McQuail's *Television and the Political Image* (Methuen 1961).

[16] Specially useful here are J. Halloran, G. Murdock and P. Elliot, *Demonstrations and Communications – A Case-Study* (Penguin 1970): and J. Lane and F. Roberts, *Strike at Pilkingtons* (Collins 1971).

distribution of crime, scandal, sport, and political gossip-writing. Here it would be important to isolate the special nastiness of English chauvinism which comes out strongly in the reporting of these loosely grouped topics. The final, most important and necessarily most precise analysis would be of the ideology carried by each 'house-style'.

The tip here comes, I think, from Marshall McLuhan, though he made gross errors in his subsequent interpretations. But the 'house-style' of a newspaper or of a periodical speaks through its layout, its juxtaposition of images and words, of colours and photographic screening.[17] Thus even where journalists and photographers (or on TV, producer, cameramen and interviewer) are highly idiosyncratic, the tone of a particular house-style unifies all the contributors in a very marked way. The discontinuities in the *Sun* between the acreage of extremely pretty girls' bodies and the spurious moral outrage of its political banner headlines provides only the most spectacular example of the unifying power of the newspaper's style. The relation of feature to advertisement in the colour supplements is another.

2 *Weekly magazines.* There is unlimited scope for entry here into the private world of a genuine popular culture (one which speaks up, interestingly, through the accurate advertisements of the local paper). I will only suggest the copying of Leo Lowenthal's classic study[18] when he contrasted the practical 'doers' who were the titanic heroes of *Colliers Weekly* between 1900 and 1920 with the playboy filmstar 'consumers' who followed between 1920 and 1940, the limits of his survey. In the same way, a contemporary study could juxtapose the heroes and heroines of pop as opposed to domestic women's magazines, and use this as a basis for a complete comparison of two issues, one of *Honey* or *19*, one of *Woman* or *Womans Own*.

3 *Radio.* The BBC perpetrated one of its blandest insults in creating its four wavelengths. It clearly thought that it would stratify content by taste and social class in the interests of

---

[17] Roland Barthes in his Elements of Semiology and more recently in *Mythologiques II* (both published by Cape, 1965 and 1972) offers a new way of 'reading' any cultural phenomena deriving from structural linguistics. It is, to my mind, a pretty arid way, emptying the phenomenon both of intention (on the part of the agent) and value, as ascribed by transmitter *and* receiver.

[18] In *American Social Patterns*, William Peterson (ed.) (Doubleday 1951).

rationalisation. No doubt good work is still done. No doubt the BBC radio is the envy of the United States. No doubt this and no doubt that. It is still true that these crude lines help to perpetrate ugly social divisions, and it would be very much to our point to conduct an analysis of content, and, harder, of tone, in such a way as to define what the BBC supposes are the lines of division, and what social myths are becoming reality *there*.

4 *Television*. There are already a lot of suggestions in the argument. A critical analysis here might look again at the styles of heroes and of social institutions (e.g. marriage and the family) and among other things notice how these alter according to the time of night (*My Wife Next Door* at 8 pm; BBC 2 plays at 10pm). The most suggestive hints of a statistical sort for this job are to be found in Hilde Himmelweit's *Television and the Child*,[19] though what is also called for is very delicate analysis of a literary-critical sort. Her classic book could also serve as the basis of another popularly contentious topic, the treatment of sex-and-violence on TV, which could attempt to give some solid ground to that fluffy quarrel. Finally the inquiry into television could launch the sort of political analysis proposed for newspapers, and explore the vague concepts of 'balance' and 'public discussion' as mediated by the small group of political commentators who do our politics for us.

The foregoing ideas apply to the library and the classroom. Far more important, however, would be the entry of students, school-children and citizens into the business of making the news for their neighbourhood to read, watch, and listen to. This essay has stressed the formal permeability of mass communications. That is to say, the technological *forms* quickly admit new kinds of knowledge and information. But the social forms – the hierarchies of decision and authority – critically limit acess to those people whom the executive choose to admit.

This state of affairs is changing. The provision of local BBC radio stations and the sudden rise of the underground and 'alternative' press emphasise to potential students and teachers that they can make their own news. Local radio has been fairly tolerant of local education – of contributions both for and from students. (Or if it hasn't, why hasn't it?) Local communities, exasperated into action by bureaucratic negligence or the monopoly of local newspapers,

[19] With A. N. Vince and P. Oppenheim (Oxford 1958).

have in many cases launched their own, dissenting broadsheets or newspapers. It is certainly imaginable that some of the commercial television stations would in a small way be amenable to working with schools and students in the preparation of off-peak programmes. The conceited and irrelevant preoccupation of the media-men with 'professionalism' in their production techniques might be an obstacle; a few programmes have shown that this is not necessarily so.[20] In any case, the general point stands. The experience in the classroom and library has to be completed by the students trying to run their own communication insruments. You learn about mass manipulation when you try to find the truth. And of course the energy and numbers of the workforce of school pupils could make an extraordinary difference in local affairs. When one thinks of the honest muckraking a few dozen persistent fifteen-year-olds could do, then one realises the giant power of the institution, of school. 'It is the role of the intellectual to tell the truth and to expose the lies of governments.'[21]

Nobody in Britain could argue that school-children should not feel the force of that statement.

I V

What is, at the end, necessary to pull all this together is a vision of an alternative, even though it will not be realised in our lifetime in Britain. Without a vision of heaven, there is no education. What would a heavenly communication system look like?

There is nothing inevitable about financing by advertising, nor about capital supply in private from the highest bidder. Finance can perfectly well come from licence revenue and direct grant. Instead of a central bureaucracy hiring its producers on alien terms (the tyranny of the slot) it is at least thinkable to have programme companies (like news agencies) in which the systems of production are in the producers' hands – producers either of TV drama or paper journalism; of sport, of regional programmes, of music. The control of such companies need not be by appointment, but by election – the election of producer and programme directors within the

---

20 E.g. a Trade Union film made by the workers and shown on Harlech TV in April 1972.
21 Noam Chomsky, 'The Responsibility of Intellectuals', in *American Power and the New Mandarins* (Chatto & Windus 1969), p. 257.

organisation, of public members by the public. The union election in the Transport and General Workers Union or the AUEW make it clear that people will vote when they feel their choices count; the widespread apathy in local and national elections is a function of powerlessness, of effective disfranchisement.

The whole emphasis, in administration and in content, needs to return to the locality, and the locality as rendering in a knowable projection the incomparably larger network of similar localities throughout the nation, so that the universal experience of demographic mobility is less embittering and vacant. Only there can a people learn the necessary scale of political amd moral reference. It is the responsibility of governments to rediscover that scale, and, if they can't, to change their institutions until they can. (The giant unions have managed it; so has the Army.) The scale and relatively loose texture of institutions are absolute; it is the only basis for an education. Without a community, there can be no education. In spite of everything, some part at least of the educational institution is capable of generating different models of a living community. Such a model should be transferable to mass communications, so that their instruments become accessible and free in the same ways as in an ideal community. Tony Benn has written, 'The public as a whole are denied access or representation in these new talking shops of the mass media as completely as the 95% without the vote were excluded from Parliament before 1832'.[22] Democratisation of the media is a first entry of a new Charter. For if we are to talk to ourselves we shall need to break with the present uniformity of the national system.

To make the break would not be to win enlightenment. The social roots of an often hateful social ideology go too deep for that. But people would then be in a position to hear themselves, and to feel power over their own lives. Having heard themselves, they might hear others. And if this is no straight road to liberal salvation, it gives the truth more chance than it gets now. As importantly, at a time of deep moral confusion, especially over what is sacred and what profane, the sharing of power, the public revelation of the sources and nature of control, will be the only way for us to recover the preservation of what is sacred in our private lives.

At the moment, we live out a constant and hateful reversal of

[22] In *The New Politics*, Fabian Tract 402, 1970.

poles, where public power lives in a mystery beyond the tabernacle, and the sanctities of our intimate relationships are defiled and paraded in public. One way at least of starting to clear up the confusion is to identify who is trying to control us, and how. It is only by being able to meet another person straightly that you can decide what you are worth to yourself.

10

Human studies and the social crisis: the problem of the past

The way in which we study humanity depends upon our view of the world, and that view is always changing. This chapter starts out from the present upheaval in the study of English literature and the humanities and attempts to strike some links with other studies.

In some ways, the changes are the same as those sketched out about English study in schools in chapter 3. English studies – the practical criticism of literature – broke through as a dominant form of intellectual inquiry in the 1930s; it provided a bold theory of society within which to place particular studies. As the movement grew it was challenged for more precise forms of epistemology and social explanation by adjacent disciplines. The studies themselves have been thrown into disorder by these challenges. In some areas they have lost their nerve and lapsed into academicism; elsewhere they have tried to jack themselves up with notions of 'scientificity' (*sic*); elsewhere again they have effected experimental liaisons with other studies, and tried – in tackling theories of communication or of social change – to incorporate and resolve the intractables implicit in the challenge of new information and frames of thinking.

The upheaval is more than local. It is deep and historical. But it provides an opportunity to redraw some of the boundaries which are placed about experience and made formal as disciplines. Now the study of philosophy (and moral philosophy in particular) is the study of thought; furthermore, to study thought is to study how thought changes and how concepts live ineradicably in their own history. We cannot without severe distortions tear the concepts out of their history. This sense – this understanding – of the embodiment of values in social institutions is largely absent in the study of the humanities and in the principles of existential freedom and individualism which support that study. For this

210

doctrine rests upon a sequence of moral negatives; it is largely to do with *not* telling people how to act, *not* coercing their beliefs, *not* interfering with their liberty. Consequently it lacks any clear sense of what we ought to do. It is unable to mediate between expressions of high moralism and of very general principles and the concrete situations of day-to-day moral and intellectual life. So it follows from such a world picture that social institutions cannot be seen to embody common values because such common values as there are, are held to be a consequence of individual choice rather than impersonal standards. The moral centrality of choice and the division such a centrality entails between fact and value is a main condition of the intellectual circumstances in which English studies are now trying to find their way.

For those circumstances – their dominant ideology, its spokes-men, milieux, institutions and conditions – rest upon an inadequate way of seeing and thinking. I shall try very briefly to characterise this way. I have already listed the defects of liberalism – the high-toned moralism whose only practical precepts can be negative – defects from which it follows that the ideology in itself can confer no universal significance on action. It is a logically antecedent state of affairs that the negative precepts rest upon a view of the individual as the realm of all value. But that individual is the product of a protestant ethic which by making salvation arbitrary divorced fact from value and virtue from happiness.[1] Kant is the most agonised visionary of this condition since by his argument the categorical imperative presupposes a moral universe without that universe having a categorical ontology. The Romantic poets variously register their dismay and delight at this unprecedented state of affairs. They render a Humean moral universe insupportable by denying the civil basis of what Hume calls the passions and what we would call wants, needs, and desires. Hume, the supreme orderer of what it was to be an eighteenth-century civil gentleman, set morality on the basis of his own cultural milieu; the colossal impact of Blake, Coleridge, Wordsworth, Beethoven, Delacroix (and 1789) made the individualist basis of the emotions utterly incongruent with universalisable rules and ends. Once there is no longer a determinate set of passions, there is no chance of devising

---

[1] A summary of Western moral history which is elegantly presented in Alasdair MacIntyre's *A History of Ethics* (Routledge & Kegan Paul 1968).

a common morality to fit those passions; if therefore men retain the earlier morality it will have to be on some different basis. The greatness – and the insufferability – of Kant is that he gave an insane or tragic grandeur to the holding of these irresoluble opposites – universality and individualism; for him as for us the most dazzling vision of human possibility is virtue crowned with happiness; but they can only be brought together by a divine power which lies clearly beyond this world and whose existence is extremely chancy, although essential to morality. The same is very synoptically true of Blake, as witness 'the tense geometry' of the *Ancient of Days*.[2] Kant, supremely, offers a version of the answers necessary when moral coherence has broken up. In such fragmentation, the problem of moral plurality must be met; claims from any one camp of moral absolutism have no plausibility. At the beginning of the nineteenth century, these conditions made for Hegel's synthesis and for the doctrine of dialectical possibilities. But the dialectic throws a long shadow both forward and back – back to the deep split between Cartesians and theists, forward to the more anodyne conflicts between empiricists and moral prescriptivists in our own time. This latter account derives from Lucien Goldmann[3] and it is he who emphasises Pascal's declaration : (fragment 353): 'On ne montre pas sa grandeur pour être à une extrémité mais bien en touchant les deux à la fois, et remplissant tout l'entre-doux' Pascal, and in England, Shakespeare, Donne, Jonson, Milton, the most amazing quartet of writers in an amazing time, all variously give meaning to the vision that a philosophy may yet recover a universal meaning from the incorrigible plurality of the world.

At the present time the differentials and divisions of labour encourage the small-scale empiricism and the private moralities which explicitly deny the dialectic victory. The claims of our time (in the industrial West) have been to achieve only local and temporary victories over reality, they have led inevitably to mechanistic accounts of human behaviour (facts) and superstitious accounts of personal morality (values); and they have rejected any bolder attemps to hold in a richer, more ambiguous relationship the

[2] Nikolaus Pevsner's phrase in *The Englishness of English Art* (Architectural Press 1956).
[3] In *Le Dieu Caché:Vision tragique dans l'oeuvre de Pascal et de Racine* (Gallimard 1967).

recalcitrant opposites of human existence. This view of things gave us utilitarianism in our public lives, and individualism in our private lives: both are now coming in for very sharp objections.

Now to say that this new emphasis is a function of the changing needs of the conditions of production is not to be crassly Marxist-determinist. Those conditions are themselves both product and expression of human ideas and relations, and refute in themselves any mechanistic explanations. Nonetheless the truth that social change in some sense turns upon the formation of consciousness in a given social group, and the process by which it constructs a novel and victorious form of thought and social control, is undoubtedly Marx's and is an essential key to understanding in the human studies. The restlessness now discernible in higher education, the efforts to redraw the lines of academic boundaries and to make them more permeable is causally related to changes in the technology and systems of social control, if not in any crude or one-to-one way. If the predicate is right that there is widespread dissatisfaction with the present divisions of intellectual labour (a dissatisfaction echoed in discontents elsewhere in society); if, further, it is true (and perhaps tautological) that intellectual change is synonymous with social change in being the product of a newly realised social group with a newly formed world-picture; if, finally, it is the high calling of the human mind (Don Quixote's not Sancho Panza's) to emulate the mind of a now absconded God by filling the space between these appalling contradictions and divisons, why then to remake English and the human studies is an effort to answer a moral, historical crisis and not simply to do a bit of curriculum development.

II

The effort, then, is part of a sporadic tendency to find a better epistemology, which will be, in turn, basis for a sufficient morality. This returns us to Hume's method: the construction of a sound morality upon a basis of human nature defined not in terms of the Augustan atheist, but in terms of what the empiricists really can fix of the limits and facts of human society and the individual psyche. But to put it more generally, the effort calls for the dissolution of the idea of privacy. That is, the work involves the study of the relations between consciousness, *alterable* contingency, and

213

the given. The idea of privacy for instance permits liberal adherents to defend religion and morality as a matter of choice; similarly the idea of historical objectivity permits Marxists – at least of a certain rigidity – to disdain the liberal view as false consciousness, a masquerade of personal freedom which conceals the real domination by vested interests, and to defend instead a view of morality as crudely determined by a reflection of productive relations. The latter view misrepresents the problem by obscuring the fact that productive relations, allegedly objective, are themselves the expression of ideas, and to speak of 'determining' in this context obscures the differences between 'determining' as causing, or as affecting, as setting limits to, or as simply preceding; and in any case 'determining' as a key concept tends to eradicate the creative complexity in which the terms of social relations and those of morality conflict and co-operate in the creation of consciousness. In the more familiar language of liberalism, what is denied is the possibility of agreement as anything other than the happy coincidence of feelings (emotivism), and what is affirmed is the necessarily individual nature of world-views and values. What I am advocating in this arid intellectual wilderness is not the (in its ancestry, liberal) chairman's resolution or synthetic mediation of these two opponents. Instead, here is an educational proposition. The focus of inquiry in a school of the humanities should be the quality of experience in an industrial culture. This is the common centre from which the participants should draw strength.

This inquiry entails the dismantling of liberalism insofar as liberalism signifies the privateness of moral values, beliefs and knowledge. To say this is not to slight or neglect the undoubted clashes of moral view which are part of our experience. But what are identified as such clashes – disputes which can only be settled by choices of allegiance to this or that moral banner – may often rest upon a mistake. In any case the disputes imply a separation between fact and value which a more adequate conceptual framework would show in many cases clearly not to be there. (That clashes do exist was the point of my quotation from Pascal, and the moral point of the study of experience is partly to identify such clashes and to recover a view of life which has the dignity to admit and include this tragic fact.)

It cannot for example be a 'private' matter of opinion whether or not there is a God, and however temporary and inconclusive the arguments may be about His existence, they entail a commitment to non-individual premises. In *that* particular case we shall probably have to settle where there is head-on disagreement simply for stopping the fight. It remains true in more worldly cases that the relativist can have a very long run for his money. He will stress how non-comparable are the social values and institutions of industrial Europe and a primitive bushman or a medieval peasant. As the anthropologists insist, you can only understand a primitive society on its own terms, not on yours. This of course is interestingly problematic in the case of newly industrialised societies, in Africa or Asia, where people *do* live within two non-comparable value-systems, and have to sort out the difficulty as best they can. But it remains the case that you cannot live as a bushman in modern industrial society. Anyone who tried would clearly be off his head. Even in a more possible mediation, as in the very interesting case of the Japanese novelist Yukimo Mishima who ritually disembowelled himself before an audience of soldiers, the clash between the Samurai values and Japan in 1970 made his suicide pitiful and not heroic. The values possible at a given time are intimately entangled with the institutions possible, and indeed understanding more of this entanglement is the point of the studies I am sketching out. So the pursuit of moral collisions seems misguided. The pursuit is perhaps partly a way of reaffirming liberal belief in the individual status of values. What seems to be preferable is to go round the back of the moral judgements in order to see what the landlord's premises are like. And it may well be that they turn out to be very rickety indeed. If they are rickety, you don't have an irreconcilable clash of opinion, you have a mistake. Take an obvious example. Most liberal ideology is committed to a belief in the autonomy of the self and its personal responsibility. At the same time, at least on its humanitarian wings, it is committed to a crudely determinist view of the environment, such that a deviant child from a poor home can hardly be responsible for its actions. Not only is there logical contradiction here (A is not −A) but even if we can get round this by pretending that the wealthy and articulate middle-class English liberal (the Henry James hero) is the embodiment of the autonomous self, that idea of the self − its identity, its springs of action, the picture it has of what it is to act at all − may turn out to be philosophically incoherent. A philosopher can reasonably reduce the self to a very small thing indeed. Thus Bernard Williams, in these speculations – pretty straightforward and accessible ones – leaves 'I' as the name of 'my self' with an extraordinarily shadowy reality.

It is not necessary to being *me* that I should have any of the individuating properties that I do have, this body, these memories, etc. And for some of them, such as the body, we may think that it is not necessary to have one at all; and, quite readily, we might not have any memories. The limiting state of this progress is the Cartesian consciousness: an 'I' without body, past, or character. In pursuing these speculations to this point, we do not so far meet any obvious dilemma or paradox – at most, there is a sense of strain, an increasing attenuation of context. A dilemma or real philosophical obstacle occurs, however, when one adds to these speculations another consideration: that it must also be true that I might not have existed. This we certainly want to agree to – few will be persuaded that their own existence is a necessary feature of the universe. Now it is clear that, if we admit the previous speculations, the 'I' of 'I might not have existed' must be the same attenuated 'I' that seemed to emerge from those speculations. For suppose we took 'I might not have existed' to mean (as it might naturally be taken to mean) that there might not have been someone who had such and such a history, such and such an appearance, etc., filling this out with a list of one's actual empirical properties. If the previous speculations in fact made sense, then this filling-out cannot be an adequate account of what it means to say 'I might not have existed'. For if, on the line of the previous speculations, I had been someone else, lived at a different time, and so forth, then it might well be true that there would not have existed someone with just the properties I actually have, and yet not be true that I did not exist – I would exist, but not with those properties. The same point can be approached from the opposite end: it looks as though we might admit that someone could exist with just those empirical properties of history, appearance, etc., that I as a matter of fact have, and yet that person not be me. So, by these arguments, 'I might not have existed' cannot mean 'there might not have

existed a person with just this specification', where the
specification is that of the properties I actually have. Nor
will any other specification of properties do better. So it
looks as though the 'I' of this statement must again be the
attenuated 'I', the Cartesian centre of consciousness. But
if this is so, what can 'I might not have existed' possibly
mean? For it now looks as though there is absolutely
nothing left to distinguish any Cartesian 'I' from any other,
and it is impossible to see any more what would be
subtracted from the universe by the removal of *me*.[4]

Similarly, in what is perhaps a much more reassuring argument,
Peter Strawson, claiming that it is hard to see what the determinist
thesis actually *is*, says that of course we treat a psychotic in a
specially 'objective' way, pulling back from normal inter-personal
relationships in an effort to explain and control the derangement.
But it doesn't follow from this that, were we to believe in a
general thesis of determinism, we should believe with similar
'objectivity' in all relationships, a state of affairs which some
socially determinist theories (Marxist ones for example) seem to
enjoin.

Neither in the case of the normal, then, nor in the case
of the abnormal is it true that, when we adopt an objective
attitude, we do so *because* we hold such a belief. So my
answer has two parts. The first is that we cannot, as we are,
seriously envisage ourselves adopting a thoroughgoing
objectivity of attitude to others as a result of theoretical
conviction of the truth of determinism; and the second is
that when we do in fact adopt such an attitude in a
particular case, our doing so is not the consequence of a
theoretical conviction which might be expressed as
'Determinism in this case', but is a consequence of our
abandoning, for different reasons in different cases, the
ordinary inter-personal attitudes.
It might be said that all this leaves the real question
unanswered, and that we cannot hope to answer it without
knowing exactly what the thesis of determinism is. For the

---

[4] 'Imagination and the Self' in *Essays in the Philosophy of Action*, P. F.
Strawson (ed.) (Oxford 1967); reprinted in *Problems of the Self*
(Cambridge 1973).

real question is not a question about what we actually do, or why we do it. It is not even a question about what we would *in fact* do if a certain theoretical conviction gained general acceptance. It is a question about what it would be *rational* to do if determinism were true, a question about the rational justification of ordinary inter-personal attitudes in general. To this I shall reply, first, that such a question could seem real only to one who had utterly failed to grasp the purport of the preceding answer, the fact of our natural human commitment to ordinary inter-personal attitudes. This commitment is part of the general framework of human life, not something that can come up for review as particular cases can come up for review within this general framework. And I shall reply, second, that if we could imagine what we cannot have, viz. a choice in this matter then we could choose rationally only in the light of an assessment of the gains and losses to human life, its enrichment or impoverishment; and the truth or falsity of a general thesis of determinism would not bear on the rationality of *this* choice.[5]

These examples turn upon the adequacy of two concepts – the self and freedom – within the moral scheme of which they are essential parts. Considering them, it is clear that philosophic discussion of the terms involved is not simply sorting out the right and wrong way to use the terms, nor settling a case of head-on moral disagreement by showing that one half of the dispute is in logical error. Far more, it is a matter of pursuing a set of suppositions which are the grounds for an evaluative disagreement, and seeing how they are necessarily bound up with a whole view of human nature, of society, and what human beings are. In looking for these bonds we would find it impossible to make the fact/value distinction even in a logical sense. That is, we couldn't separate the factual part of the statement 'he owes me a debt' from its evaluative part, even in a putatively logical way. Similarly, though more trickily, we could not separate factual and evaluative elements in 'you ought to be punished for that action' or 'this is a just society' because without the concepts of owing or obligation or justice we wouldn't have a great many social institutions. The

[5] 'Freedom and Resentment' in P. F. Strawson, cited.

concept of owing is not so much value-free or value-sodden, it is organising principle of a whole social edifice of facts and values which it becomes pointless to analyse for its relative factual and evaluative joists because they are one and the same thing. What, again, we undertake is a consideration of how we make sense of the set of institutions and what the contradictions and congruences are which they make possible in our expectations of human beings.

By this stage it is perhaps beginning to come clear how the examination of institutions is also a scrutiny of their moral coherence. The proposition that it is the function of universities to study the quality of modern industrial life turns out to mean the study of its view of human relations and the way in which this view is expressed in a variety of social institutions. The proposition itself needs, I take it, very little justification. We are surrounded by the degradations and the triumphs of industrial life; we are menaced by its runaway momentum and by the corruption, mistrust, brutality, waste and callousness which it produces. A minority of dissenters have also tried to identify their dissatis-faction with the reductive modes of thought, the over-differentiated and external models of human behaviour, the moral lassitude and loss of nerve, which are all agents in its totality. The attempt to locate such dissatisfaction, I have claimed, entails a less than specialised approach. We may usefully combine certain 'fields of knowledge', certain perspectives, as a distinctive subject. Allegedly inter-disciplinary studies are as often as not spurious, a matter of self-conscious conversation in public between this and that specialism. To think hard about the familiar philosophic issues I've mentioned – facts and values, free will and determinism, virtue and happiness – constitutes a full-time occupation, and you can't really be a sociologist or a critic *as well*. But to think on these things, with Kant or with Pascal, is to recognise their historical changefulness, the ineradicable actuality of what they say. 'Sociology may or may not be a *jeu d'esprit*, but History was once life in ear-nest.'[6] So to study anything human is to study its history; so much is tautological. To study its significance – its quality or human value – is to study how it is that a given society assigns value to human activity. Now (to say it again) this is not to give way to total relativism (the hard-nosed moral pessimist always misses this

---

[6] John Dunn's epigram in *Modern Revolutions* (Cambridge 1972).

point), for to understand the contingency of a given human significance is still to endorse the rationality of human morality, and such
endorsement gives the lie to the latter-day moral sceptics who have
reduced morality to emotivism. For not only is it the case, on this
argument, that it is of the nature of human concepts and institutions that they embody moral significances, it can only be the
case (a very knotty difficulty for sociologists) that you study them
from within the values that you hold yourself. Given Philippa
Foot's argument,[7] that 'anyone who uses moral terms at all, whether
to assert or deny a moral proposition, must abide by the rules for
their use, including the rules about what shall count as evidence
for or against the moral judgement concerned', and given also that
as she concedes 'in this sort of discussion much depends on
experience and imagination' and that 'misunderstanding will not
always be resolvable by anything which could be called argument
in the ordinary sense', given all this, the study of human experience
not only entails but *is* the study of values and their reasonableness,
and those values as having a given historical, sociological, but none
the less real (i.e. non-arbitrary) life.

Such a study is then grappling with the stuff of day-to-day life.
Its practice has as its necessary, self-justifying point, an effort of
normative redefinition. Even though we may come to the study
of literature or history or philosophy by many roads, and for many
personal reasons, it is never a sufficient account that we come simply
because we need psychological consolation from George Herbert
or a good dose of cynicism from Lewis Namier. We come with
certain needs and wants, and the earlier citations from Strawson
clear those terms of their simply determinist charge. In response
to these needs, the product of a history and culture, we identify
certain preoccupations. With these in mind we turn to the areas of
our culture which interest us –

> For an old bitch gone in the teeth
> For a botched civilisation . . .
> For two gross of broken statues
> For a few thousand battered books

and regroup the landmarks in new and more satisfying configurations. This is absolutely not to treat the culture as a

[7] In 'Moral Beliefs', reprinted in W. D. Hudson (ed.), *The Is/Ought
Question* (Macmillan 1969), pp. 196 ff.

Rorschach blot, to be assigned whatever meanings please us but to say that we take from the culture what speaks most immediately to a *situation*, as Donne was suddenly heard to do in the early part of the century, after Grierson's great new edition in 1912, as the common people of Beauvais, of Paris, of Captain Swing or of 1848 do to the present-day historian. And the proper reasons which we give for our interest represent a tension between the recoverability of the past and the way in which we have learned to see the past in order to help us live in the present. I shall take three examples of such an enterprise, two of them the efforts of two creative and critical geniuses – Lucien Goldmann and Leavis – in order to show how we might pursue our new studies in the humanities; third, I shall try briefly to offer an example of my own, deriving from theirs. I shall take Mozart as my subject.

III

'La seule manière d'approcher la réalité humaine – et
Pascal l'avait découvert deux siècles avant Engels – c'est
de dire oui et non, de réunir les deux extrêmes contraires.'[8]

Goldmann gives us a *Marxisant* Pascal, a Pascal whose life takes on a unity which has existence only 'par la puissance d'une recherche d'absolu de totalité qui se soumet entièrement à son objet et par cela même ignore tout souci subjectif de continuité extérieure et formelle.'[9] The unity in question derives from the heroic (and tragic) effort to maintain the living tension between Descartes and God. Now how far Pascal would have recognised Goldmann's description of his work is a leading question; it turns on what he wrote, on what a given intellectual milieu means by its allegations about the recoverability of the past, and on the extent to which the intellectual constructs of that later society transpire from its historically subsequent conditions. This debate about what we shall do with the past remains the central obscurity in the human studies. It may help to tackle the obscurity if I emphasise the nature of Goldmann's identification of Pascal, and of Racine. Goldmann takes Pascal as 'la première réalisation exemplaire de l'homme moderne'.[10] One could say that he puts Pascal right in the fracture which

[8] Lucien Goldmann, *Le Dieu Cachè*, p. 187.
[9] *Ibid.*, p. 188.
[10] *Ibid.*, p. 192.

marked our old friend 'the dissociation of sensibility'. He makes Pascal the first dialectician. No doubt he could not have done this without Marx. To that extent he projects backwards upon the shadows of the past an explanatory frame of illumination which sheds light in a peculiarly twentieth-century way. But equally he couldn't do this unless Pascal could be usefully and – most obviously important – *recognisably* read in this way. He therefore performs the central critical function : he identifies the significance of a great writer of the past for the present time.

In Goldmann's version Pascal defines, lives and reconciles – or not reconciles, rather holds in a terrible tension – Cartesian and Jansenist thought: modern rationalism and Augustinian asceticism. Cartesian man is 'le savant éclairé, libre de préjugés et superstitions, avançant courageusement et sans réserve vers la conquête de la vérité'; in a brilliant analysis of Goethe's *Faust*, Goldmann isolates for us, what in a literary tradition has been long acknowledged, the complaisant nullity of the thought-forms characterised by Wagner in *Faust*, the nullity of Wagner's closed belief in knowledge for its own sake. Faust himself transcends this suburban vision in such a way as to show us how the traditional scientific histories deracinate Pascal in recounting only his vast scientific achievement and so distorting the meaning of his biography. For Pascal systematically criticises the poverty of truth without human conditions. The missing capital for latter-day natural and social science is conventionally supplied by Jeremy Bentham – knowledge for the greatest good of the greatest number. Goethe's Wagner satirises the position. Pascal's effort is radically un-vulgar. He unites the undoubted power of scientific rationalism with the community of the world, but a world whose moral action can only have meaning in a beatitude forever necessary, *and* forever withheld from knowledge.

God or the world? Reason or Faith? As always, these terms have to take on highly specific meaning before we can join the argument. For Pascal, Descartes against Jansen; for Racine, the world (Néron, Athalie) against the God of Port Royal and St. Cyr; for Kant, fact against values; for Blake and Wordsworth (for Jane Eyre), the individual spirit against the moral law; for Marx, the movement of history, its physical structure and causes, against its metaphysical future (in Goldmann's phrase, 'Religion sans doute, mais religion sans Dieu'); and *l'homme moyen intellectuel* of the

222

late twentieth century is trapped and forced into arbitrary choices by a host of these unreally divided alternatives. Harried into one camp or the other (arts and science, mind and feeling, self and society) he has abandoned Pascal's tragedy which is 'l'incertitude radicale et certaine, le paradoxe, le refus intramondain du monde et l'appel de Dieu'[11] in order to try to walk normally on a one-legged morality.

Perhaps it is beginning to be clear how to complete the circle of an argument which began by criticising the rootless and atemporal terms in which we think about thought. Leavis is another major example of a man who, like Goldmann, tries to regroup certain key writers in such a way as to give their significance now, and in so doing of course to alter the significance given to now itself. A hint of what I mean comes out when Leavis directs us to a specific attention to Eliot as embodying a distinctive attitude to the past for the benefit and the better chastisement of the twentieth century. In this essay[12] he is also making specific curricular recommendations (as I shall) in pointing to the relative brevity of Eliot's œuvre as offering a unique challenge to the student of literature and of society, today. The astonishing succinctness of Leavis' outline depends in part upon a lifetime of writing about Eliot, and it's during that lifetime that one can see the development emerging which makes Leavis a contemporary version of Goldmann's Pascal, though one whose *English* differences from the Marxist tradition make him rather more congenial.

The development of Leavis' criticism is distinctly from a (to put it crudely) expressionist point of view to one more richly ambiguous and tragic in a Pascalian sense. He moves, that is, from *Revaluation*, in which poetic virtue is presented as the precise and complex registration of feeling, to his great book on Lawrence and on, among others, to the essays on *Anna Karenina* and *Little Dorrit*, in which the qualitatively changed conditions of writing about novels enforce for us a clear sense of the provisionality and essential suggestiveness of the procedure. I have to compress a whole intellectual career here, one in which the steady exploration of those key terms for Leavis 'Reality' and 'Sincerity' plays a main part, and it will have to do to say that Leavis brings to each study

[11] *Le Dieu Caché*, p. 205.
[12] In *English Literature in Our Time and the University* (Chatto & Windus 1970).

that really matters to him a sense of the sharp immutuality between the ideal of individual responsibility which the Romantics inaugurated and the chance of shared faith, standards and community. Lawrence and Eliot are the two figures who serve for him as the contemporary co-ordinates of the experience. Leavis' affirmations of creativeness with significance can only be given meaning in the discussion of particular writers, just as Pascal's meaning of God comes straight from what Augustinian Jansenists meant by God. So for Leavis the explorations of Blake's kind of creativeness tensed against Dickens', of both against Tolstoy's, figure a search to express 'the social conditions the individual needs for happiness, or fulfilment, and the determination to nourish the individual responsive moral sense that serves such fulfilment'. If, as the essays on Eliot recognise, that search is inevitably religious, it's in a tragic sense, in the sense born of the tradition inaugurated by Pascal, which holds through Kant and Marx, that religion is necessary, paradoxical, and inaccessible. Right through the essay on Eliot, Lawrence is the unspeaking other member of the dialogue;

'Who is the third who walks always beside you?'

The balancing note is there when, denying an ultimate rejection of the world, Leavis suggests that *Marina* evokes 'a significant order of reality that, in the face of transience and death, offers hope and promise without (as in *Byzantium*) ironical equivocality'. And, Leavis says, 'one doesn't need to be Anglo-Catholic, or theologically given, to find a compelling interest and a validity (the "interest" entails a response to *that*) in Eliot's religious poetry'. That 'interest' and validity are not of course of any merely aesthetic kind, but God being even more completely absconded than he was for Descartes, he stays alive in our culture in these modes of discourse, and without these modes 'rationality and intelligence are thwarted'.

The materialist would argue at this point that we have only to wait for the idea of God to become slightly more attenuated and it will altogether cease to bother men. The main point of my argument has been to refute this view. I want to conclude by very briefly offering a curricular venture of my own. The sort of study which Leavis recommends and into which I've woven Leavis' own development would only look too 'academic' – criticism of criticism – to those who go about beating the bounds between subject and subject and between the university and its suburbs, those 'whose levelling rancorous kind of a mind/never looked through a drunkard's eye or through the eye of a saint'. The point is to study how the greatest minds of an age rewrite the idea of human nature in such a way that that human nature can live better. 'Be ye therefore perfect as God thy Father is perfect.' There is no substitute for what is good. My concluding remarks about Mozart indicated in my own voice how to derive the lessons from the study of Leavis' heterodox tradition and Goldmann's Marxist one. We study Mozart because he is good (like Azdak to the advocate, we shall listen much more carefully if we know he is good). What does it mean to say he is good and how shall we perform the study in any case?

IV

He is good because he embodies the possibility of fulfilment. He holds together the centrifugal forces of tragic division. He makes possible a true vision of what human reality is like and consequently what being good is like. But of course he does this, as he must, set securely in his own time and terms. The problem is to decide which of these terms, objectively recovered, can be regrouped in such a way as to know why Mozart matters to us.

Mozart stands at another crucial stage in the development of modern man, himself no sort of a terminus. Mozart's biography and letters tell us all we need to know about the trivial oppressions of life for a subordinate official and wandering musician in the courts of the German enlightenment. But he was a member of a class both outlawed and oppressed, as well as profoundly a part of the intellectual and artistic flowering of the time. Mozart was part of the whole astonishing movement which included Schiller, Lessing, Haydn, Kant, Hegel, Goethe, Beethoven, Hölderlin. He saw – was in a position to see and was a great genius – that class societies spontaneously produce different rules and prohibitions for the different classes, so making conflict an inevitable ingredient of everyday life. He sensed and renders in his music – in piano concerto number 20, K466, or in the clarinet quintet – the more general conflict of ethics and morality, the individual and the moral law. But he also learned more profoundly than anything else the inextinguishable optimism of the *Aufklärung*, the triumph of reason over petty despotisms which were in no position to produce either a bourgeois or grand monarchic social basis. Thus *The Marriage of*

Figaro is the deepest and richest expression of the clash between rival moralities which Mozart so clearly saw was one moment of essential social change in his time. The utterly heartrending and incomparably beautiful duet between the countess and Susanna at at the end of Act III Scene x gives perfect musical expression to Mozart's perception of how an old moral and social order gives way to a new one. Mozart's clear and confident enlightenment is easily able, after *Idomeneo*, to reject the lapse into the stoic morality which characterises the early Lessing, or Schiller in *Wallenstein* and *Don Carlos*, or the whole Prussian ruling class satirised in *Minna von Barnhelm*. But as we find in K491 and afterwards in the last symphonies, the last quartets, and *Don Giovanni*, in K595 and elsewhere, this astonishing elegance and buoyant courage overcome the menacing dangers and dark threats of life without in any way diminishing their reality as powerful forces at work in life. The threat and the conviction are held in a simultaneity which in doing justice to both make it clear for us, 180 years later, that for the time being as never before, art-speech is the only speech.

This is only a hint at what the Mozart inquiry might involve. There would be, in whatever order, a reading in the most important works of the German Enlightenment – bits and pieces of the history of ideas; there would be the concomitant study of the social structure of the German states in such a way as to bring out the conflict of the available ethics and ideologies and the slow transcendence of one by another. Finally, the task would be to see how Mozart's greatness lay in his ability so to fill the terms of his ethic and ideology that he becomes the fact of its displacement and eventual transcendence. A lesser composer – a Rossini or Cimarosa – can only render a partial fulfilment of what was there to be expressed. Mozart fulfils the terms of life as it was then available to him, and without that fulfilment we could not, of course, have known that it was possible at all, which is why greatness is greatness. That is to say, Mozart's significance for us now could not crudely be a matter of his reflecting in superstructure some predetermined social base; it is rather that Mozart embodies another version of that modern man typified in this argument by Pascal, and that his version renders with unsurpassable resilience and gaiety that creativeness and renewal which is the ground of faith and reason, and which gives significance to men's lives.

Outside the whale:
the language of love and the
conversation of politics

Mozart is one possible *control* for forms of education which might go beyond the present limits and blanknesses.

> It is this deep blankness is the real thing strange.
> The more things happen to you the more you can't
> Tell or remember even what they were.
>
> The contradictions cover such a range.
> The talk would talk and go so far aslant,
> You don't want madhouse and the whole thing there.[1]

I use him not only because, as the previous chapter tries to show, he is another emblem there of modern man, but also because he is the genius he is, and a composer. 'Official' music still, in spite of the indisputable fact that it has been the greatest British cultural achievement of the past fifty years,[2] is sold very short anywhere other than the universities. The paradox is compounded by the additional fact that in more or less unofficial forms, music is easily the most living form of culture to be found both amongst downtown slum school-children and university students.

But of course Mozart could be joined as a controlling focus for a curriculum by any great creative genius: by Shakespeare, naturally; by Michelangelo, by Brunelleschi, by Brunel, by William Morris, by Dickens, by Wordsworth, by Blake (especially beside Mozart). But it would not do simply to call them genius, and have done with it. Genius is for the present day largely an excuse for present failing. 'As for living, our geniuses will do that for us.' If a very small number of men are geniuses, the present attitudes seem

---

[1] William Empson, 'Let it go', *Collected Poems* (Chatto & Windus 1955).
[2] To justify which claim, tell this register: Delius, Vaughan Williams, Rubbra, Bax, Tippett, Britten, Walton, Rawsthorne, Elisabeth Lutyens, Lennox Berkeley, and so on to the younger generation.

to go, other people can get on with keeping less admirable forms of behaviour in being. And to be told that these men *are* geniuses (and that's all there is to it) seems to be the quickest way available to make a large number of students, in and going on from school, dislike and despise these men, and move as far away as possible from admiring and imitating them. If, however, as I put it in the last chapter, the study of creative genius is the study of how a Mozart rewrites the idea of human nature in such a way that human nature can live better, then such a justification of a humane education reconnects the genius with the people. Which, providing we can say what it might mean 'to live better', that is, to live seriously and well and with all your intelligence in a world in which such living must seem really very hard indeed, brings us back to Mozart.

I placed Mozart a few pages ago on the hinge of an epoch, much as Goldmann placed Pascal in *Le Dieu Caché* at the Fall of modern man. But if Pascal, in a new theodicy, was at the Fall in that he profoundly understood what it is both to doubt and to be blessed, to desire the fruit of knowledge *and* to love and obey God – Mozart might stand for a new Redemption. He understands and imagines for us (and it is in this sense that for the time being as never before, art-speech is the only speech) the irreconcilable demands of two moralities, and is able, music being what it is, to render both at one and the same time. I think Haydn (in the quartets from opus 50 upwards) does the same. (The places of Beethoven and Schubert in this line I shall try to mark in a moment.) The two moralities are roughly those which I have spoken of in these pages as 'private' and 'public' living. This time I may speak of them less opaquely as the morality of politics and the morality of love.

The main impulse of this book has been to bring the two into immediate relation with one another. If I sense our daily politics rightly, the two moralities are thought of as irrevocably opposite and alien. One way of reading, for example, the history of the English novel in the nineteenth century – and let it be quite clear and not at all a matter of opinion, that that history is one of the very greatest peaks of cultural achievement – one way of reading it is to see its authors as watching their own finest possibilities being driven steadily into the margins of society. Those possibilities walk abroad in certain men, or in certain relationships, or in certain groups of people; time and again, the record of these works is of these men and women trying heroically to take their nobility and courage and goodness out into a society which ignores, abuses, and finally breaks them. Lydgate in *Middlemarch*, Pip in *Great Expectations*, Isabel Archer in *The Portrait of a Lady*, Maggie Tulliver in *The Mill on the Floss*, Henchard in *The Mayor of Casterbridge*, Jude the Obscure, Villette, Ursula Brangwen in *The Rainbow*, on and on. Conrad's heroes, pushed out to the most extreme limits of this society and its merchandising, come to grief in the heart of darkness, and in solitary confinement.

Perhaps Pip is the odd man out there. Certainly *Little Dorrit* itself would be, and Dickens is perhaps the English novelist who tries, like Mozart, to fill the space between the opposites. To put it my way, in his greatest books, he tries to hold together the morality of love and the language of politics.

Somewhere, David Hume makes the distinction between the two: Politics is not love; moral philosophy is not the same as political theory. In the politics of the works whose titles I have glanced at, the vindication of the individual in the face of such defeats as society exacts is found in love. Faced with the destruction of a society which increasingly divides and beats down its members, driven out of their own moral and cultural homes, then what was left for the reclamation of self was this language, and the identity of this language with the experience of love. Or, to be a good deal more precise, the experience of being in love, there being a world of difference between 'love', 'being in love', and 'loving'.

> I regained my couch, but never thought of sleep. Till morning
> dawned I was tossed on a buoyant but unquiet sea, where
> billows of trouble rolled under surges of joy. I thought
> sometimes I saw beyond its wild waters a shore, sweet as
> the hills of Beulah; and now and then a freshening gale,
> wakened by hope, bore my spirit triumphantly towards
> the bourne: but I could not reach it, even in fancy, a
> counteracting breeze blew off land, and continually drove
> me back. Sense would resist delirium: judgement would
> warn passion. Too feverish to rest, I rose as soon as day
> dawned.[3]

Jane Eyre herself is the supreme Romantic heroine: the woman

[3] *Jane Eyre*, chapter 15.

of Kant whose court of moral appeal is her own conscience and her own reason and for whom virtue and happiness, the rich, unforgettable feeling that she is at one with her world, and the *sign* that she is at one, is happy and fulfilled, is the tempestuous depth and vividness of her feelings. But more than this, she finds her own reality in the being of another – loving her neighbour, if you like, as herself. And so finding her reality confirmed by being in love, she goes beyond herself to affirm more than herself; she affirms her identity with the humanness which is found only outside herself. And this discovery of identity is the only source of life; it is the point at which 'being in love' becomes love. Love, that is, not in any generalised affection for the human race. It is not a feeling. It is a necessary state of affairs.

What can it mean to say that love is not a feeling? Something, perhaps, like what Shakespeare says in *Sonnet 116* :[4]

> Let me not to the marriage of true minds
> Admit impediments; love is not love
> Which alters when it alteration finds,
> Or bends with the remover, to remove.
> Oh no, it is an ever-fixed mark
> That looks on tempests and is never shaken;
> It is the star to every wandering barque,
> Whose worth's unknown, although his height be taken.
> Love's not time's fool, though rosy lips and cheeks
> Within his bending sickle's compass come,
> Love alters not with his brief hours and weeks,
> But bears it out even to the edge of doom :
> If this be error and upon me proved,
> I never writ, nor no man ever loved.

As feeling is presumably to be defined in relation towards an object and certainly 'alters when it alteration finds', I think Shakespeare is doing more than making familiar protestations about constancy. People may indeed stop loving one another, or may fall in love with someone else. They may, like Jane Eyre, feel the most intense feelings of their life while in love. But love itself 'alters not with his brief hours and weeks'. It is what is known when, like Levin in *Anna Karenina*, we love someone as Levin loves Kitty Schcherbatsky, and Kitty loves him.

[4] I owe much here to a conversation with Mr Gordon Reddiford.

He could not have been mistaken. There were no eyes on earth like those. There was only one creature on earth able to focus all the light and meaning of life for him. That was she – Kitty.

And in return, at their wedding:

These six weeks had been the most blissful and the most agonizing period for her. Her whole life, all her desires and hopes were concentrated in this one man, who was still incomprehensible to her, and whom she was bound to by a feeling that was even more incomprehensible than the man himself, and that alternately attracted and repelled her . . . This new life, because of its unfamiliarity, could not help being terrifying, but terrifying or not, it had already been accomplished within her soul six weeks before; what had been accomplished in her soul a long time before was merely sanctified now.

'This new life', 'accomplished in her soul', and in the first quotation, 'the focus of the light and meaning of life', these phrases signify a presence and a force which are more than a feeling. It is more like a fact, a material fact. A fact, so to speak, in modern physics. It is certainly not a state of idealisation.

To speak like this is as far away as I can make it from placing the ideal of love at the centre of some revisionist ideology. (I have in mind the mixture of accuracy and hatefulness in John Berger's remark that, 'For a woman the state of being in love was a hallucinatory interregnum between two owners, her bridegroom taking the place of her father, or later, perhaps, a lover taking the place of her husband.'[5])

Falling in love is vividly described in Iris Murdoch's work *The Nice and The Good*.[6] In a few pages near the close, she allows ready play to her signal gift as the most *recognisable* human philosopher now writing English. Briefly she brings philosophy and the novel back together where they belong. And she describes that state which continues to embody perhaps the most intense aspiration of all women and most men, whether they know it or not, 130 years after *Jane Eyre*.

[5] In *G.* (Weidenfeld & Nicolson 1972), p. 152.
[6] *The Nice and the Good* (Chatto and Windus 1969), pp. 331 ff.

> The realisation that she [the heroine] was in love with
> Ducane came to Mary quite suddenly on the day after the
> rescue from the cave, but it seemed to her then that she had
> already been in love for some time. It was as if she had for
> some time been under an authority the nature of which she
> had not understood . . .

This seems to put the matter in the same way as Tolstoy does.
While being in love causes Mary severe anguish – a condition Iris
Murdoch presents with the plainness and accessibility of which at
her rare best she is mistress – her feelings, it is clear, are not *the
same thing* as love.

> Realising that one is in love with someone in whom one has
> long been interested is a curious process. What can it be
> said to consist of? Each human being swims within a sea of
> faint suggestive imagery. It is this web of pressures, currents
> and suggestions, something often so much less definite than
> pictures, which ties our fugitive present to our past and
> future, composing the globe of consciousness. We think
> with our body, with its yearnings and its shrinkings and its
> ghostly walkings. Mary's whole body now, limp beneath
> the tall twisted acacia tree, became aware of John from
> head to foot in a new way. She imaged him with a turning
> and hovering of her being, as if a wraith were plucking
> itself out of her towards him. She felt his absence from her as
> a great tearing force moving out of her entire flesh. And she
> shivered with a dazzled joy.

There is a certain amount of strain in this passage as Iris Murdoch tries to realise the heroine's feelings; there seems to me none
at all in her moral descriptions, in her account of what it is to be
conscious – not a solid self, not a single, choosing will either, and
not a tissue of socially determined materials.

> There is a comfort in the strength of love,
> 'Twill make a thing endurable, that else
> Would break the heart.

Iris Murdoch, like any decent novelist, sees the dark and secret
side of love, which can worm its way into the bud and destroy it.
All the same, she writes that 'Great love is inseparable from great

joy', and she speaks again of love as having its peculiar authority and as pertaining in its essential nature – a nature not like that of feelings and emotions, varying with their objects – pertaining to beauty and goodness. Love is then not so much something to be experienced (as presumably a feeling is), as it is a mode of being to be learned. It is more like an art.[7]

The hero of Iris Murdoch's novel becomes the carrier of these moral truths.

> John Ducane thought to himself, why have I landed
> myself in this absurd and terrible position? Why have I
> been such a perfectly frightful ass? Why have I so
> infelicitously, inopportunely, improperly and undeniably
> fallen quite madly in love with my old friend, Mary
> Clothier?
>
> It seemed now to Ducane that his thoughts had been,
> already for a long time, turning to Mary, running to her
> instinctively like animals, like children. The moment had
> been important when he had thought about her, we are
> under the same orders. But he had known, long before he
> had formulated it clearly, that she was like him, morally
> like in some way that was important. Her mode of being
> gave him a moral, even a metaphysical, confidence in the
> world, in the reality of goodness. No love is entirely
> without worth, even when the frivolous calls to the
> frivolous and the base to the base. But it is in the nature of
> love to discern good, and the best love is in some part at any
> rate a love of what is good. Ducane was very conscious, and
> had always been conscious that he and Mary communicated
> by means of what was good in both of them.'

When all is said and done about the complex origins of love and hate, it remains both a main theme of our art and an everyday truth of experience that 'the best love is in some part at any rate a love of what is good'.

A whole area of the social imagination has kept faith with this idea, and the message of Jane Eyre is still voiced, robustly enough, in assorted reminders in women's magazines, pop songs and TV serials. That message, and the language of love generally, has no

---

[7] The main point of Erich Fromm's book, *The Art of Loving* (Allen & Unwin 1957).

doubt suffered pretty severe damage. It isn't clear, as I said before, just in what relation the expressive arts stand to the real centre of society. There is generally a gap, now wider, now narrower, between culture and being (two terms which may be roughly equated to 'manipulation' and 'expressiveness' proposed in chapter 9). When the arts and the feelings are lived as one, then you have a living culture. At the moment, this at-oneness survives in a few parts of both popular (sport, for instance) and high culture (Mozart); and it survives in the universal image of 'being in love'. Insofar as the love songs and poetry and observable mores of the time are anything to go by, that image has suffered sharp attenuation.

For my purposes, however, what is important is that this redeeming notion of love – redeeming, that is, from what is felt to be an alienating, routine, and deadly world – is set in private against the public world of politics. The idea of love is essentially linked to the idea of happiness, and both to the idea of virtue. But love in turn has become distorted by queer notions of self-denial; Freud is only the most famous of those diagnosticians of western culture who have exposed the connection between self-denial and resentment.[8] It has followed that in the lethal polarities of our consciousness and its ideologies, the idea of the hero has become severed from the idea of love. Anne Elliott puts it best and first, in *Persuasion*:

> 'Oh!' cried Anne eagerly, 'I hope I do justice to all that is
> felt by you, and by those who resemble you. God forbid
> that I should undervalue the warm and faithful feelings of
> any of my fellow creatures. I should deserve utter contempt
> if I dared to suppose that true attachment and constancy
> were known only by woman. No, I believe you capable of
> every thing great and good in your married lives. I believe
> you equal to every important exertion, and to every
> domestic forbearance, so long as – if I may be allowed the
> expression, so long as you have an object. I mean, while
> the woman you love lives, and lives for you. All the
> privilege I claim for my own sex (it is not a very enviable
> one, you need not covet it) is that of loving longest, when
> existence or when hope is gone.'

[8] See in this connection P. F. Strawson's paper, cited in chapter 10.

She could not immediately have uttered another sentence; her heart was too full, her breath too much oppressed.

What has the hero come to look like? And what are the institutions which express his values? He is the hero of Kant's *Moral Law*, the man who forces the voice of God into argument with his personal conscience. He is Mozart's Don Giovanni.

As I put it before, Mozart's greatness lay in his ability so to fill the terms of his ethic and ideology that he becomes the fact of its displacement and eventual transcendence. If Don Giovanni is hardly Kant's man of good will, what he is, is far more than the raffish and libertine aristocrat of contemporary folk tale. He is and has to be *that*, of course: various of the comic scenes turn on the caste jokes implicit in the substitutions of Giovanni for Leporello, and vice versa. But what gives Giovanni his Luciferian magnificence is the solitary recklessness of his morality. And what is unsatisfactory about his final damnation, and the way the Commandatore hauls him off, is precisely that such a morality is not adequate to argue with Giovanni's own. The punishment is sudden and arbitrary: it is not argued through in its own terms (which clearly is not a judgement to be made against either *Figaro* or *Cosi Fan Tutte*). After all, the moral extension of Kant's categorical imperative – 'All men ought to do such and such' – is presumably to say, 'Any man ought to do such and such, but if he doesn't, there's nothing you can do about it'. Don Giovanni sets up his own Moral Law, and he lives by it. He is brave, intelligent, reckless, attractive; he embodies the fighter pilot's virtues, and his pride, which in the end is mortal, is only just the wrong side of that fearless, defiant independence without which there would be no political change, and very little politics. His gay heroism and resourcefulness make him much more a brother to Figaro the manservant than to the Count Almaviva.

Above all, the Count fears to be shamed: public shame equals loss of caste. Giovanni has no such fears. Indeed and indeed, he is not afraid. But he is proud, and he is careless: he refuses to renounce freedom, even in the face of the terrible statue. Figaro, no less resourceful, does not need the same pride; like Leporello, he is a born survivor, but without Leporello's cringing perseverence. In other words, he directs his own life within the limits that life imposes. More than that, he changes the limits. Mozart's men are men of their times, and the future lies with Figaro, a natural leader of the Third Estate, if ever there was one.

What about Mozart's women? I have already mentioned Susanna's and the Countess's duet in Act 3, in which sweetness and affection are as beautifully mingled as they may well be. The affection, moreover, is not only for one another; it is, overpoweringly, for their men, and for all men. 'And much shall be forgiven her, for she loved much.' The Countess knows what it is to love not because she wants to, but because she must. It is not a feeling, it is a condition. For these women and, as we shall see, for Fiordiligi in *Cosi Fan Tutte*, it is love and not being in love which counts and which is the ground of faith and reason. Or, as it might be put, ethics precede desires.[9] Where for the men of the *Aufklä-rung* and the Romantic movement (and for the present) freedom is the central ethical fact, for the women – at least in Mozart – love is that central fact.

Cosi Fan Tutte is Mozart's most marvellous statement of this vision. It is the more comprehensive in that in this opera he is – in spite of its title – at his most severe on the men of his time, and of ours. The two men set out to test the two women's fidelity, and while in disguise, exchange *fiancées*, as objects for their courtship. Dorabella duly succumbs to the other man, but Fiordiligi, after very severe trials, only does so at the cost of great pain and guilt. All through the opera, her music has been finer and stronger (and not just more intense) than that of the other three. Her proper *fiancé*, Guglielmo, has about half her range of feeling and expression. She suffers acutely, that is, from her very strong feelings. And thus Mozart makes a rare and brilliantly accurate diagnosis of where social feelings are likely to collect and flow most strongly when Romanticism picks up speed. His men, in James' phrase, are absolute bourgeois. They combine ruthlessness and indifference to the sufferings of others, with a no less egotistical sentimentality. Public ruthlessness and private sentimentality are the two faces of our modern moralities. On the one hand, the institutionalised expression of indifference, callousness, and a tough, narrow, cognitive-bound greed by the faces of our public bureaucracies. On the other, the soft evasions and sentimentalities of so many private lives.

[9] See, for extensive treatment of this argument, Thomas Nagel, *The Possibility of Altruism* (Oxford 1970).

236

I think Mozart's music in all its forms criticises such a split. Perhaps to make the point, one could say that Beethoven, supremely, is the Kantian hero of music. In all his music, one is conscious of his *personal* struggle with conscience, with form, with thought. With Kant, it is the conception of ourselves as free which he alleges to be the source of our acceptance of the imperatives of morality, and it is the acceptance of the imperatives thus grounded by which he explains moral motivation. Schubert, instead of (like Beethoven) heroically declaiming his allegiance to this moral law, searches to get beyond it. Largely failing,[10] he writes heart-melting elegies to the world he has lost. Mozart and Haydn are still able to represent love as a social totality, and happiness as a reasonable consequence of love. This is their great triumph, and the effort of politics, and of education insofar as it *is* politics, is to find and understand examples of human culture which attain such triumphs.

The readiest examples, as well as the most complete and convincing, come from art. 'Art speech is the only speech', therefore, at least in education. In a famous essay, *Inside the Whale*, George Orwell picks out the novels of Henry Miller as the best political novels he could find in 1940, and the best because, rejecting the official postures of the continental ideologies, they spoke up for the quiet man, the man who positively refused to join the International Brigade in Spain, and went on living where he was – in this case, amongst the very seedy Parisian demi-monde.

> Nor for my peace should I go far,
> As wanderers do, that still do roam,
> But make my strengths, such as they are,
> Here in my bosom, and at home.[11]

Home is where we would all return to make our peace. The definition of a main part of culture offered by this book has been that it shall give back their home to the exiled and the lost. Inasmuch as an official education makes and refreshes the culture of its nation, this book has been about the *content* of a curriculum which would perform those offices. If it did, then the teachers and the taught would no longer be safe inside the whale, their work would be deep in the dangers of their history. To work there is

[10] Except in the C major quintet? See pp. 159–60 above.
[11] Ben Jonson, 'A Farewell to the World'.

to work in actuality: for teachers, it is to say – study this composer, these paintings, this city, this factory, this physics. For citizens, it is to say, strike now, sign this petition, stop that airport, create this new welfare. (The great political triumph these days is generally to prevent something.) Amounts of effective highmindedness are inseparable from amounts of power and cash. Edward Thompson said once, 'This is an old European country. We have seen not only the rain which the new God brought to other countries, but also the thunder and lightning – the bloody deluge'.[12] There are distinctly things to do in Britain.

The truth that the great socialists from 1848 onwards never lost hold of is that knowledge serves politics. Politics however is only the means of liberation. The truth shall doubtless make ye free, but freedom simply provides a necessary condition for a people to be able to act lovingly and know the good.

[12] In 'The Peculiarities of the English', *Socialist Register*, 1965.

Bibliography

This very select, not to say idiosyncratic, bibliography suggests ways into a definition of the main terms I use, and suggests also – at least by implication – some drastic changes in the conventional reading lists in educational and cultural studies. Obviously I don't include all the obvious primary texts: the right edition of Marx or Kant or Wordsworth, the best recording of *Così Fan Tutte*. I am concerned only to cite some of the books and articles which turn about these central concepts ('culture', 'imagination', 'ideology' and so forth) and open the discussion up in what are, I hope, new and fertile ways.

I have marked the most straightforward books with an asterisk for the benefit of those who may want to ask, reasonably, where shall we begin?

IDEOLOGY AND EXPERIENCE

Arendt, H. *The Human Condition*, Doubleday 1959.
Berger, R. and Cioffi, F. (eds.). *Explanation in the Behavourial Sciences*, Cambridge 1970
Berlin, I. *Four Essays on Liberty*, Oxford 1969.
Blackburn, R. (ed.). *Ideology in Social Science*, Fontana 1972.
Caudwell, C. *Studies and Further Studies in a Dying Culture*, Monthly Review Press, reissued, 1970.
Chomsky, N. *American Power and the New Mandarins*, Chatto and Windus with Penguin 1969.
Davies, I. 'Sociology and Culture* in F. Inglis (ed.), *Literature and Environment*, Chatto 1971.
Dunn, J. 'Identity and the History of Ideas', in P. Laslett and Q. Skinner (eds.), *Politics, Philosophy and Society*, fourth series, Basil Blackwell 1972.
Modern Revolutions, Cambridge 1972.
Gellner, E. *Thought and Change*, Weidenfeld 1964.
Gramsci, A. *The Modern Prince*, Lawrence and Wishart 1957.
Habermas, J. *Knowledge and Human Interests*, Heinemann Educational Books, 1972.
Towards a Rational Society, Heinemann Educational Books, 1972.
Theory and Practice, Heinemann Educational Books, 1974.
Horkheimer, M. *et al. Dialectic of the Enlightenment*, New Left Books 1973.

Bibliography

Kuhn, T. S. *The Structure of Scientific Revolutions*, University of Chicago; 1962.

Lukacs, G. *History and Class Consciousness*, 1919, reissued, Merlin Press, 1971.

MacIntyre, A. C. *Secularization and Moral Change,** Oxford 1967.
Marxism and Christianity, reissued, Duckworth 1968.
Against the Self-Images of the Age, Duckworth 1971.

Mannheim, K. *Ideology and Utopia*, Routledge, 1936.
Essays on the Sociology of Knowledge, Routledge 1952.

Marcuse, H. *Reason and Revolution*, Routledge 1954.
One-Dimensional Man, now Abacus, 1972.
Negations, Allen Lane, 1970.

Marx, K. and Engels, F. *The German Ideology,** ed. C. J. Arthur, Lawrence and Wishart, 1970.

Muir, K. *An Autobiography,** Hogarth Press 1940, Methuen 1956.

Plamenatz, J. *Ideology,** Macmillan 1970.

Runciman, W. G. *Social Science and Political Theory,** Cambridge 1963.

Ryan, A. *The Philosophy of the Social Sciences*, Macmillan 1970.

Thompson, E. P. 'The peculiarities of the English' in R. Miliband (ed.), *Socialist Register*, Merlin, 1965.
'Open letter to Leszek Kolakowski', in R. Miliband (ed.), *Socialist Register*, Merlin, 1973.

Toulmin, S. *Human Knowledge*, Cambridge 1972.

Williams, R. *Culture and Society,** Chatto and Penguin, 1957, 1961.
The Long Revolution, Chatto and Penguin, 1961, 1962.
'Literature and Sociology', *New Left Review* 67, 1971.
The Country and the City, Chatto, 1973.
'Base and Superstructure', *New Left Review* 82, 1973.

KNOWLEDGE AND VALUES

Anderson, P. 'Origins of the Present Crisis', *New Left Review* 23, 1964.
'Components of the National Culture', *New Left Review* 50, 1968.

Beattie, J. *Other Cultures,** Routledge 1969.

Berger, J. *Permanent Red*, Methuen, 1960.
The Look of Things, Penguin 1972.
*Ways of Seeing,** Penguin, 1973.

Bernstein, B. *Class, Codes, Control*, Routledge, 1971.

Bernstein, B. *et al*, 'Ritual in Education', reprinted in *Schools and Society*, Open University with Routledge, 1972.

Buber, M. *I and Thou*, Routledge 1937.
Paths in Utopia, Routledge 1949.

Carr, E. H. *What is History?,** Macmillan, 1961.

Chomsky, N. *Problems of Knowledge and Freedom*, Fontana, 1971.

Clarke, T. J. *Image of the People*, Thames and Hudson, 1973.

Collingwood, R. G. *Autobiography,** Oxford, 1938.
The Idea of Nature, Oxford, 1948.
The Idea of History, Oxford, 1946.

240

Principles of Art, Oxford, 1946.
Evans-Pritchard, E. E. *Social Anthropology*, reissued Oxford, 1964.
Gombrich, E. *Art and Illusion*, Phaidon, 1960.
Grene, M. *The Knower and the Known*, Faber, 1965.
Korner, S. *Theory and Experience*, Routledge, 1966.
Leach, E. R. *Revisiting Anthropology*, London, 1961.
Levi-Strauss, C. *The Savage Mind*, Weidenfeld, 1967.
    Totemism, Penguin, 1968 (with an introduction by Roger Poole)
Malcolm, N. *Wittgenstein, A Memoir*,* Oxford, 1958.
Merleau-Pouty, M. *Phenomenology of Perception*, Routledge, 1954.
    Adventures of the Dialectic, Heinemann Educational Books, 1974.
    The Prose of the World, Heinemann Educational Books, 1974.
Oakeshott, M. *Experience and Its Modes*, Cambridge, 1933, reissued C.U.P.
    Library Editions, 1966.
    Rationalism in Politics, Methuen, 1962.
Polanyi, M. *Personal Knowledge*, Routledge, 1958.
    The Tacit Dimension, Doubleday, 1966.
Poole, R. *Towards Deep Subjectivity*, Allen Lane, 1972.
Sartre, J. P. *Sketch for a Theory of the Emotions*, Methuen, 1962.
    The Psychology of the Imagination, Methuen, 1972.
    Search for a Method, Methuen, 1973.
Searle, J. *Speech Acts*, Cambridge, 1970.
Strawson, P. F. *Meaning and Truth*, Oxford, 1970.
Trotsky, L. *Literature and Revolution** (1921) Ann Arbor, 1960.
Wittgenstein, L. L. *Philosophical Investigations*, Basil Blackwell, 1953.
Young, M. F. D. (ed.). *Knowledge and Control*, Routledge, 1972.

POPULAR CULTURE AND PUBLIC COMMUNICATIONS

Adorno, T. W. *Prisms*, Neville Spearman, 1970.
Benjamin, W. *Illuminations*, Cape, 1970.
Berger, J. *Art and Revolution*, Penguin, 1969.
Cohn, N. *In Pursuit of the Millennium*, Paladin, 1970.
Craig, D. *The Real Foundations: Literature and Social Change*, Chatto, 1973.
Cullen, G. *Townscape*,* Architectural Press, 1961.
Dahrendorff, R. *Class and Class Conflict in Industrial Society*, Routledge, 1957.
Douglas, M. *Purity and Danger*, Routledge, 1966.
Fischer, E. *The Necessity of Art*, Penguin, 1963.
Garnham, N. and Bakewell, J. *The New Priesthood: British Television Today*,
    Allen Lane, 1970, Penguin 1973.
    Structures of Broadcasting, BFI Pamphlet, 1973.
Halloran, J., Murdock, G. and Elliot, P. *Demonstrations and Communications:
    A Case Study*, Penguin, 1970.
Himmelmeit, H., Oppenheim, P. and Vince, A. N. *Television and the Child*,
    Oxford, 1958.
Hiuzinga, J. *Homo Ludens*, Routledge 1949, Paladin, 1970.
Hoggart, R. *The Uses of Literacy*,* Penguin, 1950, Chatto, 1957.

Bibliography

Inglis, F. *The Imagery of Power*, Heinemann Educational, 1972.
Jacobs, J. *The Life and Death of Great American Cities*, Cape, 1962, Penguin 1969.
Lowenthal, L. *Literature, Popular Culture and Society*, Beacon, USA, 1961.
McLuhan, H. M. *The Mechanical Bridge: Folklore of Modern Industrial Man*,* Vanguard, USA, 1951.
  The Gutenberg Galaxy, Routledge, 1962.
  Understanding Media, Sphere, 1964.
McQuail, D. (ed.). *The Sociology of Mass Communications*, Penguin 1972.
Mumford, L. *The Pentagon of Power*, Secker and Warburg, 1973.
Murdock, G. and Golding, P. 'For a Political Economy of Mass Communications' in R. Miliband (ed.), *Socialist Register*, Merlin, 1973.
Namier, L. *Vanished Supremacies*, London, 1962.
Orwell, G. *Collected Essays*,* Heinemann, 1961.
Paz, O. *The Labyrinth of Solitude*, Allen Lane, 1967.
Roszak, T. *The Making of a Counter Culture*, Faber, 1970.
  Beyond the Waste Land, Faber, 1973.
Schramm, W. *et al. Television in the Lives of Our Children*, USA, 1961.
Seymour-Ure, C. *The Press, Politics, and the Public*, Methuen, 1968.
Taylor, N. *The Village in the City*,* Temple Smith, 1972.
Thompson, D. (ed.). *Discrimination and Popular Culture*,* revised edition, Penguin, 1973.
Williams, R. *Communications*,* revised edition, Penguin, 1967.
  Television: Technology and Cultural Form, Fontana, 1974.
Wollen, P. *Signs and Meaning in the Cinema*, Secker and Warburg, 1969.

EDUCATION AND THE CULTURAL SCIENCES

Allchin, W. H. *The Archetypal Context of Political Experience*, Tract, 1974.
Austin, J. L. *How to Do Things with Words*, Oxford, 1962.
Berger, J. *A Fortunate Man*, Allen Lane 1967, Penguin, 1970.
Berlin, I. *The Hedgehog and the Fox*, Weidenfeld, 1953.
  Fathers and Children,* Oxford, 1970.
Bourdieu, P. Chapters 6 and 7 in *Knowledge and Control* (q.v. under Young, p. 161.
Braudel, F. *The Meiterranean at the Time of Philip II*, Collins, 1972.
Bruner, J. *Towards a Theory of Instruction*, Belknap, Harvard, 1962.
  The Relevance of Education, Allen and Unwin, 1972.
Davies, I. Chapter 9 in *Knowledge and Control* (q.v. under Young, p. 267).
Djilas, M. *The New Class*, Allen and Unwin, 1956.
  The Unperfect Society, Allen and Unwin, 1969.
Goldmann, L. *The Hidden God*, Routledge, 1964.
  The Human Sciences and Philosophy, Cape, 1969.
Goodman, P. *Growing Up Absurd*, Sphere, 1970.
  Compulsory Miseducation, Penguin, 1971.
Gramsci, A. *Prison Notebooks*, Q. Hoare ed., Lawrence and Wishart, 1971.
Hargreaves, D. *Social Relations in a Secondary School*, Routledge, 1967.

Harrison, R. *Before the Socialists: Labour and Politics 1861–81*, Routledge, 1961.
Henry, J. *Culture Against Man*, Tavistock, 1954, Penguin, 1972.
Hill, C. *The Intellectual Origins of the English Revolution*, Weidenfeld, 1965.
Hobsbawm, E. *Industry and Empire*, Weidenfeld, 1967.
    The Age of Revolutions, Weidenfeld, 1968.
Holbrook, D. *English for the Rejected*, Cambridge, 1965.
    English for Maturity,* Cambridge, rev. edition, 1970.
    Human Hope and the Death Instinct, Permagon, 1970.
Jackson, B. and Marsden, D. *Education and the Working Class*,* Routledge
    1962.
Lacey, C. *Hightown Grammar*, Routledge, 1968.
Leavis, F. R. *English Literature in Our Time and the University*, Chatto, 1970.
    *Nor Shall My Sword: Discourses on Pluralism, Compassion, and Social
    Hope*, Chatto, 1973.
Lukacs, G. *Political Writings 1919–1929*, New Left Books, 1972.
Marshall, S. *Experiment in Education*,* Cambridge 1963.
Mills, C. Wright. *The Sociological Imagination*,* Oxford 1962.
Richardson, J. E. *The Teacher, The School, and the Task of Management*,
    Heinemann Educational, 1973.
Skinner, Q. 'Meaning and Understanding in the History of Ideas', *History
    and Theory* 8, 1, 1969.
    'Social Meaning and the Explanation of Action,' in *Politics, Philosophy
    and Society*, fourth series (q.v. under Dunn, p. 136).
Taylor, C. *The Explanation of Behaviour*, Routledge, 1964.
Winch, P. *The Idea of a Social Science*, Routledge, 1967.

MORALITY AND THE SELF

Adorno, T. W. *et al. The Authoritarian Personality*, Harper and Row, 1954.
Burke, K. *Permanence and Change*, Bobbs Merill, 1955.
Erikson, E. *Childhood and Society*,* Norton, 1950, Penguin, 1958.
    Identity: Youth and the Social Crisis, Faber, 1958.
Fromm, E. *Man for Himself: An Inquiry into the Psychology of Ethics*,
    Routledge, 1947.
    The Sane Society, Routledge, 1956.
    The Art of Loving,* Allen and Unwin, 1957.
Gerth, H. H. and Mills, C. W. *Character and Social Structure*, Routledge, 1954.
Goffman, E. *The Presentation of Self in Everyday Life*, Penguin 1968.
Hampshire, S. *Morality and Pessimism*, Cambridge, 1973.
Harding, D. W. *Experience into Words*, Chatto, 1963.
Husserl, E. *Cartesian Meditations*, the Hague, Nijhoff, 1960.
Lacan, J. *The Language of the Self*, Johns Hopkins, USA, 1968.
Laing, R. D. *The Divided Self*,* Tavistock, 1960, Penguin, 1970.
    The Politics of Experience and the Bird of Paradise, Penguin, 1966.
MacMurray, J. *The Self as Agent*, Faber, 1957.
    Reason and Emotion, Faber, 1972.

Bibliography

Mead, G. H. *Mind, Self and Society*, University of Chicago, 1935, reissued 1962.

Murdoch, I. *The Sovereignty of Good*,* Routledge, 1970.

Rawls, J. *A Theory of Justice*, Oxford, 1972.

Schutz, A. *Collected Papers*, Nijhoff, 1962.

Strawson, P. F. 'Freedom and Resentment' in P. F. Strawson (ed.), *Studies in the Philosophy of Thought and Action*, Oxford, 1970.

Williams, B. A. O. *Morality*,* Penguin, 1973.
  Problems of the Self, Cambridge, 1973.

Winnicott, D. W. *The Child, the Family, and the Outside World*,* Tavistock, 1957, Penguin, 1968.
  Playing and Reality, Tavistock, 1971. Penguin, 1974.

244